The Fool in European Theatre

Also by Tim Prentki

THE APPLIED THEATRE READER (*co-edited with Sheila Preston*)

POPULAR THEATRE IN POLITICAL CULTURE (*co-authored with Jan Selman*)

AN INTERNATIONAL COMPANION TO THE POETRY OF W. B. YEATS (*co-authored with Colin Smythe*)

FRANCIS WARNER: POET AND DRAMATIST

The Fool in European Theatre
Stages of Folly

Tim Prentki

First published 2012 by
PALGRAVE MACMILLAN

Palgrave Macmillan in the UK is an imprint of Macmillan Publishers Limited, registered in England, company number 785998, of Houndmills, Basingstoke, Hampshire RG21 6XS.

Palgrave Macmillan in the US is a division of St Martin's Press LLC, 175 Fifth Avenue, New York, NY 10010.

Palgrave Macmillan is the global academic imprint of the above companies and has companies and representatives throughout the world.

Palgrave® and Macmillan® are registered trademarks in the United States, the United Kingdom, Europe and other countries.

ISBN 978–0–230–29159–1

This book is printed on paper suitable for recycling and made from fully managed and sustained forest sources. Logging, pulping and manufacturing processes are expected to conform to the environmental regulations of the country of origin.

A catalogue record for this book is available from the British Library.

A catalog record for this book is available from the Library of Congress.

10 9 8 7 6 5 4 3 2 1
21 20 19 18 17 16 15 14 13 12

Printed and bound in Great Britain by
CPI Antony Rowe, Chippenham and Eastbourne

For Pauline, Sam and Tom

Contents

1
Fooling with Gods and Men

> If trickster stirs to life on the open road, if he embodies ambi-
> guity, if he "steals fire" to invent new technologies, if he plays
> with all boundaries both inner and outer, and so on – then he
> must still be among us, for none of these has disappeared from
> the world. His functions, like the bones of Osiris, may have
> been scattred, but they have not been destroyed. The problem
> is to find where his gathered body might come back to life, or
> where it might already have done so.
>
> (Hyde, 1999, p.11)

Playful, irreverent and frequently irrational, folly at its most serious
detonates confrontation with both society and the self. It constantly
seeks out a *persona* or mask through which it can disclaim what it
articulates. Beyond the easy, external targets of satire, the poetics of
folly operate at the heart of the body politic, questioning the cherished
orthodoxies of correctness and peering around the edges of our most
deep-rooted myths. The earliest records of the cultural life of human
societies reveal the presence of figures whose role is to provoke laughter by depicting the absurdity of the human condition; not just the
more obvious and excessive vanities and pretensions of the rich and
the powerful but that very absurdity which confronts an ever-changing,
time-bound species. These figures and the opinions typically associated
with them are constantly placed in opposition to the dominant discourses of the historical moments in which they occur and yet express
this opposition through devices that enable them to escape from the
trap of a counter-discourse. In Foucauldian terms they are not seeking
an authority for their position and therefore are not concerned with the
discourses of power through which all human life is conducted. These

figures, real or more usually fictional, are inevitably outsiders who can only articulate their views by being detached from the societies upon which they comment. Frequently, they exist in a kind of twilight of the semi-detached, uncompromised by allegiances to families, careers, ideologies, material gain and all those other considerations that contrive to cloud judgement. They are described as foolish by those who live by worldly criteria for denying themselves opportunities for prosperity and advancement. This quality of folly can be a mask worn for both disguise and protection or an essential element of personality such as naiveté or simplicity which gives to the possessor a capacity to see differently; typically to transcend the *ego*. Due to their limited interest in the material world such characters are often felt to be in closer communion with the spirit world than their fellow mortals. Some fools are professionals, earning their living (such as it is) by their wits. Some are 'naturals', foolish without artifice and unable to be anything else. Many inhabit an intermediate space between these positions, slipping between premeditated and spontaneous folly; at times worldly fools; at other times holy fools. This shape-changing, intangible quality of the trickster has made them especially suitable for the medium of theatre where rapid changes of role, disguise and the tricks of illusion are the stock in trade.

Whether in life or art, and in many circumstances the demarcation between the two is difficult to maintain with any confidence, figures going under a variety of names but manifesting congruent characteristics have been identified across the whole range of world cultures which have evolved without contact with each other. From the Vidusaka described in *The Kama Sutra* (Burton, 1994) to the Trickster of the Winnebago people of North America, from the Ananse spider trickster of West Africa to Loki, the Norse Fool and Hermes, Greek trickster of gods and men, '[m]anifestly we are here in the presence of a figure and a theme or themes which have had a special and permanent appeal and an unusual attraction for mankind from the very beginnings of civilization' (Radin, 1956, xxiii). Some vital part of what constitutes humanity is bound up in the notion of being able to laugh at ourselves. So precious is this capacity that its operation is often not left to chance but formalised in both social structures and artistic forms. A significant aspect of this operation is the placing of laughter and those who cause it at the very centre of the body politic. In former times the fool, clown or idiot has occupied a privileged position as the intimate of the most powerful person in the nation, the tribe or the village. If laughter is a necessary function for any human being, it appears even more important that those who control the lives of others should be exposed to it on a regular basis. Through laughter such guardians of our economic, social, moral and cultural life can be warned of the dangers into which they may run if they take themselves too seriously and believe in the infallibility of their own judgements. Laughter asserts another way of seeing the picture; often the view from the grassroots which can offer a different perspective from the seat of government, the boardroom or the television studio.

In his study of Winnebago trickster cycles Paul Radin discovered that the figure of the trickster was implicated alike in the affairs of gods and of men, often commuting between the two. In this regard he resembles his equivalents in many other cultures across the world and gives rise to speculations on the divinity of his origins:

> The impression one gets in perusing these various trickster cycles is that one must distinguish carefully between his consciously willed creative activities and the benefactions that come to mankind incidentally and accidently through the Trickster's activities. This, of course, raises an old question, namely, whether Trickster was originally a deity. Are we dealing here with a disintegration of his creative activities or with a merging of two entirely distinct figures, one a deity, the other a hero, represented either as human or animal? Has a hero here been elevated to the rank of a god or was Trickster originally a deity with two sides to his nature, one constructive, one destructive, one spiritual, the other material? Or, again, does Trickster antedate the divine, the animal and the human?
>
> (Radin, 1956, p.125)

The ambiguity lies at the core of the fool's representation: at once holy, heroic and idiotic; both more and less than the rest of mankind. Attempts to categorise are doomed since it is a fundamental part of the make-up of a fool to defy categories. He* lures us towards definition only to vanish at the moment when the analyst believes she is approaching an understanding. Lewis Hyde describes this characteristic in terms of border crossing:

> In short, trickster is a boundary-crosser. Every group has its edge, its sense of in and out, and trickster is always there, at the gates of the city and the gates of life, making sure there is commerce. He also attends the internal boundaries by which groups articulate their social life. We constantly distinguish – right and wrong, sacred and profane, clean and dirty, male and female, young and old, living and dead – and in every case trickster will cross the line and

confuse the distinction. Trickster is the creative idiot, therefore the wise fool, the gray-haired baby, the cross-dresser, the speaker of sacred profanities. Where someone's sense of honorable behavior has left him unable to act, trickster will appear to suggest an amoral action, something right/wrong that will get life going again. Trickster is the mythic embodiment of ambiguity and ambivalence, doubleness and duplicity, contradiction and paradox.

(Hyde, 1999, p.7)

Getting life going again is one of the key social functions of the fool and trickster. His is an art of survival, not of tragedy. In his ritual aspects he is frequently the upholder of social customs and public rites, as in his close association with European carnival. But where such rituals have ceased to carry meaning in a particular culture, the fool mocks society's adherence to stale forms and worn-out codes. He is the archetypal negotiator, searching for a new route when the traditional ones lead to an impasse. The quality that enables him to perform this function is playfulness. Where situations seem to be locked into fixed positions, the fool uses the device of play, in both senses; trying out what fiction and imagination might achieve and looking for any signs of play, that is movement in the materials presented to him. He, more than other members of his species,experiences the world as a constant process of flux, of becoming rather than of being. This is why, for the fool, certainties are always illusory and the attempts of his fellow creatures to arrive at a steady state are doomed to fail. Hyde associates the trickster, the mythical antecedent of the fool, with the development of culture wherever human societies are formed and, since culture is the process through which we make meaning out of our world and our experiences within it, culture can never be fixed or finished. To be cultured is to be continually in the process of being formed which is why one of the qualities of the trickster is to shape-shift. When we think we've grasped his dimensions, he slips from our hands like a plume of smoke in fog: 'Trickster the culture hero is always present; his seemingly asocial actions continue to keep our world lively and give it the flexibility to endure.' (Hyde, 1999, p.9) Survival is intimately connected with change; with the capacity and willingness to change in the face of a stasis which threatens the well-being of the tribe. Radin found this to be a quality common to tricksters across North America, as well as being replicated in many other parts of the world:

The overwhelming majority of all so-called trickster myths in North America give an account of the creation of the earth, or at least the transforming of the world, and have a hero who is always wandering, who is always hungry, who is not guided by normal conceptions of good and evil, who is either playing tricks on people or having them played on him and who is highly sexed.

(Radin, 1972, p.155)

These characteristics – amorality, wandering, hunger and sex – will be common features of the fools presented in these pages, as well as the conveying of a sense of the world in flux; of the need to look again at commonly held values in the light of the fool's interventions.

One of the standard means by which our world is kept 'lively' is inversion. A recurring motif in trickster behaviour is the turning of conventional wisdom upon its head. Many cultures have a figure whose primary role is to do just this. Among the Lakota people of the American Plains, the *Heyoka* is such a figure. Our fullest record of what was involved in a *heyoka* ceremony is given in *Black Elk Speaks* (Neihardt, 1959) where one such *heyoka*, Black Elk, reveals the simultaneously sacred and profane qualities of the ceremony, enabling the tribe to laugh at its deepest fears without diminishing the awe in which its deities were held. The laughter is provoked through the ritualising of the spirit of contrariness:

Heyokas often dressed in the shabbiest of clothes or wore their clothes wrong side out or turned around. Another part of their contrary behavior consisted of shivering in the sun's heat or running around nearly naked in the depths of winter. They rode miserable old ponies and often mounted them backwards, wearing boots backwards as well. Speech was also contrary.

(Janik, 1998, p.247)

Whatever cultural differences occur in the manifestation, the function sounds essentially the same as the official carnivals of medieval Europe. Here also the sacred is juxtaposed with the profane, both in order that it may be laughed at and so that its values are reaffirmed for and by the community. When Catholicism was confident of its authority, it allowed itself to be mocked within the confines of established ritual, but when challenges appeared, Protestantism and its Counter-Reformation put paid to such irreverend displays where hierarchy was mocked by inversion in forms such as boy bishops and the kings and queens of May. Sometimes there is a specific figure dedicated to inversion; more often the functon is subsumed within the gamut of trickster's repertoire. For the Lakota this figure is Coyote; for the peoples of the Pacific North-West Raven; for the Blackfeet and Crow Old Man and for the Oglala it is Iktomi, the Spider. In West Africa it is Eshu for the Yoruba and Legba for the Fon, while in Europe it was Hermes among the Greeks and Mecury in his Roman manifestation. Although the European Enlightenment inflicted serious damage upon those communal rituals which derive from pre-Christian times, elsewhere the mythical power of the trickster is still felt at times and in places today. Russell Means, an Oglala Lakota and leading member of the American Indian Movement wrote as follows in his autobiography:

> I continued to commune with the spirits as a frequent participant in Rick Two Dog's *yuwipi* ceremonies. At one of them, the spirits said a period of chaos and confusion was coming and the *Iktomi*— a being personified by the spider, who imparts wisdom through trickery – would soon return. Every indigenous people in the world has such a teacher to show them that life is tricky. The white man, unfortunately, thinks it is the devil and refuses to consider his wisdom.
>
> (Means, 1995, p.405)

From his perspective assessing the results of interactions with whites over the last two hundred years, it is not surprising that he makes this observation. But it was not always so. The trickster was once deep-rooted in European societies as well, until a combination of church and reason drove him to seek sanctuary in that last refuge of the playful, the theatre. Before that time the fool was the frequent accompaniment to power in courts both pagan and Christian; a challenge to authority and a reminder of its limitations. This role in relation to the seat of power also reaches back to mythic times. Eshu is the antagonist of Ifa and Hermes of Apollo; both gods come to understand that the maintainance of their power depends upon reaching an accommodation with the trickster. The pattern established in prehistoric myths is played out in relationships on the European stage right down to the present time. The transformative relationhip of *King Lear* is that between king and fool and the same pattern is played out within the genre of vaudeville by Vladimir and Estragon in *Waiting for Godot*. Its roots reach into the very core of Judeo-Christian tradition and iconography as interpreted by the clerics of the middle ages:

> In medieval psalters,Psalm 52 [53 in the Authorised Version] (beginning 'The Fool says in his heart/There is no god') was usually

illustrated by a depiction of King David the Psalmist in company with his fool . . .

(Southworth, 1998, p.4)

The fool is the only person whom a society can permit to challenge that which it holds most sacred because he carries within his representation the default assurance that it is 'only the fool' who has uttered such blasphemies. And yet once uttered, the words are out and with them the possibility of the need to reassess whether these sacred truths still carry authority. The challenge reinvigorates society either by confirming the potency of existing values or by demonstrating the necessity to revise them:

The curious double-act of king and fool, master and servant, substance and shadow, may thus seem as a universal, symbolic expression of the antithesis lying at the heart of the autocratic state between the forces of order and disorder, of structured authority and incipient anarchy, in which the conditional nature of the fool's licence ('so far but no further') gives reassurance that ultimately order will always prevail.

(Southworth, 1998, p.3)

This analysis, while pointing up the importance of the relationship of order to disorder, lapses into a binary distinction of the kind that the fool resists. He does indeed sponsor an antithetical view to the prevailing thesis of authority and, at times the antithesis is safely controlled according to the requirements of conservatism as suggested by Southworth. However, an antithesis does not always give way in face of the thesis but rather gives rise to a new development, a synthesis. As with the debate over carnival, so with the figure of the fool, it is not a question of being either radical or conservative but rather being both radical and conservative for the mode of 'both/and' is the one which more nearly represents the intervention of folly. Associating the trickster with the anthropological notion of dirt-work, Hyde captures this sense of unstable duality more effectively than a resort to the binary:

Where change is not in order, then, ritual dirt-work offers the virtue of non-violent stability. But where change *is* in order, dirt-work also has a role to play, for it simply isn't true that these rituals are always conservative. Dirt rituals may stabilize things for years on end, but when the order is in fundamental crisis these rituals can become the focal points for change, catalytic moments for dirt's revaluation and true structural shifts. Every so often Fat Tuesday *does* leak over into Lean Wednesday, and into the rest of the year as well.

(Hyde, 1999, p.188)

It is just such a moment that the French micro-historian Emmanuel Ladurie explores in *Carnival in Romans* (Ladurie, 1981) where 'real', bloody events were triggered by the ancient ritual. The rulers, those in charge in kingdom, work-place or family, are forever trying vainly to assert the presence of a scheme, pattern or direction to life according to their dictates but such assertions fail to take account of the human factor, or rather the foolish component in human behaviour that will forever resist the implementation of such schemes:

> Fools are characteristically unperturbed by the ignominy that comes of being irresponsible. They have a magical affinity with chaos that might allow them to serve as scapegoats on behalf of order; yet they elude the sacrifice or the banishment that would affirm order at their expense. They reduce order to chaos in a way that makes a farce of the mythical pattern. They wrest life from the "destructive element" while ridiculing the ancient dream that victory over it is possible – and while ridiculing even more the idea that victory over it may be achieved through the observance of rules of conduct.
>
> (Willeford, 1969, p.101)

Such an analysis exactly fits the function of Harlequin throughout his *Commedia dell'arte* appearances while also attaching itself smoothly to the *modus operandum* of the Madman in *Accidental Death of an Anarchist* (Fo, 1980). The Madman, the mask of Dario Fo in that particular play, draws our attention explicitly to the difference between a reformist enjoyment of scandal as proof that the system works and the revolutionary poential of folly to provoke a new order. Karl Kerényi's commentary on Radin's study draws attention to the primal significance of disorder while still insisting that there is an ultimate containment. Ironically, his very function in offering an academic commentary is itself a form of containment and perhaps hints at why an uncontained disorder would, for someone interested in systems of thought, be beyond his imaginative reach:

> Disorder belongs to the totality of life, and the spirit of this disorder is the trickster. His function in an archaic society, or rather the

function of his mythology, of the tale told about him, is to add disorder to order and so make a whole, to render possible, within the fixed bounds of what is permitted, an experience of what is not permitted.

(Radin, 1972, p.185)

However, the trickster is no respecter of 'fixed bounds' and is likely to be found at the margins where the boundary is most difficult to detect, yet alone protect. All his fundamental qualities resist the categorisations upon which borders depend: ambiguity, shape-shifting, detachment from known worlds; a creature of the twilight, borrowing alike from day and night. Whatever value we are inclined to place upon the antics of the fool, probably depending upon our own attitudes towards order, design and predictability, it is evident that the figure is, in many different cultures, closely associated with challenges to the sacredness of what a particular society holds most dear. Interpreting the purpose of that challenge seems to depend upon the position of the interpreter but that challenge is a core element whether in the mythical trickster or the latter day fool, appears to be indisputable. This in turn suggests that societies evolve by making various kinds of accommodation with those anarchic elements represented by the fool. Those which are least tolerant of such antisocial characteristics, are paradoxically most at risk of a descent into violence and anarchy. Repression and a dogged belief in progress despite the evidence to the contrary may keep folly at bay for a time but in the end, societies being composed of humans, chaos will come again. This tension between the planned, the intended and the inevitable tendency for 'stuff' to 'happen' reaches back into the furthest recesses of myth as Hyde explores:

There are designs in this world, but there are also chance events, which means design is never finished. In artistic practice open to happenstance, or in the West African arts of divination, human beings have a way to enter into the play of fate and uncertainty, and from that play this world constantly arises.

(Hyde, 1999, p.127)

The fool is a great disturber of designs in appearance, manner and speech. He is a reminder not only that the design is imperfect but that it can never be perfected and for that he has, at times and in places, been persecuted and repressed. This constant awareness of human frailty frequently positions the fool as the antagonist of authority; the enemy of the grand design. It is, therefore, tempting to depict the history of the fool in terms of an alternative, revolutionary, popular discourse; to offer it as the binary of the official discourse but, though it often manifests oppositional qualities which would qualify it for this status, such a designation is ultimately a misunderstanding. In the last analysis folly is the defiance of discourse, the refusal of category. It reminds us of the fallibility of our hopes and plans by compromising our pretensions to the divine with the untimely interruptions of our animal natures. Folly and carnival go hand in glove with the powerful for it is in the act of exerting control over other humans or over our environment that we are most vulnerable to forgetting our natures and becoming prey to antisocial desires and inhuman aspirations. This is why the fool may be subversive but he cannot be revolutionary. Revolutions involve plans and deeply held convictions about the perfectibility of human societies. Revolutionaries cannot afford to laugh at themselves but the same fervour and absence of self-consciousness that achieves revolutionary goals all too easily provokes intolerance and oppression in rulers who lack the detachment and humility that the fool provides.

The analysis of the phenomenon of foolishness within western culture begins with the figure of the philosopher- fool Socrates as depicted in the writings of his disciple Plato. From *The Symposium* (Plato, 1951) and from *The Last Days of Socrates* (Plato, 1954) emerges a picture of a man who puts his allegiance to an absolute moral imperative above and beyond the point to which 'normal' standards are applied and into the realms of folly or madness. The pursuit of wisdom at all costs is his guiding principle and the loss of his life is a vindication rather than an obstacle in that pursuit. He is acutely aware of the political consequences of this pursuit and so adopts the mask of the private man in the hope of being able to continue his social criticism from behind it:

It may seem curious that I should go round giving advice like this and busying myself in people's private affairs, and yet never venture publicly to address you as a whole and advise on matters of state. The reason for this is what you have often heard me say before on many occasions: that I am subject to a divine or supernatural experience, which Meletus saw fit to travesty in his indictment. It began in my early childhood—a sort of voice which comes to me; and when it comes it always dissuades me from what I am proposing to do, and never urges me on. It is this that debars me from entering public life, and a very good thing too, in my opinion; because you may be quite sure, gentlemen, that if I had tried long ago to engage in politics, I should long ago have lost my life, without doing any good either to you or to myself. Please do not be offended if I tell you the truth. No man on earth who conscientiously opposes either you or any other organized democracy, and flatly prevents a great many wrongs and illegalities from taking place in the state to which he belongs, can possibly escape with his life. The true champion of justice, if he intends to survive even for a short time, must necessarily confine himself to private life and leave politics alone.

(Plato, 1954, pp.37–8)

Socrates' trial has, of course, provided the very public platform which the mask of the private man disavows. The irony is compounded by the fact that he is, indeed, about to lose his life for refusing to silence that inner voice which he claims as his contact with divine wisdom. The persona that Plato projects of Socrates has come down to us as an archetype; living in poverty, detached from dominant society and discourses of his day, and offering moral insights and prophecies without regard for personal considerations. The speaking of what he perceived to be 'the truth' overrides all other considerations. As well as his function, his style or method has become equally important. With the exception of his trial which furnishes an opportunity for a set-piece defence of his life, his habitual method for revealing this truth is dialectical: he draws out his interlocutor's position and then exposes its contradiction. It is a method which relies on dialogue that feeds off the stimulus offered by the antagonist's position. It has no predetermined one of its own but develops an argument that follows the dictates of an absolute morality, a belief in good, wherever those dictates lead from that opening position. It is, therefore, the strategy of the student-centred educator who knows that people only change their positions, only open themselves to new knowledge, at the point where they feel able to accept ownership of the understanding. The core of this understanding is the willingness to use knowledge in the service of wisdom, not of power. It is this application that leads Socrates, Plato and all who have since followed them, away from politics and the fulfilment of personal ambition into a life that is depicted in terms of the ways of the world as at best unreasonable and at worst mad.

My purpose here is not to claim that Socrates is the first fool in western culture but rather to establish that many of the qualities which are associated with folly, particularly the mounting of social criticism from behind a mask or persona of detachment, are vital elements in the Socratic tradition and stem from an unfavourable comparison between politics and morality. Where Socrates, or perhaps only Plato, depart from the sphere of folly is in the desire to construct coherent alternatives to the corrupt or compromised political formations of their day. The fool tends to be more sceptical of human capability and to be content with the exposure of the folly of ambition. Nevertheless in terms of a coherent discourse it is hard to ascribe a fixed position to the Socrates who is depicted in *The Symposium* and *The Last Days of Socrates*. Rather than declaring a position, he operates as a conscience, requiring his antagonists to reveal their own positions through the responses they give to his questions. He is like a virus that attacks the weakest point of the system, forcing a breakdown in previously held certainties or the comedian who forces a confrontation between an audience and its own contradictions.

Whatever his actual or supposed importance to the society of ancient Greece, his impact on European culture in general and traditions of humanism in particular can be gauged from the manner in which he is celebrated by Rabelais in the Author's Prologue to *Gargantua*:

Most noble boozers, and you my very esteemed and poxy friends – for to you and you alone are my writings dedicated – when Alcibiades, in that dialogue of Plato's entitled *The Symposium*, praises his master Socrates, beyond all doubt the prince of philosophers, he compares him, amongst other things to a Silenus. Now a Silenus, in ancient days, was a little box, of the kind we see to-day in apothecaries' shops, painted on the outside with such gay, comical figures as harpies, satyrs, bridled geese, horned hares, saddled ducks, flying goats, stags in harness, and other devices of that sort, light-heartedly invented for the purpose of mirth, as was Silenus himself, the master of good old Bacchus. But inside these boxes were kept rare drugs, such as balm, ambergris, cardamum, musk, civet, mineral essences, and other precious things.

Just such an object, according to Plato, was Socrates. For to view him from the outside and judge by his external appearance, no one would have given a shred of an onion for him, so ugly was his body and so absurd his appearance, with his pointed nose, his bovine expression, and his idiotic face. Moreover his manners were plain and his clothes boorish; he was blessed with little wealth, was unlucky in his wives, and unfit for any public office. What is more, he was always laughing, always drinking glass for glass with everybody, always playing the fool, and always concealing his divine wisdom. But had you opened that box, you would have found inside a heavenly and priceless drug: a superhuman understanding, miraculous virtue, invincible courage, unrivalled sobriety, unfailing contentment, perfect confidence, and an incredible contempt for all those things men so watch for, pursue, work for, sail after, and struggle for.

(Rabelais, 1955, p.37)

The 'priceless drug' is better protected for being contained within such an unlikely case. Similarly, many of the most profound and uncomfortable insights into the human condition are delivered by outwardly unprepossessing characters wearing the masks of idiot, simpleton, rogue and trickster. This might be described as the whole method of Rabelais in *Gargantua and Pantagruel* which, beneath its immense rambling exterior of behavioural and linguistic excess, punctures the pretensions and vanities of late medieval Europe. Like Socrates before him, Rabelais is not afraid to expose himself to the wrath of the establishment in the quest to depict the realities of motive and behaviour among his fellow men. His attacks are not made in order to replace one corrupt system with another but rather to deplore all systems that cripple human potential through injustice, prejudice and selfishness. Being prominent among the powerful, it is not surprising that the Church figures as a prime target:

> There was a canting liar preaching at Cinais to the same tune, that St Anthony sent fire into men's legs, and St Eutropius sent the dropsy, and St Gildas sent madness, and St Genou the gout. But I made such an example of him, although he called me a heretic, that not a single hypocrite of that kidney has ventured to enter my territories to this day. I'm surprised that your king allows them to preach such scandalous doctrine in his kingdom. Why, they deserve worse punishment than those practitioners of magical arts and suchlike who, they say, actually did bring the plague into this country. Pestilence only kills the body, but these imposters poison the soul.

(Rabelais, 1955, pp.136–7)

The moral authority for this humanist stance is all the greater for the fact that Rabelais was a monk, pointing out the width of the discrepancy that had opened up in the sixteenth century between what the Catholic Church professed to be and what it actually was. Just as Socrates exposes the limitations of Athenian democracy from inside the *polis*, so Rabelais takes on the failings of the Church not as a Protestant outsider but as one who wishes to see Catholicism as the support not the antagonist of humanity. Like Erasmus and, to an extent, More, who follow him along this path, he feels it necessary to adopt this persona of near insanity in order to deliver his human truths. Given the madness of a world driven by egotism, folly is the only possible mask to adopt in order to get a hearing. The next chapter will explore in more detail some of the ways in which this type of humanism influenced the drama of the late medieval period in England. For the moment I am concerned only to establish the presence of folly as a mask at the heart of the Socratic tradition and, furthermore, as a concept fundamental to that branch of Christianity espoused by the Renaissance humanists.

This aspect of the Christian tradition owes its origin to St Paul and in particular the Letters to the Corinthians though the fool makes several appearances in the Old Testament, most notably in the person of Joseph. His famous 'coat of many colours' designates him as a fool, a keeper of wisdom and the cause of his father's favouritism and his brothers' jealousy which is exacerbated by Joseph's dreaming; the word used to describe his capacity for prophesy, another of the qualities traditionally ascribed to the fool. He sees further than his less foolish brethren, not only in the sense of knowing what will happen but aslo in his ability to spy out the real motives lurking in the minds of men as his sub-sequent career in Egypt demonstrates. Judged by the standards of the world, Paul (Saul of Tarsus) does a foolish thing in throwing away a powerful position in worldly affairs on the whim of a vision; sacrificing wealth and position to pursue the dictates of divine wisdom in the man-ner of Socrates. This dichotomy between the wisdom of the world and the foolishness of God informs the language he employs to convey the experience of being Christian. It sets up an opposition that was much favoured in the Renaissance according to the principle of inversion and which is picked up by Elizabethan and Jacobean dramatists to point the difference between witty fools and foolish wits.

> But God hath chosen the foolish things of the world to confound the wise; and God hath chosen the weak things of the world to confound the things which are mighty.
>
> (Bible, 1 Corinthians 1 v.27)

> Let no man deceive himself. If any man among you seemeth to be wise in this world, let him become a fool, that he may be wise. For wisdom of this world is foolishness with God.
>
> (Bible, 1 Corinthians 3 v. 18–19)

Pauline doctrine inaugurates a long line of literary persona who are depicted by their creators as fools in order that they may be granted the licence to speak wisdom with impunity. At times this process is aligned with a specifically religious vision, at other times the morality displayed is secular. But the types share a mutual feeling of being at odds with their times, out of step with those around them who pursue status, power or wealth. It is as if the mask of folly caused their fellow humans to shrink back from them and in so doing create the space or distance from which these fools can more clearly discern the limitations of the world. Rather than being a tributary of the mainstream of Christianity, the notion of foolish faith encompasses a core attribute of Jesus Christ. As the Son of God and the Son of Man, he commutes between the divine and the human through his ability to inhabit both worlds. In so doing he resembles the tricksters of so-called primitive societies as well as Hermes, conveyor of messages between gods and men. Christ is the archetypal fool, prepared like Socrates to die for a way of thinking, and caring nothing for the things that normal, reasonable people hold dear.

The traditions of St Paul and Socrates alike challenge the notion of a binary opposition between wisdom and folly. Their insights rather suggest some kind of dialectical relationship where folly is an indication of wisdom lurking within and the only language that wisdom can speak through is that of foolishness.

What follows is not an attempt to trace the entirety of this tradition through these secular and religious lines from their origins until the present but rather a selective consideration, mainly confined to Europe, of the influence of this area of folly and its comic representations on dramatic works with particular attention to the relationship of the fool to the dominant ideology in the world of the play. Whether by coincidence, as a result of the peculiar interests of the author, or because there is an intrinsic connection, most of this study will look at two of the periods when Europe was undergoing great ideological battles over the direction that government should take. Firstly, from the late fifteenth to the early seventeenth century when feudalism broke up and was gradually replaced by the formations that were to contain capitalism and secondly, from the late nineteenth to the mid twentieth century when capitalism was challenged by socialism. In each case it seems that when the most questions were being raised and doubts expressed about how human societies should be organised, the voice of folly, particularly in its dramatic disguise, was heard loudest and most frequently.

Because there is no such thing as an ideology of fooling, any attempt to delineate a tradition of folly is akin to seeking a leitmotif within swirling fog. In trying to develop a conceptual framework within which to set the analysis of specific dramatic works and performances, it is necessary to pursue similarities and tendencies, hints and possibilities rather than expecting to structure arguments into tidy patterns that tie up loose ends. At various historical moments it is tempting to ascribe conservative, reactionary qualities to folly and the fools who articulate its insights but this is, at least, a partial misunderstanding. The foolish muse was as active in its subversion of Catholic orthodoxies in the Middle Ages as it has been in puncturing the myths of progress in our own times. Yet to describe folly as apolitical will not do either. The interventions of fools are frequently highly charged with political intent but they are not mounted from a fixed position or in the service of the agendas of political parties. The discourses which are under investigation here are intrinsically oppositional: they oppose those processes by which people create illusions about their natures, intentions and interests. Paradoxically folly is the instrument for exposing false positions, hypocrisies and self-interest. As such it is, itself, disinterested. To achieve a state where personal interest is unable to influence the stance adopted by the foolish persona, it is essential that such a persona has no ties which could compromise that detached condition. Typically this results in the figure – clown, fool, trickster or whoever – existing in a semi-detached relation to the society upon which folly preys. This quality of detachment is peculiarly appropriate to the theatrical form because theatre is the artistic mode which most nearly invites a particular society to view images of itself for delight, education, guilt, celebration or criticism. Because theatre uses actors as its basic material it is the art which most closely resembles life. The spectators can therefore be manipulated according to the strategy and intentions of the theatrical experience into an uncritical acceptance or celebration of the fictional world depicted on stage or into a critical analysis of the society presented through the fiction. One of the most typical means for achieving the latter effect is the inclusion of a clown, fool or other kind of comic mask within the stage action who is entrusted by the playwright with carrying an alternative perspective or ironic commentary on the fictional representations. Thus a double distancing effect is produced through which the performance simultaneously confronts an audience with images of its own contradictions while enabling it to laugh at characters who are and are not representatives of itself. The theatrical mask of folly operates like the ventriloquist's dummy, expressing the outrageous opinions that draw abuse down on its head while the wearer of the mask, the fool, hides safely behind the persona.

Jung in his commentary on Radin's study draws out the connection between the mythological properties of the trickster and the manifestations of folly and carnival within the medieval Catholic church. Such antics are so fundamental to human behaviour that they survived their expulsion from the church and regrouped within a range of European theatrical genres:

> These mediaeval customs demonstrate the role of the trickster to perfection, and, when they vanished from the precincts of the Church, they appeared again on the profane level of Italian theatricals, as those comic types who, often adorned with enormous ithyphallic emblems, entertained the far from prudish public with ribaldries in true Rabelaisian style.
>
> (Radin, 1972, p.199)

The reincarnation of the trickster upon the stage is not, however, simply a matter of social convenience or changing cultural habits. There is an intrinsic connection between the operation and function of the trickster at the mythological level and of the fool at the theatrical. Just as the trickster made space for ambiguity, creativity and flexibility in the archaic societies he inhabited, so the theatre is a space where the unspeakable may be spoken and the unacceptable enacted. It is a space of play in which the most playful are the survivors:

> ...trickster intelligence arises from the tension between predators and prey. Behind trickster's tricks lies the desire to eat and not be eaten, to satisfy appetite without being its object.
>
> (Hyde, 1999, p.37)

Such a description fits Harlequin perfectly as it does the antics of Falstaff on the battlefield at Shrewsbury. Besides the trickiness required for survival, the fool also exhibits another archetypal quality of the trickster; that of not belonging in any given society. As Hyde expresses it trickster has no way of being in the world but survives by the imitative skills of the 'agile parasite', thereby calling to mind the likes of Touchstone and Schweik but also more generally alluding to the basic quality of the actor which is to imitate since she presents nothing and represents everything. Coyotes, ravens and actors, especially of the foolish variety are 'consumate survivors in a shifting world' and their main means of succeeding is through 'the playful construction of fictive worlds'. In this process their stock in trade is words and they reveal themselves as inventors of language in the course of their tales and deceits for art is lying and the lies are conveyed by words. When Feste in *Twelfth Night* is asked if he is Olivia's fool, he replies: 'I am indeed not her fool, but her corrupter of words'(III.1.34). The fool of *All's Well that Ends Well* is named Parolles ('words' in French) and when his deceits and evasions are finally exposed, rather than facing the retribution of tragedy he simply responds with:

> But I will eat, and drink, and sleep as soft
> As captain shall. Simply the thing I am
> Shall make me live. Who knows himself a braggart,
> Let him fear this; for it will come to pass
> That every braggart shall be found an ass.
> Rust, sword; cool, blushes; and Parolles, live
> Safest in shame. Being fool'd, by fool'ry thrive.
> There's place and means for every man alive.

(IV.3. 309–16)

Here is the manifesto of the trickster in a nutshell. Those codes of conduct which keep others in their fixed places through mechanisms such as the operation of shame do not apply to the fool according to his own criteria for survival and survival is always the name of his game.

He is assisted in this quest for survival, paradoxically, because he occupies no acknowledged place in any social hierarchy. Where the rest of humanity relies upon notions of status in relation to occupation and function to be accorded the means of survival, the fool relies upon the opposite. The absence of any definition of decorum in relation to the fool enables him to operate as the supreme opportunist, not knowing where the next meal is coming from but knowing, thanks to his wit, that it will surely come:

> In some of the earliest European records he is designated *nebulo*, a word expressive of his social standing; he was seen as a palty, worthless fellow, a nobody. It was not merely that his position in the feudal hierarchy was low; like the minstrels, he was altogether excluded from it. Being neither lord nor cleric, freeman nor serf, he existed in a social limbo.

(Southworth, 1998, p.1)

When this fluid, nebulous quality is transposed to the stage, it puts the fool into a special category, outside the normal discourse of characterisation. So, for instance, the Madman of Fo's *Accidental Death of an*

Anarchist is at once many people, all his impersonations, and nobody; a function not a character. When an audience is introduced to a character in a play, it waits to see what the person is like, to form a judgement based on the specific circumstances offered by the playwright. However, when the fool appears there is an instant recognition based upon a shared understanding of what fools are and what they do. Some particular characteristics may follow but these are contained within the framework of fooling. Richard Burbage in some sense disguised himself to play Othello or Hamlet, but Will Kempe was always himself whether playing Bottom or Dogberry. Willeford expresses the phenomenon thus:

> The fool we see in his special relation to dramatic convention is recognizable as a person, and he interacts with each of us, the part-fools who watch him. He is a fool only in that interaction. This is not merely to say, as one could about the hero of a drama, that he mirrors something that exists within ourselves, at least as a possibility. Rather, the fool is in a unique way both the actor and the thing he enacts. He plays roles, foolish and nonfoolish, but his doing so is at every moment a direct expression of his person and of his foolish nature.
>
> (Willeford, 1969, p.66)

This process of recognition on the part of the 'part-foolish' audience, connects to an archetypal collective unconscious that reaches back to the origins of human societies. The fool enters the stage trailing, if not 'clouds of glory', at least the murky strands of an ancient fog that reminds us of our limitations as humans and that wisdom is the capacity to see how little we can see:

> The symbol which Trickster embodies is not a static one. It contains within itself the promise of differentiation, the promise of god and man. For this reason every generation occupies iself with interpreting Trickster anew. No generation understands him fully but no generation can do without him. Each had to include him in all its theologies, in all its cosmogonies, despite the fact that it realized that he did not fit properly into any of them, for he represents not only the undifferentiated and distant past, but likewise the undifferentiated present within every individual. This constitutes his universal and persistent attraction. And so he became and remained everything to every man – god, animal, human being, hero, buffoon, he who was

before good and evil, denier, affirmer, destroyer and creator. If we laugh at him, he grins at us. What happens to him happens to us.

(Radin, 1972, pp.168–9)

One measure of the health of any society is its ability and willingness to laugh at itself and, in so doing, to grasp the paradox that it stren-thens not weakens itself according to the channels it maintains for the discourses of cleansing laughter. One such channel in European soci-eties has been the theatre, though today it might be more useful to say the processes of drama since film and television are more likely to pro-vide such channels. But whether the representation is live or electronic, the social function of the art of folly is the same. This book confines itself to the theatrical mode, not in order to priviledge it, but simply in the interests of focus and coherence. We live at a time when the price of everything, including such intangibles as health and education is endlessly scrutinised by the mass-media in a clamour that drowns any consideration of values or thoughts about what it is to be human. At such a time, the wisdom of the fool is more necessary than ever as an antidote to the short-term, business dominated plans of political economy.

To summarise the conceptual framework which I am attempting to construct to contain and support the arguments on the subsequent pages, I conclude this chapter with the analysis of Leszek Kolakowski, quoted by his compatriot Jan Kott:

The Clown is he who, although moving in high society, is not part of it, and tells unpleasant things to everybody in it; he, who dis-putes everything regarded as evident. He would not be able to do all this, if he were part of that society himself; then he could at most be a drawing-room scandal-monger. The Clown must stand aside and observe good society from outside, in order to discover the non-evidence of evidence, the non-finality of its finality. At the same time he must move in good society in order to get to know its sacred cows, and have occasion to tell unpleasant things (...) The philos-ophy of Clowns is the philosophy that in every epoch shows up as doubtful what has been regarded as most certain; it reveals con-tradictions inherent in what seems to have been proved by visual experience; it holds up to ridicule what seems obvious common sense, and discovers truth in the absurd.

(Kott, 1967, p.131)

In other words it is the fool who reminds us that it is not the unanswered questions we should fear, but the unquestioned answers.

Note

*Throughout this book the masculine pronoun will be used with the fool. This is not due to unconscious sexism but rather because historically these figures were male and will avoid ugly constructions such as s/he.

2
Fooling with Carnival and Lent

FOLY: Nay, it is I that foles can make;
For be he cayser, or be he kynge,
To felowshype with Foly I can hym brynge.
[1214–16] (Skelton, *Magnyfycence*)

When Pieter Bruegel the Elder painted *the Fight between Carnival and Lent* sometime around 1559, it was already an act of recuperation if not nostalgia. The degree to which late medieval European societies processed reality in terms of such a fight can never be accurately measured but it is evident that their Renaissance or early modern successors deployed the trope regularly as a means of understanding earlier patterns of existence. The manner of Bruegel's depiction suggests that he was concerned not merely to represent one of the dominant ways in which human existence was understood but rather to present an ironic version of the struggle. Although the fight is the foreground and chief action of the painting, it is neither the highlight, nor the point to which the eye of the spectator is drawn. Both church on the right and tavern on the left emerge out of the gloom against which the fight is played out. The joyless parade of the stock emblems of Carnival and Lent – meat and fish, body and soul – suggests that it may be time to develop different ways of responding to the demands of the flesh and the spirit. Many of those shown are taking no interest in the fight and are engaged in their own activities, including making and watching some sort of theatrical performance around the figure of a green man or Robin Hood. The visual focus of the painting is a fool with his back to the proceedings, leading a man and a woman away from the fight. Folly, it would appear, has no truck with the binary opposition that had dominated so much of medieval life in the preceding centuries. It is, however, important to note that the artist could rely upon the spectator's understanding of this struggle because it had become such a familiar conceptual framework within which cultural and spiritual life could be understood. The contradictions and paradoxes released by mankind's postlapsarian state find expression through the contrary demands of body and soul. The Fall of Adam resulted in a punishment of constant toil in this life which can only be made endurable by the consolations of the flesh; consolations which imperil mankind's chances of being redeemed on the Day of Judgement. The Catholic Church's principal way of addressing this contradiction in the medieval period was by eliding holy day with holiday so that time off from toil could become both a moment for the honouring of the saints and an opportunity to satisfy the needs of the body. Work is not present in Bruegel's painting because he is depicting the holiday balance between Shrove Tuesday and Ash Wednesday; that place in the calendar that presents most vividly the contrary impulses informing life on earth.

Bruegel's contribution through painting is matched in literature by François Rabelais' carnival epics *Gargantua and Pantagruel*, published in 1534. The mighty transitions of the sixteenth century marked in the socio-political sphere by the decline of feudalism and the emergence of an early modern version of the nation state, and in the religious sphere by the Reformation and the Counter-Reformation, witnessed, at the level of culture, at least as much looking back as forward to a period of supposed stability and abundance; to 'as plentifull a world as when Abbies stoode' (McKerrow, 1958, p.171). Mikhail Bakhtin's study of Rabelais (Bakhtin, 1984) sparked off a renewed interest in reading the late medieval period from the perspective of the sixteenth century for late twentieth century cultural critics. He reinstated carnival as the major figure defining the social rhythm of the lives of the people; lives caught, as it were, between church and market-place. Where Bruegel's depiction tends to suggest that the fight is futile with the personas of Carnival and Lent equally ridiculous in their own ways, Rabelais, according to Bakhtin, offers, through carnival, an alternative world to the daily life of toil endured by most of the population; rituals of festive pleasure that both endorse and subvert the dominant ideology of Catholicism and baronial authority. Bakhtin's interpretation of Rabelais extends the notion of carnival far beyond the specific moments marked out for celebration by the medieval church calendar. For Bakhtin carnival is an alternative mode of existence that becomes both means and emblem of popular resistance. The extent to which his interpretation of medieval society was actually a projection of his subject position within the absolutist Soviet state can be endlessly and inconclusively debated, but more certain is the evidence that some remaining cultural artefacts of the period offer us about the ways in which medieval people understood the meaning of their lives. A key element in this picture is the carnivalesque and its attendant mode of laughter:

> The serious aspects of class culture are official and authoritarian; they are combined with violence, prohibitions, limitations and always contain an element of fear and of intimidation. These elements prevailed in the Middle Ages. Laughter, on the contrary, overcomes fear, for it knows no inhibitions, no limitations. Its idiom is never used by violence and authority.
>
> (Bakhtin, 1984, p.90)

The idiom can, however, be used *against* authority not so much through overt opposition that is readily identified and therefore easily destroyed, as by the more oblique strategies of play, irony and allegory where ridicule is unleashed against targets who are removed historically or geographically from the direct contact of daily, contemporary experience. This is, pre-eminently, the indirect mode of the theatrical which presents a mingling of fiction and reality through the devices of representation and disguise.

This chapter will explore the notion of the fight between Carnival and Lent as a way of analysing some examples of English theatrical production from the fifteenth and sixteenth centuries. In particular, the focus will fall upon the role and function of the fool and its association during this period with the figure of the Vice; an association which supports the integration of folly with the concerns of the flesh and hence with carnival. Taking up Bakhtin's notion of the carnival as a 'second world' which parallels the official discourse, I shall begin an examination of what happens when elements from this second world penetrate the dominant. When folly interacts with what passes for wisdom in the official world, does it foster ideological alterations in the relationships between people or does it lose itself amid the self-interested transactions of the everyday? Does the dissolution of the binary line between Carnival and Lent which becomes increasingly evident through the sixteenth century, result in a more dynamic, mobile society, heralding the arrival of modernity, or does it signal the defeat of the festive and the rout of folly? 'Merry England' as a totalising concept to account for an age when communal social structures supported an entitlement for all people to experience festive release may be a myth spawned by nostalgia and fear but what is incontrovertible is that such festive spaces were once clearly marked on the calendar as moments when certain types of behaviour, frequently involving the exercise of folly and performance, were permitted if not actively encouraged. If it was, indeed, a second world, it was one which had a firm idea of its legitimate territory and of what belonged to its expression. An increasingly important aspect of this expression was by theatrical means which in England meant the growth of the Mystery Plays, especially associated with the Feast of Corpus Christi, the Morality Plays which indicate a wide range of performance contexts, and the interludes that are particularly associated with presentation in the great houses of the Tudor period. Theatrical activity is play; time off from reality; an alternative space, itself a kind of second world with its own codes of conduct. We might reasonably expect, therefore, that it shares much in common with carnival, at least in terms of its meaning and reception by popular audiences.

One of the earliest sites for the performance of folly was purpose-built for a different purpose: worship. The Feast of Fools (Feste's Feast commonly held on Twelfth Night) was the occasion on which a bishop of fools was elected to conduct a mock or inverted mass. A popular English variant for a time was the boy bishop whose election was associated with the Feast of St Nicholas. Notwithstanding the myriad local variants scattered across Western European Catholicism from the twelfth century onwards, these rituals are marked by certain common features such as the election by the lower clergy of one from amongst their ranks to serve for a day as their 'bishop' and to lead them in a parody of the liturgy. The activities provoked by this ceremony frequently lead to admonitions and attempts to reign in excess from the senior clerics. However, the principle behind the Feast of Fools was generally endorsed by the church hierarchy during this period whether out of expediency or through a recognition of the value of these activities in cementing the faith among the lower orders:

> The reversal of roles enacted by the Bishop of Fools – where the lowly appropriate for themselves the seat of the powerful for one day, wear their garb, and mimic their authority with irreverence – is a multifaceted phenomenon of human ritual and performance.
>
> (Cochis, 1998, p.101)

It is important to note that the purpose of the ritual is not to achieve a realistic impersonation of the everyday roles but to subject those roles to the effects of folly; to show how a 'mad' or 'foolish' bishop would look and behave were the sacred and the serious to be usurped by the foolish and the comic. Of particular interest to the thesis of this book is the occurrence of the festive, transgressive 'other' at the heart of the sacred ritual; not so much a fight *between* Carnival and Lent as an intuition about the dialectical nature of their relationship. Here the second world is manifested within the official discourse of the Catholic liturgy. Carnival's excesses are a counter-narrative to the church's regular proceedings but they are organised as a reflection upon those proceedings. Parody must always pay due regard to that which is being parodied or its effect is lost. Harder to discern is the distinction between the Feast as a sanctioned release from pious devotion (time off for good behaviour) and an expression of a vital element within the sacred itself. Is this carnival controlled by the Church as a means of buttressing its own authority by demonstrating its capacity to laugh at itself or is it a revelation (as Erasmus would have it) of a quality at the heart of the Christian experience?

> Christ too, though he is the wisdom of the Father, was made something of a fool himself in order to help the folly of mankind, when he assumed the nature of man and was seen in man's form; just as he was made sin so that he could redeem sinners. Nor did he wish them to be redeemed in any other way save by the folly of the cross and through his simple, ignorant apostles, to whom he unfailingly preached folly.
>
> (Erasmus, 1971, pp.198–9)

This reading is much more that a celebration of the paradox of the 'King of the Jews' for it places folly at the core of human experience; it is not possible to be fully human without an exposure to folly. Both individuals and institutions cannot renew themselves unless they contain within themselves the means to laugh at themselves. Here there can be no *between* in Carnival's relation to Lent, no either/or between body and soul but only the discovery of the one in the other – King Lear in the Fool and the Fool in King Lear (see Chapter 5).

Among English Mystery Plays, the First and Second Shepherds' Plays in the Towneley cycle have long been regarded as one of the high points in the artistry of this genre. They are among the revisions offered by the Wakefield Master, writing during the first half of the fifteenth century. The qualities in the craftsmanship of these plays have been noted elsewhere (Brown, 1983; Hetterman, 1981; Meredith, 1994; Richardson & Johnston, 1991; for example) but their particular interest for the argument of this book lies in the ways in which the foolish or comic has been integrated into the sacred or serious; how theatre turns Christmas into carnival and how, at the core of the carnival experience, an intimation of the sacred is released. In many ways the Second Shepherd's Play offers a clear illustration of Bakhtin's notion of a second world. Of its 754 lines, only 116 are based on the annunciation of Christ's birth to the shepherds in the biblical source. All that precedes the latter can be regarded as a popular insertion into the authorised material of a Mystery Cycle whose performance marked the coming together of the dominant forces of the Catholic Church, providing the ideological basis and the official approval for the work, and of the trade guilds which supplied the means of production by which the cycles reached performance. Just as the Feast of Fools sprang from the official liturgy as a way of both mitigating and reinforcing the hierarchical distinctions of the Church, so the popular revisions to the Mystery Plays served at once to parody the biblical accounts and to demonstrate their continuing significance in the contemporary worlds depicted in these plays.

The opening sections of the Second Shepherds' Play not only establish the three shepherds as easily recognisable types inhabiting the same world as the audience for the play, they also introduce a discourse of popular resistance. The First Shepherd in particular voices his discontent at the abuses heaped on working men such as himself by the servants or hangers-on of the gentry. This description of a corrupt or fallen world operates simultaneously on several levels. Literally it shows that the state of the world requires a miracle such as the birth of Christ to redeem it from the sinful behaviour of its inhabitants while, within the double time of the action, it also demonstrates that Christ's birth did not achieve widespread reform of earthly morality but only promised a better life in the hereafter alike to the shepherds of first century Palestine as to those of fifteenth century Yorkshire. Nevertheless, it does not take a great feat of imagination to picture the empathetic response that these words may have elicited from a popular audience in holiday mood. As Robert Weimann has indicated, the amount of interaction between performers and spectators can only have enhanced the level of involvement and identification with the dramatic action (Weimann, 1978, pp.85–97). The message of Christ which was enacted to a greater or lesser extent in all carnival performances was that of inversion: the raising of the humble to the place of honour and the sending away of the wealthy, empty-handed. The complaint with which the play begins is answered at the end by the revelation of Christ's birth being granted first to the shepherds because of rather than despite their lowly status in worldly terms.

However, the efforts of the Wakefield Master amount to much more than making the content of the story accessible and relevant to a wide cross-section of the local population. The insertion of the counter-narrative of Mak and Gyll is a burlesque of a nativity built around the metaphor of Christ as the lamb of God. In this carnival version Mak plays the role of Joseph and Gyll is Mary, with the lamb of God being a stolen sheep. Joseph is transformed into a thief and trickster, the Virgin Mary into a fecund hag who produces children at least once a year and even the innocent lamb becomes a fat, foul-smelling ewe. The stage-craft of the pageant further laminates one reality onto another with the hut of Mak and Gyll doubling as the stable in Bethlehem (appropriate setting for a sheep) and the actors of Mak and Gyll doubling as Mary and Joseph (if the latter was impersonated). Alternatively it might be that the actor of Mak makes a swift costume change to reappear as the Angel while the shepherds sleep, repeating his earlier appearance among the sleeping trio; once to remove a sheep from their care and a second time to direct them to the lamb who will perform the role of good shepherd in rounding up the lost souls of humanity. The shepherds are and are not themselves throughout for in the final 'official' scene they are simultaneously the shepherds at the first Nativity, Yorkshire shepherds in the year of the play's performance and poor folk to whom Christ's birth is announced afresh each year; quarrelling, hungry, oppressed and oppressing workers and innocent souls in receipt of divine revelation. The Wakefield Master crafts the plot not only to achieve the relatively simple task of paralleling the biblical story with a burlesque contemporary version but also to enable the burlesque to live in the biblical and the biblical in the burlesque. The rejoicing over one lost sheep that is found mirrors the joy of finding the Son of God cradled among the beasts. The moment of transition from profane to sacred, from contemporary realism to symbolic representation is handled with multivalent subtlety:

> *I Pastor*: Syrs, do my reede.
>   For this trespass,
>   We will nawther ban ne flyte,
>   Fyght nor chyte,
>   Bot have done as tyte,
>   And cast hym in canvas.

[623–628] (Happé, 1975, p.289)

The logic of the grim lives represented until this point in the play would lead to the hanging of Mak as a sheep stealer but instead the shepherds are touched by the divine spirit of forgiveness while the actors of their roles are equally touched by the spirit of game or holiday and opt to toss Mak in a blanket. Even in this moment the artistry of the burlesque holds for the punishment meted out to Mak, itself a substitute for death, is also a method used to induce birth. Beside prefiguring the news of Christ's birth the ritual also conforms to the carnivalesque practice which Bakhtin identifies in many instances in Rabelais where violence leads directly to regeneration. Mak is thus a type of mock scapegoat or winter king who is beaten out at the darkest moment of the year in order that new life can emerge as the light grows stronger. His 'child' and the baby Jesus are alike addressed by the term 'day-star'. Something of the complex response of an audience to such a moment as the transition from the tossing of Mak to the appearance of the Angel is captured in the relationship which Bakhtin proposes between laughter and seriousness:

> True ambivalent and universal laughter does not deny seriousness but purifies and completes it. Laughter purifies from dogmatism, from the intolerant and the petrified; it liberates from fanaticism and pedantry, from fear and intimidation, from didacticism, naïveté and illusion, from the single meaning, the single level, from sentimentality. Laughter does not permit seriousness to atrophy and to be torn away from the one being, forever incomplete. It restores this ambivalent wholeness.
>
> (Bakhtin, 1984, pp.122–3)

The Second Shepherds' Play does not contain one character who corresponds to a fool or even to a vice though Mak clearly displays some of the latter's features, notably his transparent attempt to disguise himself and his voice and his use of magic to bewitch the shepherds into deep sleep. But he is included in the pattern of redemption in a way that would not be open to a vice. Rather the play is structured throughout to explore the relationship of folly to the sacred; to discover the foolish in the divine; to reveal the laughable paradox of divinity set amongst the humble creatures of the stable. Christmas in medieval European society was both religious festival and carnival feast; the solemnity and anticipation of Christmas Eve giving way to the laughter and excess of Christmas Day. Birth and renewal at the darkest moment of the year is a joke that laughs at the paradox at the core of survival.

The Wakefield Master's interventions into the text of *Mactatio Abel* also demonstrate his vision of the burlesque at the heart of the serious. Faced with the story of the first fratricidal murder of Abel by Cain, a parable for the divided nature of mankind with one part belonging to God and the other to the devil, he sets about establishing an atmosphere of carnivalesque irreverence and implicating the audience in the fatal action through the direct address of Cain and the machinations of Garcio, Cain's servant. His opening address to the audience not only sets a tone of obscene farce but also establishes him as a satiric commentator, half implicated in the action, half observer of it from outside:

> *Garcio*: All hayll, all hayll, both blithe and glad,
>   For here com I, a mery lad!
>   Be peasse youre dyn, my master bad,
>   Or els the dwill you spede.
>   Wote ye not I com before?
>   Bot who that ianglis any more
>   He must blaw my blak hoill bore,
>   Both behind and before,
>   Till his tethe blede.
>   Fellows, here I you forbade
>   To make nother nose ne cry;
>   Who so is so hardy to do that dede
>   The dwill hang hym up to dry.
>
>   [1–13] (Happé, 1975, pp.79–80)

Like the character who clears a performance space at the start of a mummers' play (though whether precursor or inheritor is a moot point), Garcio imposes himself upon the audience both to claim their attention and to signify what kind of attention is required. The audience is associated with Cain who is already introduced as 'bad', by its similar propensity for making noise and its punishment will be intimately connected to what Bakhtin labelled 'the lower bodily stratum'. Garcio's arse is proffered like a hell-mouth from Bruegel or the place wherein Cain will later hide unsuccessfully from God. The carnivalesque intimations which cling to Garcio are further underscored by his initial dialogue and interaction with his master, Cain:

Cayn: Gog gif the sorow, boy; want of mete it gars.
Garcio: Thare provand, sir, forthi, I lay behind thare ars,
            And tyes them fast bi the nekys,
            With many stanys in thare hekys.
Cayn: That shall bi thi fals chekys.
Garcio: And have agane as right.
Cayn: I am thi master; wilt thou fight?
Garcio: Yai, with the same mesure and weght
            That I boro will I qwite.

[44–52] (Happé, 1975, p.81)

His sarcastic inversion of the feeding of the oxen and horses by placing food at their backsides is given further substance by his defiance of
hierarchical rule in returning the blows doled out to him by his master.
Whilst associating him with both fools and regenerative scapegoats as
victims of violence, the refusal to accept this treatment passively inaugurates a feast of fools where hierarchy is overturned. Cain, like the
shepherds, is presented through a sort of double vision or simultaneous
reality; both the first murderer of the biblical story and the oppressed
fifteenth century tenant attempting to cheat a greedy and venal church
of the tithes due it by tradition. Like the devil himself, he is both arch
enemy and freedom fighter. This quality of doubleness is thrown into
relief by the antics of Garcio who is both his servant and moral commentator on him. Weimann highlights the significance of Garcio within
the development of the *platea* as a space of negotiation between stage
fiction and audience reality but he overstates his place in a coherent,
developmental progress:

> It is here that Garcio (by recalling the speech of Jack Finney and
> anticipating that of the Vice) provides a significant link between
> the medieval traditions of the folk and the popular culture of the
> Renaissance.
>
> (Weimann, 1978, p.139)

Weimann's thesis is predicated upon a notion of theatrical chronology
which organises a tidy sequence of folk play, Mystery, Morality and
Interlude culminating in the glories of Shakespeare. More likely was
a much more disorderly or random appearance of overlapping forms
where Garcio (and figures like him) embody the ethos of Bakhtin's

second or parallel world that offers a vision from the perspective of fulfilling bodily needs superimposed on the orthodox narratives of the Bible:

> ...the unofficial folk culture of the Middle Ages and even of the Renaissance had its own territory and its own particular time, the time of fairs and feasts. This territory, as we have said, was a peculiar second world within the official medieval order and was ruled by a special type of relationship, a free, familiar, marketplace relationship. Officially the palaces, churches, institutions, and private homes were dominated by hierarchy and etiquette, but in the marketplace a special kind of speech was heard, almost a language of its own, quite unlike the language of Church, palace, courts, and institutions.
>
> (Bakhtin, 1984, p.154)

The particular originality of the Wakefield Master and those like him was to import this language into an institutional context – the institution of theatre. The special excitement or possibility of the medieval and Renaissance theatre is that it becomes the meeting place, or perhaps battleground, for the contest of these two discourses and the ideological positions that underpin them.

Garcio's appearance at the end of the episode continues to undermine Cain's hope of pardon and his escape to a higher physical level leaves Cain and the audience in the same place to share God's curse until redeemed by later events in the cycle. Garcio's role does not undermine the orthodox moral of the story but it does complicate the audience's reception of it. From an event in the distant past of biblical history, it becomes as well a contemporary moment that evokes the political and moral controversies surrounding the payment of tithes and the abuse of authority. In 'carnivalising' the official discourse the Wakefield Master has begun to explore the ways in which figures associated with folly mediate the action to the audience. The likes of Mak and Garcio are more than prototypes for Feste and Lear's Fool, however, since they are the means by which dominant ideology is subjected to the humanising processes of laughter and irony by which contradiction is revealed.

Weimann's attachment to a linear teleology reaching towards the golden vision of Shakespeare tends to provoke an overemphasis on the differences between the mysteries and the moralities (Weimann, 1984, p.98) at the expense of a comparison of the ways in which they each present the relationship between Carnival and Lent. The further significance of this way of depicting the actuality of human life is nowhere more vividly illustrated than in *Mankind*, traditionally labelled a morality play but also exhibiting many of the traits of an early version of an interlude in terms of setting (the interior of a tavern or else an inn yard), the fluidity of the interactions between actors and audience with the Vice and his cohorts regularly entering and exiting among the spectators as well as making both general and specific reference to them, and the small company of travelling players which was to become a characteristic of the later form. Notwithstanding these aspects of production, the narrative is unambiguously that of the morality play with the struggle for the soul of mankind at its centre. That this struggle is a theatrical version of Breugel's depiction is made clear upon Mankind's first appearance:

> *Mankind*: My name is Mankind. I have my composition
> Of a body and of a soul, of condition contrary.
> Betwixt the twain is a great division:
> He that should be subject, now he hath the victory.
>
> [ll.194–7] (Lester, 1981, p.14)

Mankind is the representative within the drama of the audience, all of whom are implicated in this battle as Mercy makes explicit at the opening of the play or 'game': "O sovereigns! I beseech you your conditions to rectify" (p.13). This trope which permeates the drama of late medieval England with increasing intensity is here located within the contrary being of every man. Life on earth is defined as contradiction since man's soul, destined for heaven or hell, has to endure the corruption of the flesh during his (*sic*) brief stay. The flesh requires a different type of nourishment from the soul; feasting rather than fasting; lewd songs rather than prayer; sexual gratification rather than abstinence. Those virtues which are the soul's allies would have us prepare for the life to come through asceticism and contemplation while those vices which adopt the body's cause would have us live this life to the full at the extremity of our senses. Though the struggle itself may be articulated in the starkest binary terms, the context for the battle is replete with paradox. If the inspiration for the morality plays was to awaken sinful men to the need to prepare their souls for eternity, the choice of the form, play, was one that ensured that the advocates of the spiritual life, in this instance Mercy, would have to achieve an away win. As is made clear throughout, play, or 'game' as it is most often called, is the province or natural habitat of the vices. Attendance at a theatrical spectacle which is constructed as agit-prop on behalf of the soul thus requires something of an ambivalent attitude on the part of the audience from the outset. This notion is exploited fully in the action of the play where the theatrical energy and rapport with the audience is located among the representatives of the flesh. The occasion of the performance is itself festive: either part of the Christmas indulgence or Shrove Tuesday's Carnival and the location was most probably a tavern; a place specifically given over or licensed to support the desires of the flesh. The practice of playing is itself associated with holiday and idleness; a dangerous distraction from the daily requirement to earn bread through honest toil. Yet this Lenten prescription is the consequence of man's fall from grace; a punishment for sins against God whereas festive leisure might be regarded as a reminder of the nature of life before the Fall, like Christ's reference to the lilies of the field: 'they toil not neither do they spin'. Though there is certainly no suggestion of anything laudable, still less graceful, in the actions of Mischief and his henchmen, they do perhaps point to another possibility, another aspect to existence; that very aspect which has brought the audience into contact with these players in the first place. This sense of two worlds in one extends beyond content into the genre itself where the profane operates within the sacred and the sacred within the profane:

> ...the notion of carnival is present in both the uncontroversial, restricted sense (the play alludes to Shrove Tuesday and Christmas customs) and in the elaborated Bakhtinian sense: it is a Janus-faced play in which a stilted, courtly style (aureation) is explicitly associated with the Church as a temporal authority, and set against an 'underworld' of festive, tavern, comic infernal and excremental language which parodies the 'high' language. Usually treated as a morality play, it is more usefully seen as compounding two genres, one official, the other unofficial, by punning between the morality play structure (the fall, repentance and salvation of mankind) and a festive structure (the battle between the licence of Christmas and the prohibitions of Lent).
>
> (Gash, 1986, p.82)

This idea of the simultaneous operation of two different kinds of reality is amply illustrated in the opening dialogue between Mercy and Mischief around the subject of the Day of Judgement. Where Mercy offers authority's orthodox allegory of the separation of the corn from the chaff, Mischief, himself apparently looking for work as a winter corn-thresher, responds at the literal, realistic level where not only is the chaff not to be burnt but used as animal feed, but even the straw is valuable as fuel. There are clear class implications at work in the exchange for the cleric, comfortable in this life and so with an eye on the next, may be in a position to waste the chaff and straw but the peasant has to be mindful of the value of commodities in the here and now. Though Mischief may be a corrupter of Mercy's words, those words may themselves be an indication of social division reflected in the discourse of Carnival and Lent. It is just possible that this kind of class division, later to be replicated in the Elizabethan playhouse, is beginning to establish itself among the audiences for this play since Mercy refers to the audience in two categories: "O! ye sovereigns that sit, and ye brothern that stand right up" (Marshall, 1997, pp.189–202).

Much of the stage business which takes place between Mankind and Nought, New Guise and Nowadays, such as the beating with the spade, conforms to the set-piece farcical insertions of moralities and interludes. Here Mankind attempts to deal with the regular, even routine, temptations of daily life. The encounters with Mercy and Titivillus are of another order and it is they who prove too strong for Mankind with their respective forces of good and evil. Given their roles in the scheme of salvation, it is a bold stroke of the playwright to present them in certain ways as mirror images. It is more than likely that the original performance conditions required the same actor to play both parts. The connection is further enhanced by Mischief's early description of Mercy in terms of a mummers play character: 'Yowur wytt ys lytyll, yowur hede ys mekyll'. As well as associating Mercy with the beheading game that Mischief engages in later on, the reference to a big head will echo in the memory of the audience when the same actor dons the head of a giant puppet to perform the role of Titivillus, the focal point of the carnival presentation. Mankind's daily life oscillates between the carnival foolishness of the body as represented by the earthy vices and the Lenten devotions of the soul as endorsed by Mercy. But the special moment in the presentation, the moment that the audience is required to pay for is the appearance of the diabolical Titivillus. His effect upon the spectators is complex, combining terror with the capacity to dismiss fear through laughter. Yet more complex is his relationship to Mercy since the power of Mercy to command Mankind to the path of salvation depends upon the latter's belief in the power of Titivillus to damn him. This perception of the interdependence of good and evil, processed here in terms of a fight between Carnival and Lent, goes some way towards explaining medieval drama's predilection for inversion; for finding folly at the heart of wisdom and wisdom as the defining characteristic of folly. God's 'other' is Lucifer and the spirit of resistance which 'foolish' characters reinterpret as a demand for social justice, paradoxically owes its origins to the first rebellion:

> It is only by referring to the dialectical structure of Christmas against Lent that we can point to the play's ambiguity – an ambiguity which as we have shown was fundamental to festive practices themselves.
>
> (Gash, 1986, pp.93–4)

It is, I believe, this quality of ambiguity that operates at the core of what Bakhtin called 'popular-festive forms' and endowed them with that potency and vitality that made them a progressive force for social renewal and even, at times, transformation:

> ... popular-festive images became a powerful means of grasping reality; they served as a basis for an authentic and deep realism. Popular imagery did not reflect the naturalistic, fleeting, meaningless, and scattered aspect of reality but the very process of becoming, its meaning and direction. Hence the universality and sober optimism of this system.
>
> (Bakhtin, 1984, pp.211–12)

Though the last sentence may betray a Marxist affiliation that contemporary reality tends to belie, there is in this analysis an attempt to capture the spirit that some of the works of English medieval theatre might have evoked in their original audiences; a spirit that had much in common with Erasmus' notion of folly as a fundamental element of human society.

The prominence of the Vice in the plays commonly labelled Tudor Interludes has long been noted:

> In a number of plays his [the Vice's] is the only part which cannot be doubled. He strives to make a quick rapport with the audience and was probably costumed so extravagantly (making great play with his ludicrous wooden dagger) as to have an immediate effect upon the audience, who would know how to respond to his tricks as soon as he appeared before them.
>
> (Weimann, 1978, p.156)

This is, however, a double-edged importance. Though the Vice is entrusted with more dramatic functions than any other character in most moralities and interludes, he is also more readily identifiable and therefore containable. As Happé points out, the audience knows what to expect; the Vice has become something of a theatrical cliché. With this development comes the risk of a loss of that very ambiguity that was the source of his capacity to disturb and surprise. Part of this process is signalled in Weimann's reduction of the figure to structural functions:

> If, therefore, the varying structural functions of the Vice are taken into account, at least three aspects must be examined more closely: the Vice as protagonist and opponent to the figures of Virtue; the Vice as intriguer and manipulator of the representatives of humanity; and the Vice as producer, manager, and commentator.
>
> (Weimann, 1978, p.156)

While this works well enough as a generic description that covers the different emphases placed on the various figures who function as or are actually labelled the Vice, it is in danger of compartmentalising and then explaining away the peculiar power of the figure; a power invested in his capacity for foolish rebellion, for inevitably and ultimately futile resistance. In the event, the development of the interludes, responding to changes in both presentational practices and social climate, resulted in just such a fragmentation. The move from the community performance practices of the mystery plays to the professional touring of small companies meant that the 'serious' and comic plots became separated so that actors could double the parts. While this increased scope for performance irony in some cases, it also signalled the emergence of plays that could respond to the diverse tastes of a more socially divided audience. A play as early as Henry Medwall's *Fulgens and Lucres* (1515) already exhibits this tendency to view different parts as being appropriate for different tastes within the audience:

> For some there be that lokis and gapys
> Only for suche trifles and iapys,
> And some there be amonge
> That forceth lytyll of suche madness,
> But delytyth them in matter of sadness,
> Be it never so longe.
>
> [30–5] (Happé, 1972, p.84)

Although Medwall has rightly been praised for the skill with which he uses the two comic servants, A and B, both to cast the wooing main plot into ironic relief and to exploit the metatheatrical joke of multi-layered fiction, there is already a sense in which the common engagement of a community with the rituals of survival, characteristic of the mystery plays, has been lost in the transition to a more secular and socially specific form. As far as the Vice is concerned, many of the dramatic functions identified by Weimann have been retained but some of the moral functions have lapsed. The three tier universe of heaven, earth and hell configured in the pageant arrangement for the mystery plays led, as Weimann has effectively shown, to an important demarcation in the activities variously appropriate to *locus* and *platea*. In this arrange-ment the *locus* is the site of authority; the theatrical space that becomes the equivalent of altar or pulpit from whence the official message or approved story can be declaimed. By contrast the *platea* is frequently employed as a counter-narrative space from which an ironic perspective on the 'main' events can be cast. It is also a space less firmly demar-cated for the stage fiction where interventions from the real world of the audience, scripted or improvised, can be launched. It is the domain of the fool, servant or vice; figures who operate both in and out of the fiction emanating from the *locus*. Though the physical (and usually the moral) demarcation is lost in the more fluid stage space of the interludes and later of the Elizabethan court and public theatres, this tradition of exploiting levels of theatrical reality or building ambivalence into the layers of the fiction persisted and was reflected in the proximity of the actor to the audience. Characters who inhabit the *platea* or, later, forestage, manipulate the theatrical paradox whereby drawing attention to the unreality of the fiction being staged behind them strengthens the audience's capacity to believe in what they are seeing and to connect it to their own experiences:

> Their [those characters who are descended from the Vice] dramatic function is not a farcical one, but involves that special relation-ship with the audience which results from a *platea*-like position and allows the statement of generalized truth in a choric mode. Theirs, indeed, are "countervoices" – voices from outside the representative ideologies – ushering in a contrapuntal theme, some countervision which, even in a comic context, cannot be easily dismissed in its thematic implications for the main plot.
>
> (Weimann, 1978, p.159)

The question lurking beneath Weimann's analysis of this transition from the late medieval to the early modern is whether the 'counter-vision' offers an alternative – Vice or Virtue; Carnival or Lent – or a dialectical vision of the plebeian, parodic 'Other' at the core of the 'representative ideology'? To the extent that Barber is right when he asserts that

> ... the clown or Vice, when Shakespeare started to write, was a rec-
> ognized anarchist who made aberration obvious by carrying release
> to absurd extremes. The cult of fools and folly, half social and half
> literary, embodied a similar polarization of experience.
>
> (Barber, 1963, p.5)

to the same extent the observation denotes both the loss and the gain from medieval practices. Anarchists tend to lose much of their capacity to surprise and reorder the world once they are recognised and figures such as Mak and Garcio rather than polarising experience, imbued it with a sense of disturbing ambiguity (not only this but also that).

Barber's relentless insistence upon the festive, though opening up a discourse that has enabled subsequent scholars, directors and performers to locate Shakespeare within a popular (albeit nostalgic) tradition, has also tended to obscure some of this quality of ambiguity and neutralises something of the threat that carnival carried towards the state:

> The scenes of the Jack Cade rebellion in that history are an aston-
> ishingly consistent expression of anarchy by clowning: the popular
> rising is presented throughout as a saturnalia, ignorantly undertaken
> in earnest...
>
> (Barber, 1963, p.13)

Much hinges on Barber's telling adverb 'ignorantly' and the extent to which Cade in *Henry VI Part 2* uses his 'ignorance' as the mask behind which he hopes to enact his carnival transgressively without incurring the ultimate sanction of the state. Stephen Longstaffe has sought to read the presentation of Cade against the grain of the dominant by invoking the presence of Will Kempe as the actor of the role of Cade and thereby suggesting that there is an enhanced space for ambiguity lurking in the signifying gap between actor and character:

> But the alternative that I wish to explore is that Cade can be per-
> formed as deliberately signalling at its outset that the rising is ludic
> and ludicrous, carnivalesque, aware of its own contradictions, and
> that Kemp as a performer could well have dialogically provided a

presentation of Cade the character, in which the two senses of the word 'clown' interacted so as to cast doubt who was who.

(Longstaffe, 1998, p.21)

The only problem here is with the notion of 'alternative' as though the spectator must opt for a reading that either presents Cade as a dangerous and barbaric threat to the state or as the self-conscious master of ceremonies, presiding over a seasonal carnival. Whatever Kempe may have made of him within the 'reality' of the playhouse, within the fiction of the drama Cade is both of these possibilities. In the medieval spirit that combines both Garcio and Cain, Cade temporarily thrusts carnival into the heart of the state and makes a theatrical show out of authority. By exposing his own blatant theatricality, or having it exposed by Kempe, Cade reveals the suspect base upon which rank and power is built.

The entire episode of the Cade rebellion is framed in terms that would have been familiar to the audience from any exposure to medieval drama. When the rebels first appear, one reference instantly places them, both theatrically and morally: "Come and get thee a sword, though made of a lath" [IV.2.1]. They are committing the treasonous act of taking up arms but simultaneously characterising themselves as representatives of the faction of the 'old Vice' of the Moralities with his 'dagger of lath'. They are performing the uprising like an old play, already aware of the ending even in the beginning. They know that they are enacting a fantasy, embodying Utopian contradictions, by imagining that their actions might return the realm to some mythic condition that predates hierarchy and social distinction: "Well, I say it was never merry world in England since gentlemen came up" [IV.2.8-9]. 'Merry world' is a euphemism for carnival, now imagined as a permanent state which nonetheless still carries a contradiction between the inversion of established order and its obliteration:

> *Cade*: My father was a Mortimer –
> *Dick*: [*Aside*] He was an honest man and a good bricklayer.
> *Cade*: My mother a Plantagenet –
> *Dick*: [*Aside*] I knew her well; she was a midwife.
> *Cade*: My wife descended of the Lacies –
> *Dick*: [*Aside*] She was, indeed, a pedlar's daughter, and sold
> many laces.

[IV.2.37–44]

If Cade's ambitions were really egalitarian, the last claim he would wish to make would be that of nobility. In fact, he never escapes from a self-image as a king of Carnival or Lord of Misrule whose reign is predicated upon its brevity; its function as an interruption to the rule of law which thereby reminds subjects of the necessity of traditional governance. As Longstaffe suggests the audience at no time during these scenes loses sight of the playful dimension underscored by the antics of Kempe's interpretation of the role:

> So for the first scene, imagine Kemp/Cade flanked by Dick and Smith, who address their undercutting comments to an audience, on stage or off, joining Cade's illusion-breaking parody of a claim to the throne with their own parody of supporting such a claim, which effectively establishes 'Cade' as a commoner, and the rising as predicated upon a carnivalesque doubleness, whose keynote is their ability to moralize two meanings in one word.
>
> (Longstaffe, 1998, p.28)

The convention of the 'aside' needs qualifying as applied to the performance of carnival. Whereas in a 'straight' theatrical performance it is a means of revealing a reality beyond the fiction in which the scene is presented, usually to allow for the play of irony between action and audience, in carnival this alternative perspective is part of the action itself. In medieval performance the audience are at once in the presence of God and of the particular member of the guild who always plays God; so here there is both Cade and Kempe; within Cade both the clothier and the pretender to the throne; within Kempe both the actor performing the role of Cade and the *extempore* stand-up comedian. Because there are at least two simultaneous performances, it is possible to laminate the grotesque onto the serious and turn death into a laughing matter. If there was any doubt about whether this degree of self-consciousness is present in the composite 'Cade', one exchange places the issue beyond uncertainty:

> *William Stafford*: Jack Cade, the Duke of York hath taught
> you this.
> *Cade*:   [*Aside*] He lies, for I invented it myself –
>
> [IV.2.149–50]

Stafford, bound by the constraints of the historical narrative, cannot operate like Cade who slips between levels of identity from moment to moment depending on the particular phase of the carnival that he is enacting. In the theatre identity, like death, is always temporary and the clown is adept at making a plaything of both:

Cade: I charge and command that, of the city's cost, the pissing-
         conduit run nothing but claret wine this first year of our
         reign. And now henceforth it shall be treason for any that
         calls me other than Lord Mortimer.

Enter a Soldier running

Soldier: Jack Cade! Jack Cade!
Cade: Knock him down there. [*They kill him*]
Smith: If this fellow be wise, he'll never call ye Jack Cade more;
         I think he hath a very fair warning.

[IV.6.3–10]

This is the mode of slapstick and even in death the hapless soldier is used as the butt of humour. Indeed, the scene plays as if the only point of his entrance and death is to make a joke and to demonstrate the absurdity of Cade's pretensions. Yet within the stage fiction a man is wantonly slain. This death is not just the regenerative violence that Bakhtin identifies throughout Rabelais, it is also loss of life like Cain's murder of Abel.

The rebellion finishes as abruptly and easily as it had begun for Cade created it as a carnival intermission, a utopian possibility of time out from the real world. All the iconography of his death is presented as the ultimate contrast to his life. Instead of a carnival of the streets with plenty and holiday, Shakespeare presents a starving man invading the private space of a private, bourgeois man. The conservative, complacent Squire Iden in the Eden of his Kentish garden restores normal service to the realm after the intermission of rebellion. He represents those most English of virtues, knowing his place and being contented with his lot:

Sufficeth that I have maintains my state,
And sends the poor well pleased from my gate.

[IV.10.22–3]

Perhaps there lurks here some premonition of William Shakespeare, gentleman, throwing in his lot with the Stratford bourgeoisie from the secluded bower of his garden at New Place.

In *2 Henry VI* carnival, in the form of Cade's rebellion, oversteps the mark, betrays the playful laws of carnival and mistakes itself for an intervention into the course of history, a challenge to the workings of the everyday world. It has the uncanny appearance of a theatrical rerun of events some ten years earlier when carnival in the French provincial town of Romans ended with bloody consequences in 1580 as related in the meticulous work of the micro-historian Emmanuel Ladurie (Ladurie, 1981). He charts the gradual build up of social tension in Romans and the wider region as a result of growing economic and religious divisions. The Mardi Gras Carnival became a means of acting out these tensions symbolically through the rivalries of the confraternities, conforming to the 'safety-valve' version of the function of carnival, the second life of the people. But in 1580 the popular factions used the occasion of the carnival to challenge the authority of the aristocratic and bour-geois elements in ways which caused the latter to respond by using the cover of the carnival with its pseudo-military configurations to slaughter the leading personalities of the opposition and restore 'order' through the reestablishment of their Lenten authority. Unlike *2 Henry VI* where Cade's discourse is isolated from the main political characters, Ladurie was struck by the way in which Carnival was a discourse understood by all sections of Romans society and therefore capable of operating as a kind of social cement until the mortar was torn off by the transgression from the symbolic into the realm of the concrete:

> Even in Romans, division did not exclude synthesis. Paumier and Guérin were mortal enemies; still they communed intellectually through a Carnival folklore which constituted their 'code', linguis-tically speaking. They played contradictory roles in the Carnival, but it was the natural element for them both. Despite their rivalry to the death, they were cultural brothers.
>
> (Ladurie, 1981, p.338)

In both fact and fiction the position of carnival became increasingly problematic as the sixteenth century was drawing to a close. The notion of a separate or parallel space in which carnival could operate without consequence that Bakhtin highlights as the essence of Rabelais' nov-els looks increasingly like an act of nostalgia for a more certain world of religious and social fixity. In that more confident polity, communi-ties could afford to accommodate the inversions and parodies of power relations which are the stuff of carnival whereas the insertion of the carnivalesque into the frayed social fabric of the early modern period provoked responses that compromised the continuing tolerance of car-nival as a form susceptible to political exploitation. James Scott clearly recruits carnival into the ranks of popular resistance in his analysis of the significance of the events in Romans:

However much the aristocrats and property owners of Romans may have wished to orchestrate Carnival into a ritual reaffirmation of existing hierarchies, they failed. Like any ritual site, it could be infused with the signs, symbols, and meanings brought to it by its least advantaged participants as well. It might symbolize the folly of disorder or it might, if appropriated from below, break out of its ritual straightjacket to symbolize oppression and defiance. What is striking historically about carnival is not how it contributed to the maintenance of existing hierarchies, but how frequently it was the scene of open social conflict.

(Scott, 1990, pp.180–1)

But importantly it was a 'scene', a place where social conflict could be performed. If the laws of theatre and the conventions of carnival were transgressed, it ceased to be available to communities as either a ritual of affirmation or of resistance. Once carnival forgets its place, loses that 'doubleness' so characteristic in late medieval drama, and inserts itself into the daily political discourse; becomes as it were the 'Other' of the dominant ideology, it ceases to function as a communal regenerative force and is reduced to the factionalism of partisan interests.

I have located the primary source of the double perspective within the figure of the Vice and his many associates. In works such as *The Second Shepherds' Play* and *Mankind* this figure or his current representative is more than simply the diabolical antagonist of God. Although finally he serves to endorse the Christian message in his defeat, the manner of his presentation ensures that he becomes the focal point of many of the contradictions that result from inhabiting a mortal body subject to change and decay. This particular quality of doubleness in medieval drama seems to be constantly underemphasized by critics in search of a progressive or modernising teleology. Ruth Lunney at least adapts the discourse to provide a space into which Marlowe rather than Shakespeare can be presented as the sophisticated innovator:

In the morality tradition the framing techniques – whether they are found in explicit commentary or direct address, or in other aspects of the playworld – supported a single authorised version of the action.

(Lunney, 2002, p.103)

In the sense that the Vice does not finally triumph and succumbs to his role in the scheme of redemption, Lunney is, of course, right. But every word written has been 'authorised' or we would not be reading it today. Furthermore the effect of this playing outside the frame of the 'game' – a kind of double play or play at once within and without 'the play' – is to suggest to the audience that the orthodox Christian message can never be unproblematic, fixed or certain as a consolation. Lent will, in fact, never shed its dialectical other of Carnival. The very qualities which Lunney identifies as distinguishing Marlowe from his medieval antecedents are the ones which he inherits and remakes according to the changing world whose experiences require new theatrical modes of expression:

> Complication, shift, and contradiction: these strategies begin to dismantle the traditional structure of framing rhetoric and to transform theatrical experience. They dislodge the Vice from his interpretative role, casting him adrift to continue the organising of mischief. They unsettle preconceptions, converting a world that recalls the predictable world of the moralities into one that challenges accustomed ways of feeling and responding in the playhouse. In this process, both sides of the morality contrast are subverted.
>
> (Lunney, 2002, pp.112–13)

Whilst these 'strategies' do indeed apply to the world that Marlowe presents, the analysis that dissipates the effect of the Vice upon the audience through the splitting of functions and the insistence upon a moral binary renders the experience of the morality far more 'predictable' in the academic's study than would have been the case in performance.

Such division of function applies much more to Shakespeare's *Richard III* which largely avoids these ambiguities and paradoxes by locating his protagonist uncomplicatedly within the devil's faction. Richard knows exactly who he is and makes sure that the audience shares this understanding fully from the outset:

> And therefore, since I cannot prove a lover
> To entertain these fair well-spoken days,
> I am determined to prove a villain,
> And hate the idle pleasures of these days.
>
> [I.1.28–31]

There is no ambiguity in this statement of position. Richard appoints himself to a role familiar to the audience who will now know what to expect from him, somewhat akin to the later direct address from Prince Hal which reassures the audience as to the ultimate outcome of the *Henry IV* plays. Richard's function as villain consigns him to hell in a fixed moral scheme inherited from the morality plays. However, in no sense can he be considered a carnival figure. Indeed, his opening address places him as the enemy of 'the idle pleasures' associated with holiday festivity. He is a Machiavel, rather than a Lord of Misrule. Even his choice of mask which might recall carnival behaviour, is the Lenten appearance of an ascetic:

> And thus I clothe my naked villainy
> With odd old ends stol'n forth of Holy Writ
> And seem a saint, when most I play the devil.

> [I.3.336–8]

But this is a devil of individualism rather than a disciple of the Deadly Sins. He may share ambition and a propensity for playing with Jack Cade but little else. Though preserving the theatrical form, Shakespeare pours new wine into the old bottle. Richard plays with the gullibility and frailty of all whom he encounters, armed with an absolute cynicism which holds him aloof from forming any relationship with another human. In this particular respect he stands outside the network of developing relations even though it is his actions which are largely responsible for those relations since Shakespeare's innovation is the transforming of the Vice into the protagonist. Many of Richard's strategies are taken from the handbook of folly:

> Thus, like the formal Vice, Iniquity,
> I moralize two meanings in one word.

> [III.1.82–3]

but the single-mindedness of his pursuit of power ensures that he has no shred of the empathy which is fundamental to the performance of the true fool who values being human over being powerful. Although he acts outside any network of relationships or loyalties, bringing destruction onto the houses of York and Lancaster alike, he is the only active agent in the play until the belated stirrings of the alliance which forms around Richmond. As medieval theatre has already demonstrated in full measure, it is the active agency of the devil's disciples that proves most attractive in performance, especially when combined with the dramatic irony that arises as a result of the direct address of the Vice to the audience. If the dominant moral scheme is to be upheld, the Vice must be defeated but the handling of this defeat has to take account of the theatrical dominance of the figure lest morality triumphs at the cost of theatrical effect. Part of Shakespeare's response to this paradox is to anticipate a lessening of Richard's authority by indicating an emerging self-doubt; in modern terms the psychology of individuality challenges the abstract scheme of the morality plays. Richard is clearly and absolutely the Vice but he is also an individual, particular human being operating in a specific political context:

> ....But I am in
> So far in blood that sin will pluck on sin;
> Tear-falling pity dwells not in this eye.
>
> [IV.2.63–5]

The choice of the word 'sin' suggests that Richard is well aware of the morality he is defying even as he characterises himself as impervious to its claims. Shakespeare will return much later to exactly the same image but when it is articulated by Macbeth it carries with it the full force of self-alienation and the sense of a wasted life that is the core of the tragedy:

> ....I am in blood
> Stepp'd in so far that, should I wade no more,
> Returning were as tedious as go'er.
>
> [III.4.136–8]

A much closer parallel exists between *Richard III* and Marlowe's *Dr. Faustus*. Like Shakespeare, Marlowe relies heavily upon the inherited traditions of the morality plays and in each case the devil's disciple is defeated at the climax of the play. When Margaret predicts the outcome to Richard's reign of terror:

> Earth gapes, hell burns, fiends roar, saints pray,
> To have him suddenly convey'd from hence.
>
> [IV.4.75–76]

She uses words that are a reprise of Faustus' own vision in the moment of his demise:

> Ugly hell gape not! Come not Lucifer;
> I'll burn my books – ah Mephostophilis!

> [V.2.187–8]

Where Richard is the monolithic figure of the Vice, spiced with a little humanity, Faustus is hopelessly torn between the human and the diabolical. He is both man and devil as Marlowe locates the whole moral scheme within his person rather than, like Richard, making him more simply an agent within the greater scheme. The difference between the two is signalled in their respective languages of psychosis: 'Richard loves Richard, that is, I and I' [V.3.184]. He is immune from contact with any well-spring of humanity through the totality of his self-absorption whereas Faustus is conceived from the outset as a man wrenched from the paths of human development but conscious always of what it is costing him as a human being. Fittingly his last word is 'Mephostophilis', plausibly translated as 'I Faustus lover of myself'. But Mephostophilis has never accounted for the totality of Faustus' being in the way that he has of Richard's. Faustus has embraced a full range of human feeling and activity, including folly and the carnivalesque. He is in Lunney's term a 'debateable' character (at least until the very last moment):

> The 'debateable' character may assume the position of the Vice as focus of audience expectations and chief interpreter of the playworld, but this represents a significant displacement of framing perspective: where the Vice inverts playworld values in order to affirm them, the 'debateable' character is detached from, and often at odds with, the 'authorised' values of the playworld.

> (Lunney, 2002, p.145)

Such detachment from the dominant ideology is clearly invested in the spirit of folly as it occurs in the morality plays. The novelty of Marlowe's strategy is the placing of the debate within the breast of the figure who represents mankind; in this case, Faustus. As the representative figure for mankind begins to give way to a specific example of the species, that example includes the spirit of folly; the capacity to play and to treat playfully the most sacred aspects of his existence. Barabas is recognisable within the tradition of the Vice as one who sees through the follies of worldly values and desires from his perspective of outsider and villainous 'other'. Faustus, however, chooses to remove himself by opting for detachment and folly but surrenders that place in the end as a consequence of his fatal desire to 'resolve me of all ambiguities' rather than to live with them. Insufficient folly rather than an excess of it is his undoing.

The conclusion to *Richard III* underlines the force of the morality play in determining its structure. Richmond, England's saviour, is hardly conceived as a realistic character but much more as a symbolic one. He performs a role like that of Mercy in *Mankind*, speaking in an equivalent formal manner in contrast to the speech of his antagonist:

> Let them not live to taste this land's increase,
> That would with treason wound this fair land's peace.
> Now civil wounds are stopp'd; peace lives again.
> That she may long live here, God say Amen.

> [V.5.38–41]

In Shakespeare's version of the morality play, it is the land itself, England, that performs the role of Everyman, passively acted upon by devil and God, Richard and Richmond. In this instance the emergence of the new individualism does not threaten the traditional moral structure with the same degree of seriousness as in Marlowe's play. In both cases, however, the structure holds. Later with a play such as *King Lear*, the outcome is more doubtful.

In *Richard III* Shakespeare separates the diabolical from the comic and loses the doubleness of the medieval presentation of vice and folly. Distinct genres of tragedy and comedy are emerging where these functions will be handled more discretely. For example, in *Much Ado About Nothing* the diabolical is scaled down to the ridiculously mechanical operations of Don John while the comic is separately entrusted to Dogberry and his accomplices. Towards the end of the sixteenth century Europe is offered, in life and in art, several instances of the destructive power of carnival as challenge to the social order to which Shakespeare responds by separating carnival from political agency and restoring to it the nostalgic energy of 'merry England'. Paradoxically, once carnival has been made safe, it loses its theatrical force and is replaced by the notion of folly operating at the core of the dominant ideology as the protagonists, Hamlet, Lear and, in a particular sense, Prospero, perform as the clowns of themselves.

3
Fooling with Falstaff

> ...he's not in hell: he's in Arthur's bosom, if ever man went to
> Arthur's bosom.
>
> *(King Henry V*, II, 3, 9–10)

One way of looking at the plays Shakespeare wrote before 1599, to whatever genre they have subsequently been allotted, is as depictions of two worlds which operate in ironic counterpoint but ultimately as discrete entities unable to take on the discourses of the other. In this process the carnival world of disorder and inversion is presented as sub-plot, as time out from the 'real', serious concerns of the important, heroic characters. Even when the whole play is an escape from the real, as in the case of comedies like *A Midsummer Night's Dream* and *Much Ado About Nothing*, the structure of carnivalesque sub-plot is maintained through the antics of Bottom and the mechanicals and Dogberry and the watch. In both these cases the attempts of these figures to insert themselves into the main plots of their plays is at best awkward, at worst painful.

Not all dimensions of this structural parallelism are literary; some are performative. There is a recurrent pattern in which the character who was almost certainly played by Will Kempe tries with varying degrees of lack of success to involve himself with the main or serious plot. The clown, the jig-maker and inheritor of Tarleton's reputation for stand-up improvisations threatens at moments to wrest the play from the grasp of the playwright before bending his art to the service of the recent phenomenon of the literary text. The separation of plot and sub-plot with the confining of the clown to the latter is in itself a device for limiting the damage that improvisation might perpetrate upon the unguarded text once performance commences. By this means the popular audience gets its variety while the educated audience can condescend to their tastes before returning to the main event.

This pattern can be discerned in many plays of the period 1576–1642 in England but this chapter is primarily concerned with those written by Shakespeare before 1599: the date which is commonly felt to mark a hiatus in his development signalled by the external events of the move from the Theatre to the Globe and from Will Kempe to Robert Armin in the personnel of the Lord Chamberlain's Men. In particular the focus is on the two plays of *Henry IV* and forms and functions of carnival in relation to the workings of the state. Inevitably much of the argument revolves around the character of Sir John Falstaff and his impersonation in the performance of Will Kempe. Many of these arguments can be remade with reference to other plays of Shakespeare and to the works of other playwrights. However, the 'fortunes of Falstaff' offer a particularly sharp insight into the way in which the parallel universe of carnival does and does not influence the discourses of power in the Tudor state.

Like a latter day Vice figure from a morality play or the spirit of carnival itself, Falstaff appears fully formed at the start of *Henry IV Part 1*. Despite attempts to link him to historical and contemporary figures, he defies ancestry. Although he can, and does, die, he cannot be born; he just is. Enter Falstaff trailing clouds of anarchy from the lost world of a Rabelaisian medieval fantasy. As long as his sphere of activity is confined to Eastcheap that fantasy can be maintained, albeit at others' expense. When circumstances force Falstaff from his home territory, the (all) licensed premises of the Boar's Head, his defeat at the hands of reality is assured. Nevertheless, using all the tricks associated with theatrical performance, he gives that reality a good run for its money. His element is performance, so where better to practice it than the playhouse? The structural device which ensures that Falstaff's role in the play amounts to more than 'mere' entertainment and time off from the serious business of the plot, is the pairing or paralleling of him with his *alter ego* in the main story, King Henry IV. They operate as rival fathers for the affections of Prince Hal, defying the simplistic binaries of good and bad; each in their way a 'bad' example for the Prince, destined to be the very emblem of kingship. The presence of Falstaff, wittingly or otherwise, constantly reminds Hal of the precariousness of power and the illusory nature of the absolutes by which it justifies itself. While Falstaff is the motley or May King – the carnival figure who rules for one festive holiday in the year, the actual king is haunted by the shadow play of his illegitimacy, frequently acknowledging that it is the devices of the playhouse in performance and costume that keep him in power. Were he to be himself he would be executed as an usurper but so long as he plays the role of king that representation can keep the truth at bay. There is in their rotting, diseased bodies an uncanny similarity between Falstaff and Bolingbroke, each falling short of their fantasies: Falstaff's of a kingdom of perpetual carnival ruled by his *protégé*, Hal; Bolingbroke's of a penitent monarch redeeming the Christian world and purging his own guilt by dying in Jerusalem. The actual death of Henry IV prefigures the symbolic death of Falstaff through his rejection in the process of the transformation of Hal to Henry V.

François Laroque's reading of the *Henry IV* plays, though helpfully highlighting Falstaff as an emblem of carnival, does scant justice to the complexity of the pattern of relationships:

> The Falstaff scenes in *1&2 Henry IV* provide the spectator with a dramatic counterpart of Pieter Bruegel's famous painting 'The Battle of Carnival and Lent'. As I shall show, Shakespeare's ten-act play is shaped by an underlying opposition between those two principles.
>   (Laroque, 1998, pp.83–4)

Whilst Laroque makes a compelling case for the importance of the two principles for a reading of these plays, his notion of opposition is misleading. After all at the climactic Battle of Shrewsbury Falstaff and Bolingbroke not only 'fight' on the same side but moreover save their respective carcasses by means of a trick, a device of the playhouse: in one case by 'playing dead' and in the other by a deception of the wardrobe department. Here, even more than in its medieval origins, the relationship between Carnival and Lent is not so much that of binary opposition, more of a dialectic whereby the contradictions of each bring forth the existence of the other: negating carnival 'produces' Lent, the contradictions within which can only be resolved or at least contained by carnival. The carnival antics of Falstaff, culminating in his impersonation of Henry IV on the licensed premises of the Boar's Head, offer a distorted mirror image of Bolingbroke's player-king reign. Hal's accession to the throne is not only the rejection of Falstaff but also that of his father, the king of shadows. However, the distancing of himself from his two 'fathers' and his self-fashioning as Henry V does not involve a single-minded embracing of Lent. As king he has a clear understanding of the importance of performance in the maintenance of his authority as his disguise on the eve of Agincourt reveals.

However, in asserting the connections between Falstaff and Rabelais, Laroque is on firmer ground:

> By creating a character like Falstaff, Shakespeare comes as close as he possibly could to Rabelais's particular style of comedy which, as we know, centres on the body and on the belly as well as on the world of the tavern and of the carnivalesque celebration of life.
>
> (Laroque, 1998, p.83)

The creation of Falstaff amounts to much more than a 'style of comedy' for he brings with him into the world of the English History plays an alternative to the political discourses which constitute their dominant themes. Shakespeare's technique of parallelism ensures that this alternative amounts to more than light relief or fodder for the groundlings. By means of the device of the two, parallel fathers a whole set of insights which emanate from the inverted world of carnival threaten to undermine the ideological basis of the 'serious', political world of the play. Although ultimately contained, at their height the words and behaviour of Falstaff almost expose fatally the sham at the heart of the display of regal power. The tighter the parallel between Falstaff and Bolingbroke, the more nearly monarchy starts to resemble the playhouse antics of the clown.

Before this can happen Falstaff has to establish his credentials as a spirit of carnival descended from the Vice of the morality play. His first appearance, sprung fully-formed and without history, like the personification of the spirit of carnival, is like that of Sloth dragged reluctantly from his 'sunny bank' and heightened by the contrast with the busy scene of timetables and plans which precedes it. Carnival is essentially a phenomenon existing outside time – time off or holiday time. Its purpose is the instant gratification of the senses rather than the deferred gratification of those who make plans. Hal's question underlines the point:

> What a devil hast thou to do with the time of day?
>
> (1.2.6–7)

Falstaff has very little to do with time as other men experience it. He lives according to his body clock, acknowledging only a cycle of sleeping, waking, eating. His life is a waist of time, converting energy to food in an inversion of the workaday processes by which the rest of humanity is enslaved. This mode of inversion, a habitual feature of carnival, notably during the Feast of Fools, is adopted by Falstaff at every opportunity, both in his role-play and in his reversal of intended meaning:

> By the Lord, I'll be a brave judge!
>
> (1.2.62)

His mistaking of the role of judge for that of hangman points to the inappropriateness of his contemplating the task of judging his fellow men against criteria of legality and absolute morality which, as Vice, fool, and essence of carnival, he is never likely to recognise. He could only be judge if Hal were to reign over a carnival kingdom, exchanging the golden crown for the *papier mâché* version of the May king; a delusion he persists in until his rejection at the end of Part 2. Clowns and fools as judges belong in Utopia or the fables of Bertolt Brecht. Falstaff as judge would prove a close relative of Azdak since both share an obsession with food and drink and reject any notion of absolute principles such as justice. In the *Henry IV* plays carnival does not replace the workaday world of political intrigue, of winners and losers; rather it serves to remind the audience of the shallowness and insubstantiality with which that world is organised. Falstaff, unlike Azdak, never crosses the border into the 'real' world so his vision of life under King Hal remains a fantasy. The permanent rule of carnival is an oxymoron. It exists through being distinct from what happens on 'normal' days. Hal understands this with icy clarity as his assurances to the audience at the close of the scene make unambiguous. The days he passes in the company of Falstaff are his own period of carnival, indulged in now because kingship will not permit it later:

> If all the year were playing holidays
> To sport would be as tedious as to work;
>
> (1.2.199–200)

Falstaff's triumph is confined to the days of his governance, holidays, and to the places licensed to allow people to take time off from their cares – in this case the Boar's Head. Attempts to expand his carnivalesque dimensions at the expense of a proper observance of Lent associate him squarely with diabolical behaviour of the kind we witnessed in the play *Mankind*:

Jack! How agrees the devil and thee about thy soul, that thou soldest him on Good Friday last, for a cup of Madeira and a cold capon's leg?

(1.2.111–13)

The offence against the expected behaviour during Lent not only associates Falstaff with the Vice of the morality plays, it also associates him with another activity incurring official disapproval during Lent, playing. Performance – that staple of carnival – lies at the core of this play and links the destinies of Hal who performs the role of Prince Hal, dissolute companion to a reprobate, Bolingbroke who won the crown from Richard through playhouse tricks and holds on to it at Shrewsbury with another, and Falstaff whose whole being and survival is dependent on his capacity to switch role, alter character, at a moment's notice. Notwithstanding his substantial bulk Falstaff is in many respects a shape-shifter. References to him and to his actions highlight his function as trickster. Nowhere is this clearer than in his discomfort and subsequent recovery over the post-mortem on the Gadshill debacle. Like the archetypal trickster he seems to be found out, his verbal disguise penetrated, but, in the moment that the official discourse triumphs over him he is able to use his wit to restore his position beyond the borders of containment. Excess, be it physical or verbal, is once more rampant:

By the Lord, I knew ye as well as he that made ye. Why, hear you, my masters, was it for me to kill the heir-apparent? should I turn upon the true prince? Why, thou knowest I am as valiant as Hercules: but beware instinct – the lion will not touch the true prince; instinct is a great matter. I was now a coward on instinct: I shall think the better of myself, and thee, during my life – I for a valiant lion, and thou for a true prince.

(2.4.263–71)

As usual in performance very little is what it seems and the irony of Falstaff's verbal gymnastics is that it exposes again the thinness of the ice on which legitimacy skates. For the audience, as for Falstaff, its sense of nationhood is founded on the myth of the 'true prince' who can be transmuted into the heroic king. Although neither Shakespeare (nor Will Kempe) is yet ready to place carnival or folly at the heart of power, he is willing to rehearse the possibility through the device of the 'play extempore'. Furthermore he sets the mock or parody version of the interview between king and prince before the 'real' one, thereby qualifying or alienating the actual event for an audience who still has the rehearsal in mind:

> *Fal*:   Well, thou wilt be horribly chid tomorrow when thou comest to thy father; if thou love me practise an answer.
>
> *Prince*: Do thou stand for my father and examine me upon the particulars of my life.
>
> *Fal*:   Shall I? Content! This chair shall be my state, this dagger my sceptre, and this cushion my crown.
>
> *Prince*: Thy state is taken for a joint-stool, thy golden sceptre for a leaden dagger, and thy Precious rich crown for a pitiful bald crown.
>
> (2.4.368–77)

At a stroke the improvisation draws the parallel between Hal's two fathers and reminds us that the emblems of state are merely playhouse properties translated into the theatre of politics and bearing authority only so long as citizens, like an audience at a play, invest them with the authority of their imaginations through the suspension, temporary or permanent, of disbelief. At this moment Shakespeare is able to have it both ways: the parallels are drawn between Bolingbroke and Falstaff and Hal maintains his slippery nature in gliding between the two but, simultaneously, there is no danger of the tavern being mistaken for the court. Like the playhouse, the tavern is licensed premises. The premise which is licensed is that behaviour which would elsewhere incur serious penalties, is here indulged in the spirit of carnival.

The transformation of the tavern into the court is the stock in trade of a theatrical tradition which evolved from the inn yard and now thrived under the protection of the monarchy. The discourses of the play reflect the situation of public performance in Elizabethan London; tolerated because of its special relationship to the court (here represented by Hal) but relegated to the margins beyond the City limits (the Eastcheap of the play). By drawing attention to the crudeness of the impersonation and by keeping the tavern audience on stage, Shakespeare is able to maintain the carnivalesque as the dominant discourse into which the themes of state intervene through the controlled device of role-play, itself a means of representing reality frequently associated with carnival. The role of Bolingbroke is the thinnest of veneers covering the histrionic appetite of Falstaff. It is another instance of Brechtian (Kempean?) performance where the audience is never allowed to overlook the presence of the performer who regales us with insights into his method:

Falstaff: Give me a cup of sack to make my eyes look red, that it may
　　　　　be thought I have wept, for I must speak in passion, and I will
　　　　　do it in King Cambyses' vein.

(2.4.379–82)

Falstaff's excesses extend to his Thespian mannerisms, thereby reinforcing the connection between Bolingbroke and acting which resurfaces
in the 'real' interview in the following scene. Again the deep structure of the play is based on parallelism with Falstaff and Bolingbroke
both using the devices of the playhouse; the former as a May king for
a single day, the latter as the means of obtaining and retaining power.
Shakespeare takes up the theme of politics as performance with which
he played so extensively in *Richard III*:

King: And then I stole all courtesy from heaven,
　　　　And dress'd myself in such humility
　　　　That I did pluck allegiance from men's hearts,

(3.2.49–51)

But in revealing his strategy he also reminds us of the illegitimacy of
his position which not only tells us of his barely suppressed guilt but
also encourages us to make a comparison with Falstaff: rival 'fathers'
for the affections of Hal, himself in the process of performing the role
of dissolute companion. As elsewhere in Renaissance theatre, the political victory goes to the most convincing player. As Ladurie painstakingly
depicted, carnival and playhouse part company at the point where playing leaks out into the 'real' world; where the conventions which govern
holiday behaviour are employed to secure power in the everyday world.
This propensity for performance anticipates the strategy adopted by
both Bolingbroke and Falstaff at the Battle of Shrewsbury. They each
employ tricks of the playhouse to ensure personal survival, renewing
the age old link between carnival, folly and life.

The tavern, unlike the palace, is a place accustomed to the conventions of play where there is little danger that Falstaff's impersonations
will be mistaken for 'the thing itself'. Just as cushion and dagger are
grotesque emblems of that which they purport to represent, so the material reality of Falstaff constantly overwhelms the roles he adopts: be it
King or Prince. In the play *extempore* the person without a character or
mask to adopt is at a loss for words, naked before the costumed players.
So Hal moves swiftly to exchange roles with Falstaff so that he no longer
suffers the disadvantage of playing himself. He deposes Falstaff hastily

in a move which prefigures his premature self-coronation in Part 2. His unease at playing himself stands in marked contrast to the verbal excess which he pours over Falstaff's head from behind his mask. The opportunity to participate in the playing unleashes his carnival vocabulary to charge rampant through the fields of Rabelais and Bruegel:

> *Prince*: Thou art violently carried away from grace, there is a devil haunts thee in the likeness of an old fat man, a tun of man is thy companion. Why dost thou converse with that trunk of humours, that bolting-hutch of beastliness, that swollen parcel of dropsies, that huge bombard of sack, that stuffed cloak-bag of guts, that roasted Manningtree ox with the pudding in his belly, that reverend vice, that grey iniquity, that father ruffian, that vanity in years?

> (2.4.440–9)

Although ironically it is only the 'real' Hal who could attempt an answer to this question, that he can depict Falstaff thus is further proof that he understands the man and can confine him to the discourses of carnival. He is the talisman of Hal's carnival years, his intentionally misspent youth, but his influence can have no currency in a life beyond those discourses. The employment of images recognisable to the audience as belonging to carnival are an assurance that Falstaff will be contained in that element. Hal explicitly associates him with the bygone world of the medieval morality play:

> *Prince*: That villainous abominable misleader of youth, Falstaff, that old white-bearded Satan.

> (2.4.456–7)

The role of monarch enables him to rehearse the inevitable confrontation when carnival in the shape of Falstaff will be reminded that it has no place in the serious world of Tudor absolutism:

> *Falstaff*: ...banish not him thy Harry's company, banish not him thy Harry's company, banish plump Jack, and banish all the world.
> *Prince*:   I do, I will.

> (2.4.472–5)

The repetition betrays the rising panic in Falstaff while the change of tense in Hal's reply shows him answering in the present as his father and in the future as himself. His immanent departure from the scene of carnival is further signalled by the knocking of the outside, the other world, instantly contradicting the notion that Jack Falstaff represents 'all the world', on the door of the tavern by that most anti-carnival of figures the sheriff, seeking to curb the excesses of the Vice even on his home territory. Hal, however, is not yet ready to renounce his youth and, besides, the setting is inappropriate for the betrayal of the spirit of carnival. Instead Falstaff has to make shift to survive in the bleak, violent world of the new pragmatism inaugurated by Bolingbroke and soon to be implemented by his sons. The 'battle' between Carnival and Lent now moves to the battle-field, a movement from fertility to death where there may be space for folly but where there will be no festivity. The abstract glories of the military ideal clash uncomfortably with the material demands of the grotesque body:

> *Falstaff*: Rare words! Brave world! Hostess, my breakfast come!
>   O, I could wish this tavern were my drum.
>
> (3.3.204–5)

Outside the safe haven of the tavern the means by which he secures his breakfast is fatal to the prospects of others. In time of war folly has terminal consequences for those who are its victims:

> *Falstaff*: I have misused the King's press damnably. I have got in exchange of a hundred and fifty soldiers three hundred and odd pounds.
>
> (4.2.12–14)

He secures his personal comfort by transforming a group of fighting men into a collection of skeletons performing a dance of death; emblems alike of human insanity and mortality:

> *Falstaff*: A mad fellow met me on the way, and told me I had unloaded all the gibbets and pressed the dead bodies.
>
> (4.2.36–8)

This is the grotesque carnival of death depicted by Bruegel and Bosch with Falstaff as Mad Meg bestriding the corpses in grim pursuit of profit and survival. In doing so he is acting as an agent of the established order which sought to cleanse the kingdom of these subversive vagabonds as Stephen Greenblatt has pointed out (Greenblatt, 1985, pp.18–47).

But this does not account for the full effect of Falstaff's action which offers a sustained challenge to the conventional myth of medieval chivalry. Unlike the rebels who offer a challenge based on the same ideological paradigms as operated by the state, Falstaff's views and behaviour cast doubt on the most basic assumptions of power and authority. In both his personal behaviour and in the conduct of his men, he produces a counterfeit battle order; a grotesque representation of the glories of warfare, grounded in the typically carnivalesque preoccupation with the needs of the flesh. He remains true to carnival's function of inversion, being instrumental in interrupting the nobility's obsession with power or honour to remind the audience of what war means at the grassroots. Shakespeare situates him where he can simultaneously expand the scope of England's history beyond the confines of the court while still offering a commentary on its machinations. His friendship with Hal, whether real or imagined, is the fuel which drives the engine of his fantastic vision of an alternative kingdom in which only the laws of carnival are upheld. It is the achievement of the play's structure to suggest at moments that this vision is no less substantial than the one which governs a regime where the best actor or, at least, the one who best understands the rules of the playhouse controls the political action. However, it is clear that the tide of history is flowing against this vision; that its moment is passing before our eyes. This transience is not located solely in the aging, mortal spirit of Falstaff but also in the historical moment which is witnessing the passing of carnival as a significant factor in popular social life.

A paradox lurks here which is foregrounded in Falstaff's soliloquy on honour. His pragmatic materialist deflation of the ideal sounds the death knell for a code of life even as it does for its representative, Hotspur. The image of Falstaff desecrating his corpse with his dagger, supplies the emblem for the eclipse of the age of chivalry. However, the new age of absolutism, depicted anachronistically in the state's treatment of the rebels, will ultimately expel carnival from its streets and marketplaces for fear of becoming the subject of its mockeries and parodies. The earlier certainties of the morality plays must now give way to the relative values of political reality which holds power rather than right supreme. If Falstaff is identified with the Old Vice, he belongs in a genre and in a world that has passed, even as his own words signal that passing. The paradox of 'double' time is a constituent feature of both history plays and the mysteries. The audience is simultaneously confronted with two worlds: their own and that of the play's setting, be it first century Palestine or fourteenth century England. This quality of doubleness creates the ironic space in which the playful, foolish figures can commute between the contemporary audience and the world of the stage fiction. In the case of Falstaff there is a particular poignancy to the paradox, given that the 'merry world' over which he presides, though at its height at the period in which the plays are set, was already under severe attack in post-Reformation England. His banishment from the court of Henry V is therefore a retrospective premonition; a most foolish conceit.

But first he is once again used by Shakespeare as the means by which English history is experienced at the grass-roots, the opposite end from the fantasies of heroism perpetuated by the aristocracy. To do this the playwright can call on the tradition which combined the characters of the Lord of Misrule and the servant of the Devil in the single figure of the clown. Falstaff generally inhabits the world of mischief as festive inversion; here, however, his diabolic aspect is prominent:

Falstaff: I have led my ragamuffins where they are peppered; there's not three of my hundred and fifty left alive, and they are for the town's end, to beg during life.

(5.3.36–8)

The Vice uses the disguise of Sir John Falstaff even as he used the figure of the King in *Richard III*, behind which to work the villainy that undoes mankind. Just as Will Kempe presents the character of Falstaff while never letting the audience lose sight of the actor as company clown, so the character of Falstaff, relishing the possibilities afforded by the playhouse, performs as both clown and Vice even though he would rather think of himself as the former, 'kind Jack Falstaff', while Hal opts to depict him as his *alter ego*, 'that old white-bearded Satan'. His soliloquy on 'honour' reveals him to be at once of the Devil's party, rejecting the moral basis for action, and of the clown's, preferring the physical certainties of the body's comfort in typically Rabelaisian style.

However, his most sophisticated encounter with the main or serious plot revolves around the notion of 'counterfeit' which is used to bring Falstaff and Bolingbroke, clown and king, into an ironic parallel. Both look to preserve themselves from the dangers of battle by means of counterfeits:

> *Douglas*: What art thou
>   That counterfeit'st the person of a king?
> *King*:   The King himself, who, Douglas, grieves at heart
>   So many of his shadows thou hast met,
>   And not the very King.

(5.4.26–30)

This bald lie from the perpetrator of the strategy whereby the rebels expend their energy chasing shadows (the King's actors), while ensuring his own survival by cheating death, tightens the link between himself and Falstaff since both employ tricks of the playhouse. Bolingbroke visits the wardrobe department which delineates social function through costume. Falstaff opts for the device of playing dead, a counterfeit within a counterfeit since the 'really' dead victims of Shrewsbury will soon be back on their feet to take a bow:

> *Falstaff*: 'Sblood, 'twas time to counterfeit, or that hot termagant Scot had paid me, scot and lot too. Counterfeit? I lie, I am no counterfeit: to die is to be a counterfeit, for he is but the counterfeit of a man, who hath not the life of a man: but to counterfeit dying, when a man thereby liveth, is to be no counterfeit, but the true and perfect image of life indeed.

(5.4. 112–19)

So theatre is the counterfeit of reality, the one defying time and death where the other is bound by both. The carnival spirit of play, enshrined in the figure of the fool, sets a premium upon survival, of triumph over death as performed ritualistically through the restoration of St George's head to his body by the Doctor in the Mummers Plays as we saw recalled in the clownish antics of *Mankind*. At the climax of his powers at the end of *Part 1* Falstaff escapes all confinements, even those of the senses:

> *Lancaster*: Did you not tell me this fat man was dead?
> *Prince*:   I did, I saw him dead,
>   Breathless and bleeding on the ground. Art thou alive?
>   Or is it fantasy that plays upon our eyesight?
>   I prithee speak, we will not trust our eyes
>   Without our ears: thou art not what thou seem'st.
> *Falstaff*: No, that's certain, I am not a double-man: but if I be not Jack Falstaff, then am I a Jack: there is Percy [*throwing the body down*] !

(5.4.131–9)

Hal's announcement that Falstaff is not what he seems is easy enough to endorse. More difficult is the attempt to encompass all that Falstaff represents at this moment. The play upon 'double' is multivalent for, like a rolling snowball, he has gathered identities throughout the play and his final entrance reveals him as two men, Falstaff and Hotspur, his own double in the sense of his ghost, as large enough to be two people, as both clown and vice, and ultimately as both the character Falstaff and the actor Kempe. He is the trickster, the shape-shifter, crossing and recrossing the boundaries between life and death even as he has moved throughout the play between the fool, Jack Falstaff, and the false knight, Sir John Falstaff.

He represents the one point of danger, of potential disruption to the ethical and political assumptions upon which the rest of the characters build. Both from his situation within the text and from his impersonation by Kempe, Falstaff performs the function of an interpreter of history for the benefit of the common man. In this role he offers a double vision, a shadow play from the ground up, raising the thought that the 'serious' plot is just another version of play and that the instinct for carnival may subvert the schemes of the great. Any carnivalesque tendencies latent in Bolingbroke's *penchant* for theatre or his son's desire to play with commoners never threaten to unravel the robes of state, for these are strategies by which the powerful maintain themselves in power. They play at carnival to balance their Lenten selves: this is indeed the safety-valve version of carnival made manifest. It is only the presence of Falstaff that reminds us of the possibility of alternative purposes for the species.

Such reminders grow increasingly faint throughout *Part 2* where Falstaff's marginalisation is the echo of Hal's transformation into first Prince Henry and finally Henry V. The *Henry IV* plays are the proverbial game of two halves where carnival holds its own to emerge with a triumph of sorts at Shrewsbury as Falstaff 'scores' on the stroke of half-time but Lent asserts its power with increasing confidence throughout *Part 2*, building up to the decisive moment of Falstaff's rejection. The pivotal dramatic moments around which *Part 1* is shaped reveal the subtle interpenetrations between Carnival and Lent, resisting any tidy separation of the respective worlds. Eastcheap can at a stroke become Lenten ('I do. I will.'), while the deadly climax at Shrewsbury is transformed into a carnivalesque charade. However, in *Part 2* there is a progressive separation of the two worlds until the distance that carnival must travel to meet the dominant discourse of Lent is too great to be accomplished. The emphasis of this play is upon the way Hal grows into his power and authority even as life and energy ebb away from Falstaff.

Initially the worlds seem held in the pattern of mutual tension familiar from *Part 1*. Falstaff's meeting with the Lord Chief Justice occurs in a London street; neutral, fluid territory where confrontation can be deflected and exit strategies negotiated. Even here Falstaff retains the theatrical privilege of framing the encounter within his own discourse, once more occupying the liminal space between action and audience to assert his interpretation of the way the world works. In some measure Falstaff is conceived as a combination of the Vice from the morality plays and the fool or strolling player of popular tradition; at once endearing and dangerous; by turns amoral and immoral. In *Part 2* this balance is tipped decisively towards the latter. His soliloquy at the close of Scene 2 associates him explicitly with the diseased personification of Gluttony as time is already starting to be called on his reign as carnival king. The emphasis on the decrepitude of the body further links him to the fate of his parallel figure in the serious world, Henry IV. Both the 'mockery' monarchs, the shadow kings of carnival and Lent are nearing the end of their offices. Falstaff's ambition to 'turn diseases to commodity' sets him alongside the defeated Pandarus in the camp of Vice:

> *Pandarus*: Till then I'll sweat and seek about for eases,
>   And at that time bequeath you my diseases.
>
> (*Troilus and Cressida* V.10. 54–5)

Although the structure of the *Henry IV* plays, unlike *Richard III*, has developed away from the morality play, the tone of *Part 2* regularly reminds the audience of that model. Hal distances himself from Falstaff even as Mankind sought ultimately to align himself with heavenly rather than diabolical influences:

> *Prince*: Well, thus we play the fools with the time, and the spirits of
>   the wise sit in the clouds and mock us.
>
> (II. 2. 134–5)

It is not only in the 'real' world that time is being called on Falstaff. The stink of his mortality reeks in the nostrils of his carnival acquaintance as well. The representatives of the 'lower bodily stratum' well know that they are not exempt from the physical effects of time and the moral effects of salvation as the time of day about which Falstaff was formerly so careless reels him towards the abyss:

> *Doll*: Thou whoreson little tidy Bartholomew boar-pig, when wilt
>   thou leave fighting a-days, and foining-nights and begin to
>   patch up thine old body for heaven?

> (II. 4. 227–30)

The phrases Doll uses to characterise Falstaff maintain the close connection of his person to those aspects of life that the audience recognise as belonging to carnival. But Bartholomew Fair belongs to a particular moment of the festive cycle and that moment, like Falstaff's zenith has passed. The underlying structure and the verbal echoes of the morality play signal his imminent departure from the busy world of the major players some time before his official expulsion. 'Falstaff's curious out-of-the-way journey to Gloucestershire on his way north from London' (Oliver, 1971, p.lv) becomes in effect a brief time out before the great reckoning; a place where the memory of carnival rather than the thing itself can still hold sway, undisturbed by the changes of the wider world. Here Falstaff's self-image is unlikely to be challenged by Shallow or Silence, anxious to profit in reputation from an association with the famous knight. In these scenes carnival slips from being a force of energy in a parallel world to being merely nostalgia for an imaginary time past. Falstaff surrounds himself with shards of his own decomposing persona; parodies of the different elements which together combine to form his own excess. For the man who has lived 'out of all reasonable compass' the space in which he can operate with impunity is becoming increasingly confined. The exploitative relationship between Falstaff and Shallow, becoming strained as the credibility of the former evaporates, is a forerunner of the more fully developed version of *Twelfth Night* between Belch and Aguecheek. In both cases the larger than life figure is sustained in his excesses by the smaller than life figure's willingness to live vicariously as the shadow or zany of the spirit of carnival.

The final, desperate journey from the remotest backwater to the heart of the kingdom is propelled by the fantastic contradiction contained in Pistol's announcement: 'Sir John, thy tender lambkin now is King' (V.3.113). All that Shakespeare has shown us of Hal since the second scene of *Part 1* has demonstrated that he understands fully the incompatibility of carnival with proper government. Hal can be Falstaff's 'tender lambkin' or he can be king of England; he can never be both.

> *King*: I know thee not, old man. Fall to thy prayers.
>   How ill white hairs becomes a fool and jester!

> (V.5.47–8)

The 'I' who knows not Falstaff is Henry V. The Hal who might have acknowledged an acquaintance has been relegated to a figure in a dream which is now 'despised'. Shakespeare uses his familiar device of the dream once again as a way of depicting a phase through which characters grow in order to attain maturity. In this phase carnivalesque behaviour often figures prominently. His instructions to Falstaff, like Doll's more kindly meant advice, are to behave in a manner appropriate to his time of life but Falstaff has only one time of life from first appearance to last. Like the figure of the Vice he is an emblem of a way of life and, as such, is trapped forever within it. In theatrical terms it is as if Burbage is gradually finding himself in the role of Henry V while Kempe, famous clown in his own right, cloaks Falstaff with his own personality.

Henry IV Part 2 lacks much of the dramatic tension of *Part 1* because that tension derives from the encounter between Carnival and Lent; between the clash of different aspects of the human personality. As long as there were opportunities for Falstaff's view of the world to undermine the dominant discourse as in his soliloquy on 'honour' and his shadow play at Shrewsbury, there was a possibility that he could perform a transformative role by offering a critique of power to the audience, but once the two worlds become firmly separated in *Part 2*, he can only provide a distraction from the world of power rather than a threat to it. Whatever the chronology of their creation, *Henry IV Part 2* and *The Merry Wives of Windsor* share a depiction of Falstaff that keeps his carnival instincts securely within the confines of his own fantasy, unthreatening to those he seeks to manipulate. This sense of a diminution in his powers is further exacerbated between *Henry IV Part 2* and *The Merry Wives of Windsor*. In the later stages of the former Falstaff has succeeded in defrauding Shallow of a thousand pounds whereas in the latter his hopes for retrieving his finances at the expense of the 'merry wives' result in ignominious failure. Not only has Falstaff's sphere of operations shrunk from the carnival kingdom of Prince Hal to the bourgeois hearths of a provincial town, but these operations pose no threat to the equilibrium of this closed environment. So palpable and gross are the attempts of Falstaff to ingratiate himself into the favours of the wives that they create a suspicion that he only embarks upon them in the expectation of failure. Developing the emerging theme from *Part 2*, he now represents the most obvious aspects of the Vice and in rejecting him Mistresses Ford and Page reject the ancient morality of his passing world with scorn and ridicule:

Mrs. Page: Why, Sir John, do you think, though we would have thrust
virtue out of our hearts by the head and shoulders, and have
given ourselves without scruple to hell, that ever the devil
could have made you our delight?

(V.5. 147–51)

They lose nothing by their banishing of 'plump Jack' whereas when
Falstaff dared Hal to 'banish plump Jack, and banish all the world' the
dramatic tension in that moment suggests that Hal has a real choice to
make and, although it is already clear what that choice will be, there is a
sense of loss involved in it. Hal may not lose 'all the world' but he does
turn his back upon a substantial slice of medieval life.

However laughable Falstaff's pretensions as a lover, he does have one
card to play – his status as a knight which might conceivably prove
attractive to an upwardly mobile bourgeoisie.

Mrs. Ford: O woman, if it were not for one trifling respect, I could come
to such honour!
Mrs. Page: Hang the trifle, woman, take the honour. What is it?
Dispense with trifles – what is it?
Mrs. Ford: If I would but go to hell for an eternal moment or so, I could
be knighted.

(II.1.43–8)

In a society where the woman takes her status from the rank of her
husband, marriage above one's station offered the one route to improvement. Unencumbered by an existing marriage, Maria in *Twelfth Night*
transforms herself from waiting-gentlewoman into Lady Belch. Given
Ford's pathological jealousy, she does not lack an excuse for being
tempted. That she is not, further delineates the decline in Falstaff as an
emblem for an attractive, alternative life. This motif also places Falstaff
in an ironic parallel with the juvenile lead and traditional centre piece
of the comedy, Fenton. Page attempts to prevent his daughter's marriage
to Fenton on the grounds that, like Falstaff, he is an aristocrat looking
for the means to maintain a debauched life-style. The growing confidence of the bourgeoisie in this period is signalled by the determination
with which it protects its financial interests even in the face of the
temptations of social climbing. The happy outcome to the play depends
upon the audience believing in Fenton's conversion to the cause of love.
Otherwise the parallel with Falstaff holds; except that he succeeds in
capturing the Page fortune where the old, fat man fails. He triumphs in

the instant of Falstaff's public humiliation, yet the possibility remains that they shared the same aim.

Although in form the Herne the Hunter masque resembles a carnival, its purpose, as Jonathan Hall assesses, points in the opposite direction towards a narrow, Lenten morality:

> Fenton is integrated, and so, in a sense, is Falstaff, but only after a series of shamings. The first two take the form of expulsions from the domestic space, and the last is public. The reinvention of a theatricalized and thoroughly controlled carnival in a public space for this last shaming is important. It is a carnival memory, with its old connotations of fertility now reduced to mere foolishness or baseless fear. And it is conjured up out of this folk celebration and fear by Mistress Page herself for her more narrow moralizing purpose.
>
> (Hall, 1998, pp.142–3)

We have seen Falstaff fall victim to the masquerade of others previously during the Gadshill episode, so being the butt of others' stratagems is not a new experience for him. There is, however, a vital difference between the two charades and that difference is not in the credulity of Falstaff for he falls for both of them. It is rather that in *The Merry Wives of Windsor* he accepts the moral premise of those who seek to discomfort him. His ultimate defeat is signalled by his acceptance of the moral codes of his bourgeois antagonists:

> *Falstaff*: I was three or four times in the thought they were not fairies; and yet the guiltiness of my mind, the sudden surprise of my powers, drove the grossness of the foppery into a received belief, in despite of the teeth of all rhyme and reason, that they were fairies. See now how wit may be made a Jack-a-Lent, when 'tis upon ill employment!
>
> (V.5.122–9)

Falstaff willingly internalises his function as butt of public ridicule and, in nominating himself as a Jack-a-Lent, submits to the rule of Lent. If the 'fortunes of Falstaff' can be read in terms of a battle between Carnival and Lent, the conclusion of this play signals the victory of the latter. He becomes increasingly associated with a world that has passed until he passes from our sight as the emblem of an antiquated piece of folk lore. Once a present threat to the fate of the kingdom, he is now indeed the 'stuff of dreams'.

4
Fooling with Love

For the rain it raineth every day

[*Twelfth Night*, V.1.378]

Shakespeare's comedies, by which I mean those plays which conform to a structural pattern of disruption to social equilibrium, potential disaster and conclusion in marriage and restoration – covering plays as diverse in tone as *As You Like It* and *Measure for Measure* – take as their theme the discrepancies between an ideal view of love and the reality of the workings of desire within the human animal. There is a gap, which many do not mind, between the position the protagonists of a comedy occupy and the position they suppose themselves to inhabit. This gap is the space which is frequently delineated by the words and actions of the clown or fool in these plays. It is, however, necessary to determine who fulfils this function play by play since the one who reveals the discrepancy may not be the designated clown while the process of revelation may be conscious or unconscious. This allows for the possibility of more than one character being entrusted with aspects of the function. In terms of Chapter 2 both Carnival and Lent are unreal positions, false descriptors of the human condition, and those characters who cleave too hard to one or other of those poles are likely to find themselves the butt of the knowing mirth of those who exploit such lack of self-awareness, both on the stage and in the auditorium. It is often a part of the fool's strategy to share the joke with the audience as it unfolds, from his semi-detached position mediating between the stage fiction and the auditorium reality.

This pattern is established in early comedies such as *The Two Gentlemen of Verona* and *Love's Labour's Lost* and is maintained in later plays with increasing sophistication and complexity as the consequences of the gap produce fissures in the fragile social relationships. In *The Two Gentlemen of Verona* this gap assumes the proportions of a gulf, such is the degree of unreality with which the ideal is invested. Shakespeare introduces two strategies for undermining unreal aspirations, both of which he consistently employs throughout his subsequent career. First, he offers an alternative perception which is the province of 'lower' or 'popular' characters: clowns, fools, peasants and artisans. In this play the function is entrusted to servants of the gentry, Launce and Speed; a device inherited from the Roman comedy. Secondly, those characters most prone to idealism undo themselves through their own actions. They perform the fools or shadows of their own persons. The spectacularly unreal Proteus, already given away to the audience by his name, is the prime but not the only example in *The Two Gentlemen of Verona*. As Weimann has demonstrated (Weimann, 1978, pp.255–60) both Speed and Launce function to co-opt the audience into a shared view of the discrepancies between ideal and real which beset the protagonists. This is more than a matter of theatrical convention although the asides and direct address do reposition the audience in relation to the fiction of the play's story. The preposterous sentimental pretensions of their masters and mistresses are refracted to the audience through the consciousness of the servants in ways which ensure that a particular attitude to the fiction is encouraged among the spectators. Launce, Speed and, to a lesser degree Lucetta, each both frame and mediate the action which they are simultaneously a part of and outside. Weimann explains this doubleness in terms of a partial separation of the character from the actor in the manner of Brecht. Once a character articulates a self-consciousness about the theatricality of the fiction in which s/he is involved, the audience is reminded of the processes which go into the making of a play in a way which encourages them to see clear daylight between actor and character. This tendency is exacerbated in cases where the role is being performed by an actor famous for a certain style of playing which extends beyond the bounds of any one character. In this instance, the first appearance of Launce, detached from the plot and engaging in a stand-up comedy routine with his hapless dog, offers only the thinnest of veils between the stage-play world and an exhibition of the talents of Will Kempe. Kempe and Launce between them serve to remind the audience that there is an everyday, familiar world beyond the confines of the plot's artifice. In this world the materiality of human desire and its consequences for behaviour are readily recognised since its inhabitants are not insulated by wealth or position. Codes of courtly love and friendship belong to those with the leisure to create such fantasies, divorced from the reality of the fallen state of being human. Shakespeare's stage-craft, anticipating the pattern of scenes in *Henry IV Part 1*, ensures that the audience experiences both worlds juxtaposed for maximum effect. The first scene of Act II frames the courting of Silvia by Valentine within the asides of Speed. Valentine, as his name suggests, represents the very epitome of the ideal of love; an ideal that does not, however, answer to all the material needs of the body:

> *Speed*: Ay, but hearken Speed, sir: though the chameleon Love
>   can feed on the air, I am one that am nourished by
>   my victuals; and would fain have meat.
>
> [II.1. 162–64]

Speed's closing remarks refer not only to the position of the character within the drama but also to the concerns of the actor and the audience in the world beyond the theatre. Where Valentine is a character created entirely to serve the fiction of a tale of love and friendship, his servant operates simultaneously within and without that world.

Besides, as it were, locating Valentine firmly within the fantasy, these lines also serve as the prologue to the parting of Proteus from Julia which immediately follows. Where Valentine's name announces his function in the story, Proteus' warns the audience of the gap between human intention and human reality. Even without any assistance from the materialist perceptions of Launce or Speed, the audience cannot miss the blatant discrepancy between his name and the quality of 'my true constancy' which he assures Julia is his defining virtue. Again the dramatic tension is created from the disparity between the ideal and the real of human nature. In terms of the pattern of the morality plays which lies behind Shakespeare's comic structure, man is caught between his aspiration for godliness and his fallen nature as animal. It is almost, but not quite, a rerun of the battle between Carnival and Lent. The parallel can only be partial because both these positions, as future plays will show, are prone to their own undermining, internal contradictions. Panthino enters to hurry Proteus on his way and, when the same character is used to bring Launce's monologue on his departure to an end in the following scene, it is evident that the two partings are being set before the audience for comparison. In relation to the plot of the play, Launce's speech serves a double function; at once burlesquing the courtly manners of Proteus by relocating the trope of departure into the popular sphere – a reverse proceeding to the play *extempore* in Eastcheap which was placed before the 'serious' event of the royal interview – and at the same time indicating that for all its humour, Launce's farewell to his family expressed at its core an emotion whose integrity is beyond the reach of his master. At the generic as well as the thematic level, it is a complex moment in the theatre. Kempe as performer of the chief clown parts is given his Tarletonesque moment to entertain the crowd through direct address in a style which on one level seems to have little to do with the rest of the play, somewhat like Mak in *The Second Shepherds' Play*, while simultaneously drawing the audience's attention to the frailty of Proteus' self-knowledge through the contrast with his own well grounded emotional condition. As a 'clownish' servant to Robert Dudley, Earl of Leicester, during the 1580s, Kempe may well have been able to base some of the insights into love among the nobles upon personal observation.

Act III, scene 1 demonstrates the complex range of Launce's functions within the comic structure, both residual and current. He has by now witnessed the machinations of his master to replace Valentine in Silvia's affections. Anticipating Dogberry in his mangling of the language, he cuts through Proteus' circumlocutions to break the news to Valentine:

> *Launce*: Sir, there is a proclamation that you are vanished
>
> [III.1.216]

Knowingly or not, he hits upon the more appropriate word since it is Proteus' fondest wish that Valentine might vanish and leave the field clear for the play of his own desires. From his position within the fiction, Launce can, at best, use whatever indirect means are available to him to offer a critical perspective on the action. However, once freed up from the fiction to speak from outside it directly, he exploits his mask of folly in order to put moral distance between himself and Proteus and thereby maintain his position as confidant of the audience:

> I am but a fool, look you, and yet I have the wit to
> think my master is a kind of a knave;
>
> [III.1.261–2]

He goes on to articulate his more earthy but realistic passion for a milk-maid in terms that reassure the audience of his place in a pattern of desire which can lead not to treachery and frustration but to fertility. Lest we get too comfortable in our relationship to him, the entrance of Speed reminds us of his ambiguous heritage:

Speed: How now, Signor Launce! What news with your mastership?
Launce: With my master's ship? Why, it is at sea.
Speed: Well, your old vice still: mistake the word.

[III.1. 277–80]

As Weimann, Spivak (Spivak, 1958, p.202) and others have noted there is
a pun on 'vice' alluding to Launce's derivation from the Old Vice of the
morality plays. Like Launce that figure was distinguished by his habit of
direct address to co-opt the audience to his opinion. But the moral universe of Shakespearean comedy is different. While Launce and the vice
figures of the moralities share a tendency towards the carnivalesque and
a grounding in material reality, the world upon which he comments is
devoted to the pursuit of human desires rather than spiritual salvation.
Although he may not quite be occupying the moral high ground, his
position alongside the audience enables him to look at the stage fiction
from the foothills of irony and scepticism.

   Another type of folly, destined to become the stock in trade of
Shakespeare's comedies is introduced in this play: disguise. The characters who adopt a disguise put themselves behind a mask from which
they can enjoy the freedom to express views that might put them at a
social disadvantage or even physical danger if they were to express them
in their own persons. The typical working of the device entails the hero-
ine of the piece disguising herself as a young man in order to reduce the
danger she will find herself in when having to go out into the world.
In *The Two Gentlemen of Verona* it is employed as a prototype for the
more sophisticated versions that follow later. Although Julia takes on a
physical disguise she never adopts an alternative character. There is no
alter ego in the manner of Rosalind/Ganymede or Viola/Cesario. When
Julia uses asides to invoke the sympathy of the audience at her betrayal,
she does so as herself and all the content concerns her plight as Julia.
When Silvia asks her about Julia, there is an occasion for a theatrical
joke that makes her all the more present for the audience:

> *Julia*: ... for at Pentecost,
>   When all our pageants of delight were play'd,
>   Our youth got me to play the woman's part,
>   And I was trimm'd in Madam Julia's gown,

[IV.4. 156–9]

The apprentice playing the role of Julia has just undergone exactly this
experience and has now reverted to his proper shape after time off

disguised as a woman. One of the follies encouraged by theatre is that of the shape-changing gender disguise. Here there is only the ambivalence of Julia and the boy-actor of her role whereas subsequently this will give way to the triangular relationship of two characters and an actor. Were she to develop an alternative character in the style of *As You Like It*, it is difficult to see how such a consciousness could be accommodated to the outrageous happenings of the last act of this play. It is significant that Launce and Speed are absent from a denouement which includes the attempted rape of Silvia by Proteus, immediately followed by her being offered to Proteus by Valentine as a reward for the former's repentance. To close off this fiction with a 'happy' ending – the double coupling of the protagonists and the return of the outlaws to the orbit of civilised society – Shakespeare could ill afford any reminders from Launce or Speed of the improbability of this outcome. Had either been present, it is difficult to imagine that they would have refrained from ironies destructive to the homogeneity of the fabulous conclusion: 'One feast, one house, one mutual happiness.' The triumph of form over character is an enduring feature of Shakespeare's comedies but nowhere is the discrepancy more blatant than in this play. The gap between the ideal and the real is so wide that in resorting to the former, Shakespeare has had to exclude the latter entirely from the final portrait.

Whilst *Love's Labour's Lost* continues the theme of the battle between the ideal and the real, one fool is now located inside the idealised fiction while another takes up the more accustomed position of outsider. In this play the function of critiquing folly is given both to Berowne who is located, albeit ironically, within the orbit of Navarre's fantastic academy and to Costard, the clown, whose words and actions undermine those idealistic pretensions. In keeping with the greater sophistication resulting from the multiple ironies of this play, the initial aspiration to promote Lent over Carnival, as Longaville expresses it: 'The mind shall banquet, though the body pine' [I.1.25] is merely the pretext for announcing the major battle, once again, between courtly love and the realities of the mortal world beyond. The pre-Reformation ideal of the monastic life, echoed in the fight for the soul of man in the morality plays, is now reduced to a metaphor for the hopeless discrepancy between our words and our deeds; in Berowne's phrase: 'Necessity will make us all forsworn' [I.1.148]. What Berowne articulates Costard demonstrates as once more desire disrupts the ideal, this time even before the first scene is out. Throughout the ensuing action Costard performs the function that Shakespeare will regularly assign to the clown or fool, that of exposing the hypocrisies and contradictions at the heart of the stage action. He is, in effect, the channel through which the audience's view of that action is directed so that we acquire the habit of watching as if we, too, are of the fool's party. In exposing the affectations and vanities of Armado, Nathaniel and Holofernes he is doing little more than we could do for ourselves. Their differences are highlighted in the pageant of the Nine Worthies where his performance of Pompey is held together by his insistence on maintaining the division between actor and character, so that there is no cue for the audience, on or off stage, to mock the discrepancy between actor and role as in the case of the other performers.

> *Costard*: If your ladyship would say, 'Thanks, Pompey,' I had done.
> *Princess*: Great thanks, great Pompey.
> *Costard*: 'Tis not so much worth; but I hope I was perfect.
>   I made a little fault in 'Great.'
> *Berowne*: My hat to a halfpenny, Pompey proves the best Worthy.
>
> [V.2. 551–6]

Whilst his wit and self-awareness in contrast to the other inhabitants of his *milieu* make him an obvious candidate for the approbation of the nobility, his entrance onto the stage of their affairs whether intentional or not (anticipating in lighter vein the action of Dogberry and the Watch in *Much Ado About Nothing*), is more disquieting particularly for Berowne who is moved from subject into object of mirth by Costard's disclosure of his love letter. The clown's exit line when Berowne urges his dismissal to the King so that there is no further disruption to the story Berowne wishes to fashion, draws our attention to the upside down world where moral laws are framed according to social position:

> Walk aside the true folk, and let the traitors stay.
>
> [IV.3.209]

C.L. Barber summed up the sense of satisfaction that his role in the performance can bring to audiences:

> He is a thoroughly satisfactory "downright" style of clown, ironical about the follies of his betters half out of naïveté and half out of shrewdness. His role embodies the proverbial, homespun perspective Berowne can occasionally borrow.
>
> (Barber, 1963, p.109)

This observation on Berowne, however, is too limiting. He is not, after all, a double act with Costard but rather offers a different kind of perspective on the operation of the comic form. Where Costard's function of clown endows him with that degree of separation necessary for his delineation of human failings, Berowne's intellectual capacity enables him to stand outside the comedy which he inhabits. In this way Shakespeare makes a start at finding ways of diminishing some of the severe contradictions between form and character that are so blatant in *The Two Gentlemen of Verona*. Uncannily anticipating the current fashion for the recuperative powers of mirth, 'I'll jest a twelvemonth in an hospital', Berowne draws the audience's attention to the effect that bringing an announcement of death into the conclusion of the play has had on it:

> Berowne: Our wooing doth not end like an old play;
> Jack hath not Jill: these ladies' courtesy
> Might well have made our sport a comedy.
> *King*: Come, sir, it wants a twelvemonth and a day,
> And then 'twill end.
> *Berowne*: That's too long for a play.
>
> [V.2.466–70]

Too long indeed for a so-called 'happy comedy' but the late romances will develop forms that can encompass some of the dual demands of art and life. In this instance Shakespeare is having his cake and eating it. For while Berowne's intervention shows that the story of these lives cannot be contained within this comedy, his observation does and does not end the play. The interruption of the Worthies' pageant allows Armado to restore the balanced songs of spring and winter in the manner of a traditional epilogue to the performance of a comedy. In such a way the conclusion of *Love's Labour's Lost* is and is not like 'an old play'. Shakespeare is able to play self-consciously with the confines of his art because he can use the devices of folly to highlight its contradictions.

The stories that form the stuff of the comedies are based on the anarchy of desire that undermines the attempts of man to organise life according to the dictates of reason and order. Characters propose courses of action or understand where their best interests lie, only to discover that they have been pushed to the brink of disaster by the promptings of desires that they are unable to control. The structure of the come-dies is grounded in the belief that marriage is the ideal institution for reining in desire so that it can be channelled into productive, socialised forms. The most vivid, destructive manifestation of desire is the notion of love at first sight with the power to overturn previous relationships and tear up the bonds of loyalty and hierarchy. In *A Midsummer Night's Dream* Shakespeare embarks on an exploration of the effects of desire and its disorders at every level of the multiple plots: Oberon and Titania, Theseus and Hippolyta, Lysander and Hermia, Demetrius and Helena, Pyramus and Thisbe; the latter being the only constant pair whose desires are thwarted by an external force of nature in the form of a (wo)man eating lion. Imagination is the quality that gives to human life both its savour and its danger as well as the capacity without which there can be no theatre. Imagination does not divide the artist from the ordinary mortal; rather the artist is one who seeks to control its work-ings through the creation of art instead of allowing it to run amok in daily life.

In a play where almost every other character is defined by her/his rela-tion to the operation of desire, it fits the paradigm for the clown or fool that he, in this case Bottom, should be largely immune to its debilitating tendencies. He operates not outside the social but rather the psycholog-ical orbit of the play in order that he can occupy a position from which to demonstrate another way of being. This demonstration is particularly powerful because the plot places him, potentially, in the greatest dan-ger of losing himself to imaginary forces, first in the guise of Titania's asinine beloved, and subsequently as the tragic lover Pyramus. It is the dominant structural irony of the play that those with the least cause fall most prey to the tricks of imagination while he upon whom imagination works hardest to impress, emerges unscathed from its assaults:

> His imperviousness, indeed, is what is most delightful about him with Titania: he remains so completely himself, even in her arms, and despite the outward change of his head and ears; his confident, self-satisfied tone is a triumph of consistency, persistence, existence.
>
> (Barber, 1963, p.157)

Everywhere else in this play characters are being enjoined to look with the eyes of another in order to share the same view. Here Bottom's refusal to see in himself what is only visible to Titania enables him to combat physical transformation with psychic constancy:

Titania: And thy fair virtue's face perforce doth move me
　　　On first view, to say, to swear, I love thee.
Bottom: Methinks, mistress, you should have little reason for that.
　　　And yet, to say the truth, reason and love keep little company
　　　together now-a-days.

[III.1.128–32]

It is in remarks like this that Terry Eagleton's view of Bottom and Puck as opposites needs to be tempered. On the thematic level of imagination this is undoubtedly true:

> The ass's head is thus appropriate: like an animal, Bottom is unable to be either more or less than he is. He is thus the polar opposite of Puck, who has no existence outside his theatrical incarnations; Puck cannot be merely one thing, Bottom can be no more than one.
>
> (Eagleton, 1986, p.25)

But because Puck is the floating essence of irrationality and arbitrariness and Bottom is the embodiment of earth-bound, plodding logic, in combination they offer a critique of human behaviour, sharing a scepticism at the follies played out before them ('Lord, what fools these mortals be!'). Paradoxically, it is only the farcical, cold, mechanistic actions of Puck that allow for the sentimental conclusion demanded of romantic comedy. Where imagination is tempered by reality, the ending of the 'old play' was thwarted:

> Jack shall have Jill;
> Nought shall go ill;
> The man shall have his mare again and all shall be well.

[III.2.461–3]

Driving the fantastic patterns woven by rampant desire through the anarchy of the green place is the inescapable reality of animal desire. But in the moment of fulfilling Titania's desire for sexual intercourse with a donkey Bottom appears to the audience as most securely himself. Afterwards the first promptings of his ego propel him (Kempe like?) towards disclosure through the medium of popular culture: 'It shall be call'd 'Bottom's Dream', because it hath no bottom'. However, he immediately realises that the territory of the unconscious is best kept private and the inveterate showman buries the experience with 'not a word of me.'

This is the wisdom which confines the imagination to its proper sphere without which there can be no awakening from the dream. Just as earlier clowns brought the fantastic ideals of those around them into sharp relief with behaviour grounded in reality, so Bottom renders unto the realms of the imagination no more than is appropriate for an artisan's survival.

Once again using the devices of metatheatre to resist oversimplifying the ending of the comedy, Shakespeare exposes the performance of *Pyramus and Thisbe* (*Romeo and Juliet* revisited in burlesque) to a double irony. The play is doomed because the players have too much respect for the power of illusion but the remarks of the audience sound crassly condescending in the mouths of those who have so recently been victims of an overdose of it. Here Shakespeare reverses the scheme of *Love's Labour's Lost*, not ending like an old play with the actors' Bergomask but returning us to the imaginary world of fairyland. If Bottom and Puck can be thought of as the presiding geniuses of the play, it is perhaps appropriate that a wedding celebration should err on the side of illusion since much of it may be needed to navigate the years ahead. The return of the audience to the real world from the imaginative experience of the theatre is likened by Puck to awakening from a dream. Puck, or perhaps rather the actor playing Puck, somewhat disingenuously invites us to consign the whole experience to the unconscious. But theatre, like dreams, can have a nasty habit of invading our waking lives and making asses of us all.

The epithet is better suited to Dogberry than to Bottom. The only feature of clowning that attaches itself to him is that residual characteristic of the Vice, the corruption of words. With Dogberry, however, it is not a matter of occupying the liminal gap between signifier and signified, but simply the reversal of intended meaning through using the wrong word. If this habit is intended to point to a world turned upside down, it is, perhaps, fitting that Dogberry is the unwitting instrument by which it is set back on its feet. *Much Ado About Nothing* is truly much ado about noting in a play where the principals struggle to notice what is in front of them. Shakespeare exploits the irony of the somnolent Watch who are the only characters who see people for what they are: 'What your wisdoms could not discover, these shallow fools have brought to light.' Folly seeing where wisdom is blind is a typical trope of the comic mode but here it is reduced to the almost mechanical resolution of the plot. The obligations of office weigh too heavily upon Dogberry to permit the lightness of wit and this Dull has to cope without the bright foil of Costard. Unlike many of the other comedies there is no deep contradiction between aspiration and desire, soul and body. There are only temporary, self-inflicted barriers to fulfilment. Without a vital function in offering complex seeing, clowns and protracted disguises are notable absentees from this play.

Though the clown's role is limited in *The Merchant of Venice* and Launcelot Gobbo is almost entirely absent from the later action, he is given a crucial function in the presentation of the underlying conflict of the play: this time not so much the contradiction between aspiration and desire as the clash of two worlds, declining and emergent and the contradictory value systems that they each espouse. So used are we to conjuring up a picture of Shylock at the mention of the play's title, that it is easy to forget that it refers not to the Jew but to Antonio, the Christian and the merchant. It is the latter's inability to reconcile his personality with his profession that leads him into the courtroom and the immanent appointment with Shylock's knife. He is trapped like a spider at the centre of its own web; tied by the bond of friendship to subsidising Bassanio's romantic adventure and called to account by the mercantile bond entered into with Shylock, the honouring of which is critical to his credibility as a merchant. The clash of two world orders is announced in the cryptic sentence uttered by Shylock to Bassanio that 'Antonio is a good man.' Christian morality and early modern capitalism meet head on in this phrase and Antonio is impaled on the two prongs of the double meaning. The same contradiction is explored in Brecht's play *The Good Person of Szechwan* where he adopts the device of the split character (Shen Te/Shui Ta) to present it.

Launcelot is the character who confronts the audience directly with the contending demands, adopting direct address to articulate his own dilemma as servant which is a mirror or parody of that which faces Antonio:

> ... to be rul'd by my conscience, I should stay with the Jew my master, who (God bless the mark) is a kind of devil; and to run away from the Jew I should be ruled by the fiend, who (saving your reverence) is the devil himself.
>
> [II.2.21–5]

In form his struggle is the same as that of Man in the morality plays with the Good Angel at one ear and the Bad at the other. As servant to Shylock he has entered into a bond to serve him and his defection to Bassanio is the first breaking of the bonds owed to Shylock. Jessica follows, breaking the filial bond, before Portia breaks the legal bond by arguing against its spirit upon a technicality as Eagleton points out

(Eagleton, 1986, pp.35–40). The law is made by and for Christians and Launcelot's decision to leave Shylock prefigures the latter's fate while drawing our attention to the political realities of the early modern world that have rendered the old moral certainty a thing of the past. Launcelot tries to face both ways: at once modern in the equivocation with which he dispenses with the medieval bond of servitude and loyalty, yet, in defecting from money-lender to impecunious aristocrat, pledging his alliance to the old codes of honour and friendship. David Wiles drew attention to his close ancestry in the Vice tradition (Wiles, 1987, p.8), more helpful about where he came from than where he is going to. As is often the case with the clown/fool figures, their partial displacement from the activities of the present can be read as an indication that they belong in appearance and sentiment more to the past, but in social and psychological terms point to the future. Contradiction inhabits every aspect of form and function and is announced, in the case of Launcelot Gobbo, like Falstaff, even in his name, where the hurtful jab of his needle's point is belied by his slothful flesh. He is in his small role a barometer for the fortunes of the rest, though his attachment as Vice to the fortunes of Bassanio may be taken as an ambiguous indicator of the latter's fate beyond the range of the play. The 'triumph' of Portia over the 'villain' Shylock and his exit, beaten, preserves the comic form that is subsequently restored, but no more resolves the contradiction for the wider world than does the expulsion of the Puritan at the close of *Twelfth Night*. Usury had arrived with a vengeance and capitalism's revenge was merely postponed. Like his predecessor Launce, Launcelot Gobbo is withdrawn from the closing moments of the tale not, this time, because his presence might disturb the formal demand for suspension of disbelief but rather because romance has displaced contradiction.

There is a powerful critical orthodoxy surrounding the character of Touchstone in *As You Like It* that presents him as a significant innovation in the dramatic practice of Shakespeare. The advent of Robert Armin to replace Will Kempe in the Lord Chamberlain's Men has provoked an overstatement of the discontinuity in the evolution of clown to fool that is the result, in part, of the divorce of the figure from his consistent function as the purveyor of contradictions between the ideal and the real:

Touchstone is literally new, the first of the court jester figures Shakespeare later develops in Feste and Lear's Fool, a figure in *AYLI* very probably drawing on the talents of Robert Armin, the new fool for the Globe Theatre, whose past as apprentice goldsmith may be invoked by Touchstone's name – the touchstone identifies what is valuable.

(Lutkus, 1998, p.468)

The specific claim to novelty focuses upon the perceived detachment and objectivity of the role of professional fool. However, as we have already noted, there is a strong tendency for the clown figure to occupy a liminal space between fiction and audience from the outset. It is not obvious that Touchstone whose devotion leads him to accompany Celia and Rosalind into the forest, is any more detached from the pattern of relationships than Launcelot, even though the latter is described as a servant. Robert Goldsmith, following Barber, builds his thesis around the notion of the 'wise fool' as a new and largely separate category of character within Shakespeare's *oeuvre*:

> With the advent of Touchstone, the witty stage fool came completely into his own, divorced alike from the Vice and the clown. Shakespeare had come to realize, as Chapman and Jonson never did, that the comic spirit breathes most freely in the person of a somewhat detached observer.

(Goldsmith, 1974, p.31)

Detachment, however, comes in several forms and 'the comic spirit' is by no means the sole preserve of the character invested in motley. In staking out the territory for the exclusive possession of the 'wise fool' Goldsmith encourages others in the belief that folly with its alternative perspectives on human behaviour, is to be contained within that person's job description:

> Until he came to write *As You Like It* Shakespeare had created fools only dimly aware of their folly, if at all. Dogberry has no idea that he is comical. Touchstone intends to be.

(Latham, 1975, p.lii)

The editor of the Arden edition thus enshrines the orthodox view, thereby begging the question of which characters in previous plays might be designated as fools. She singles out the easiest target for comparison, Dogberry, without raising more interesting and ambiguous cases such as Launce, Costard and, in his own way, Bottom. This is not to deny the importance of Touchstone to his play but rather to qualify the notion that his appearance constitutes some sort of hiatus in Shakespeare's evolving practice. Many of his perceptions relate to the familiar function of using physical, material reality as antidote to the idealist aspirations of those around him. Within the fabulous world of Arden (Eden), he is the voice of the audience etched with the experience of post-lapsarian mortality:

> *Rosalind*:   O Jupiter, how weary are my spirits!
> *Touchstone*: I care not for my spirits, if my legs were not weary.
>
> [II.4. 1–2]

In a play which draws upon the conventional worlds of pastoral and romance, leading to the self-conscious artifice of Hymen's concluding appearance to satisfy 'our' desire for happy, orderly endings to comedies (as we like it), Touchstone keeps his feet firmly on the ground while acting as a lightening-conductor for our disbelief at the fantastic unfolding of events. He is a mocker of pastoral convention through his comments on the reality of rustic existence even as he mocks an idealised view of love which floats free from its initiating impulse in sexual desire. But his observations are not detached since he is linked via the 'bodily lower stratum' to the pattern of social relations upon which the *denouement* is predicated. This pattern is presented in the form of a spectrum with Silvius/Phebe at the idealised end, Touchstone/Audrey at the material end and Orlando/Rosalind occupying the space of the fulcrum in a balance of soul and body.

Detachment is much more the quality that clings to Jaques than to Touchstone. Where the latter is bound by the desires of the body, the former seeks to free himself from their dictates by the application of a melancholy critique of human activity. His name is both ironic and appropriate, signifying the place where the excess and waste of the body is expelled. In his wish to assert the novelty of Shakespeare's practice in this play, Barber elides some crucial differences between the attitudes of Touchstone and Jaques:

> In *As You Like It* the court fool for the first time takes over the work of comic commentary and burlesque from the clown of the earlier plays; in Jaques' praise of Touchstone and the corrective virtues of fooling, Shakespeare can be heard crowing with delight at his discovery. The figure of the jester, with his recognized social role and rich traditional meaning, enabled the dramatist to embody in a character and his relations with other characters the comedy's purpose of maintaining objectivity.
>
> (Barber, 1963, p.228)

The phrase 'the corrective virtues of fooling' shows that Barber is happy to ascribe to Shakespeare the idea that there is a moral purpose to folly that is allied to a campaign to reform the condition of the world. This is, however, not Shakespeare's position but Jaques'. Barber indeed makes the same error as the melancholy man in ascribing this intention to the fool:

> *Jaques*: Invest me in my motley. Give me leave
> To speak my mind, and I will through and through
> Cleanse the foul body of th'infected world,
> If they will patiently receive my medicine.
>
> [II.7.56–61]

Jaques would abuse the licence of the fool to take upon himself the function of the priest; not content with demonstrating the follies of the species, he would presume to tell it what to do to improve itself. He has his own agenda and would use the role of fool to inflict it upon his unfortunate victims. As an evangelical therapist, he would preach moral rearmament rather than engaging his fellow beings in Socratic dialogues designed to expose contradiction as a prerequisite for self-transformation. The pulpit not the forum is his preferred territory. His speech on the seven ages of man demonstrates his inability to accept the reality of mortality while the theatrical metaphor is used to insulate himself from his own shared fate in the process. The lines are a manifestation of the illusion of detachment as exposed in the action that immediately follows their utterance. Although the play's events may endorse the words of the song: 'Most friendship is feigning, most loving mere folly', except for Jaques the other characters are prepared to risk it since friendship and loving are aspects of being human that give this mortal existence a sense of purpose and richness. The fool participates in the knowledge that the behaviour is foolish whereas Jaques uses the same perception to justify his detachment from the life of man.

A by-product of the obsession with Touchstone as the sole repository of wise foolishness in *As You Like It* has been the neglect of the extent to which Rosalind performs the same function. Unlike previously disguised heroines or, for that matter, Viola, she uses the mask of Ganymede not merely as a protective disguise but to release the playful, foolish aspects of her personality. In true Socratic vein her encounters with fellow creatures in the forest reveal the discrepancies and contradictions inherent in their attitudes as in her comment to Jaques: 'I had rather have a fool to make me merry than experience to make me sad, and to travel for it too!' [IV. 1. 25–7]. Most importantly her disguise gives her licence to inherit the function of the Vice and to become the play maker like Mischief and Richard III, in both her own drama with Orlando: 'I will speak to him like a saucy lackey and under that habit play the knave with him' [III.2.291–92], and in that of Silvius and Phebe: 'I'll prove a busy actor in their play' [III.5.55]. Her frequent recourse to the theatrical metaphor begins to detach her from her own role so that she can be both in and out of the fiction. This pays Shakespeare particular theatrical dividends in the scenes with Orlando where simultaneously she is, and is not, his Rosalind. This liminal condition of being and non-being is highlighted by the complexity of the gendered representation confronting the audience where a boy actor impersonates Rosalind who impersonates the male Ganymede who spends much of his time on stage impersonating Rosalind. One effect of the strategy is to point up the discrepancy between an idealised view of courtly love as endorsed by Orlando, and the material reality of its operation as underlined by Ganymede: 'But these are all lies: men have died from time to time and worms have eaten them, but not for love' [IV.1.101–3] The detached Jaques will therefore have nothing to do with love while the cynical Touchstone will acquiesce to the demands of the flesh by exploiting the gullible Audrey. Rosalind, however, internalises her own fool in a manner that enables her to embark, in full knowledge of the dangers, upon the voyage of love. In this play marriage is not only the conventional structural device required to conclude the comedy, it is also, in the case of Orlando and Rosalind, a means of reconciling the ideal with the real, of containing if not confronting the contradiction. The idea of the protagonist playing the fool in her/his own drama is a thread woven throughout the fabric of Shakespeare's canon but here the device has changed from the incorporation of the Vice as in *Richard III* to the taking on of characteristics derived from the fool. This anticipates a major strategy of the tragedies where folly becomes a principal mask with which the protagonist negotiates encounters with a hostile environment. The two strands of the 'wise fool' inaugurated by Touchstone, and the protagonist as fool announced by Rosalind are destined to achieve their union and apotheosis in *King Lear* via a rehearsal in *Hamlet*.

Meanwhile the discrepancy between the ideal and the real grows ever wider and moves in the so-called 'problem' plays from the vexations of irrational love to a matter of life and death. In Angelo and Isabella two protagonists who put the claims of the ideal beyond the reach of reality's compromises, clash with nearly fatal consequences (Edwards,

1968, p.117). If sexual desire was only one element provoking the activities in Arden, in Vienna sex, the having or not having, is all. Inevitably this pits the formal, official discourse against the popular; the Lenten Angelo against the carnivalesque Pompey: 'Does your worship mean to geld and splay all the youth of the city?' [II.1.227–8]. In this play there is no middle ground between the two; no Berowne or Rosalind with the self-awareness to attempt a balancing of their contraries. Whatever the current political correctness may require him to speak, Pompey knows that the dictates of the flesh will always ensure a profitable 'trade':

> *Pompey*: I thank your worship for your good counsel; [*aside*] but I shall
> follow it as the flesh and fortune shall better determine.
> Whip me? No, no, let carman whip his jade;
> The valiant heart's not whipt out of his trade.
>
> [II.1. 249–53]

The gap between counsel and action is a running theme of this play and nowhere illustrated more fiercely than in the blatant discrepancy between word and deed revealed in the unlocking of Angelo's desire. Pompey who is the closest character to a clown that this play offers, demonstrates a level of self-knowledge beyond the reach of the deputy whilst typically enlisting the sympathies of the audience through his direct address to it outside the frame of the ideology promoted by the chief protagonist. Whereas the struggle between the flawed ideal and the earth-bound real is the stock in trade of his comedy, Shakespeare develops the scope of the onstage stage manager, the 'play maker', well beyond that of Rosalind. The Duke with his 'disappearance' and disguise lures Angelo into betraying the full contradiction between the absolute of the law and the contingent of humanity. His strategy is itself an admission that he has hitherto been unable to address that contradiction and so he resorts to fooling (in both senses for he fools Angelo) in order to achieve that socialisation of desire that he could not bring about in his own right. He clearly knew all along about Angelo's past history with Mariana which raises a question about the extent to which he engineers the whole crisis that constitutes the action of the play.

It becomes increasingly apparent that the Duke relishes the freedom of his role as 'fixer', made possible by his self-imposed detachment from Viennese society: 'My business in this state/Made me a looker-on here in Vienna' [V.1.314–15]. It is as if he can only see how people are when he is free of the responsibility for responding to their behaviour; in other words, the typical situation of the fool:

Duke: ... and hear, by this is your brother saved, your honour untainted, the poor Mariana advantaged, and the corrupt deputy scaled

[III.1.235–56]

This brisk summary of the intended outline of events is, however, antic-ipating the action of *The Tempest*, thwarted. The Duke is not God and is therefore unable to read the souls of his fellow men. He does not allow for the possibility that some men's natures are irredeemably fallen: Angelo does not keep to the bargain with Isabella when he believes he has got what he wants. The corruption inaugurated by his giving way to sexual desire has already corroded his wider moral sense. The pattern of the morality plays has been turned through 180 degrees; the maker of the 'game' is now not the Vice but rather an anti-vice who may not be able to secure salvation for fallen man but can at least protect us from the worst consequences of our follies: 'Craft against vice I must apply' [III.2.270]. It is the craft of improvisation that is called up as he exploits the outrageous convenience of the execution of the Claudio look-alike, Ragozine. However, it is not the creaking of the plot as much as the intentions of the Duke which give cause for disquiet as events unravel. There is a danger that the Duke as fool may simply become the foolish Duke:

Duke: But I will keep her ignorant of her good,
To make her heavenly comforts of despair
When it is least expected.

[IV.3.107–9]

Not only does this suggest that his pleasure at remotely controlling the fate of his subjects may be bordering on psychological torture but also that, with the final moments in mind, the Duke may be softening Isabella up so that, overwhelmed with gratitude, she accepts his offer. The difficulty has been created by the device of the split character; his freedom to manipulate as the 'friar' not answerable to the power brokers of Vienna, is immediately compromised when he assumes his own per-son as the Duke or, as Lucio not altogether unjustly terms him: 'the old fantastical duke of dark corners' [IV.3.156]. The response that Isabella might make to a proposition from the 'friar' is not necessarily the same as that which the Duke would elicit. The fool, by dividing actor from role, constantly has the advantage of operating on two planes of reality (or perhaps more accurately, in the context of a theatrical performance, three). But while this may prove to be a 'device to make all well', it also raises serious doubts about the split figure's reintegration into society as himself for what now constitutes that 'self'?

The problem of the discrepancy between the conventional demands of the comic form and the reality of human experience which dominates the conclusion of *Measure for Measure* is confronted even in the very title, albeit ironically, of *All's Well That Ends Well*. Bertram, like Angelo, is another protagonist upon whose nature nurture appears unable to stick. His flight from Helena who, unlike the Duke, is always herself no matter how she disguises that self, is a flight from marriage as the accepted social conduit for sexual desire and therefore a flight from the required ending of the comedy. Thus the play shares with *Measure for Measure* a sense of being open-ended, of closure resisted even beyond the epilogue of the jig. In other ways, however, *All's Well That Ends Well* harks back to the earlier worlds of the folk and morality plays, though there is an important and complete separation of the Vice from the fool. From the outset Parolles who resembles New Guise from *Mankind* with his love of fashion, is associated in word and deed with the Vice ('and though the devil lead the measure, such are to be followed' [II.1.54–5], 'The devil it is that's thy master' [II.3.245]) who leads Bertram to his destruction. His antagonist in the moral scheme is Lavatch, the clown who is never deceived about the character or function of his opposite:

> To say nothing, to do nothing, to know nothing
> and to have nothing, is to be a great part of your
> title, which is within a very little of nothing.

> [II.4.23–6]

He underlines the association of Parolles with the devil through the reiteration of 'nothing', the zero that signifies the diabolical. While the unmasking of Parolles, emphasising the hollowness of his words (*paroles*) belongs in the morality scheme, his response to the experience is distinctly modern:

> Rust, sword; cool, blushes; and Parolles live
> Safest in shame; being fool'd, by fool'ry thrive.
> There's place and means for every man alive.

> [IV.3.326–8]

In heaven there is the ultimate distinction of sheep from goats but on earth no such discrimination operates. His false military posture has been exposed but he'll create another role by means of folly itself, though it be a type of fooling that grows more and more distant from that which is articulated in the diminutive body of the 'wise' fool, Armin:

> . . . I am for the house with the narrow gate, which I take to be too little for pomp to enter; some that humble themselves may, but the many will be too chill and tender, and they'll be for the flow'ry way that leads to the broad gate and the great fire.

> [IV.5.47–52]

There may not be quite as many of the 'many' as inhabit the world depicted by the Porter in *Macbeth* but there is now no possibility of the whole cast tripping off to redemption in an all encompassing conclusion. Where once the Vice stood alone outside the moral pattern of the morality play's ending, there is now an increasing number of characters who belong in his faction; so much so that the fool, transformed into his opposite, may be in danger of occupying that place of isolation.

Isolation, indeed, effectively describes Feste's situation in *Twelfth Night*. The figure alone on stage at the end to sing the epilogue has been anticipated throughout by a refusal to tie him into any of the social patterns that account for others. In contrast to Touchstone he has no place in the collective pairing off that characterises the formal conclusion of the comedy. Though officially of Olivia's household he is frequently absent and commutes to Orsino's court, searching for payment for his songs. The notion of detachment which I have traced as an increasingly significant aspect of those who perform the functions of fools, achieves its most extreme expression in the persona of Feste. He has face to face encounters with all the major characters of the play: Orsino, Olivia, Viola, Sebastian, Malvolio, Sir Toby and Sir Andrew, and is at ease in the company of none of them. It is as if his ability to perceive their limitations or the dangers of their situations holds him back from engaging whole-heartedly with their hopes and desires. Like Puck he can see 'what fools these mortals be' but unlike Puck he is acutely aware that he is one of them himself and has to live with them in spite of what he knows.

The other aspect of this detachment or isolation reflects how far the figure of the fool has travelled from his starting point in the late medieval world as a version of the Vice who is in turn associated with the pleasures of the flesh and their manifestation in carnival. The tension between Carnival and Lent personified in the antagonism between Sir Toby and Malvolio is the dominant theme of the entire play. Announced even in its title, for the Twelfth Night after Christmas is the Feast of Fools when social order is inverted and lords and ladies wait upon servants, the play traces the consequences for the orderly running of the world when those trusted with maintaining order, Orsino and Olivia, give way to their desires; in this instance desires which carry more than a hint of inherent social disorder in the revelation of their homosexual and lesbian tendencies. Illyria seems a country in the grip of uncontrolled, carnivalesque desires in which even the apparent agent of order, in both his social function as steward and in temperamental proclivity as a kind of Puritan, is caught up via the self-love which propels him into the fantasy of Count Malvolio. It is doubly ironic that it is Sir Toby who highlights the discrepancy ('art any more than a Steward?' [II.3.108], since as a knight and as Olivia's uncle he is unmindful of the demands of order and since he becomes the means by which order is transcended by elevating Maria to Lady Belch. In this aspect as in others it is Feste who stands alone to comment on the follies of defying the social claims of order and the natural claims of mortality. In a play which presents a series of characters at war with themselves over the rival claims of Carnival and Lent, it is left to the fool to articulate the delicate balance of these contrary impulses.

On his first appearance Feste offers Maria 'a good lenten answer' and follows up by showing that he knows what Maria's intentions are towards Sir Toby, paralleling those of Malvolio towards Olivia. When he expresses the familiar inversion of wisdom and folly it serves as more than the cliché of his profession but rather announces the structural principle of a play where inversion is the norm: Sir Toby and Sir Andrew invert work and holiday; Malvolio would invert service and dominance; either wilfully or strategically Orsino, Olivia and Viola invert the gendered desire. When Feste inverts his role of fool by playing priest, it is announced visually and verbally to the audience and his interchange of voices highlights the blatant theatricality of the proceeding. In the spirit of Socrates his dialogues are used to expose the contradictions and excesses in the behaviour of those upon whom he exercises his wit. Olivia's initial unbalance is in the excess of formal mourning that she proposes to mark the death of her brother. The counter to this behaviour comes from within her own beliefs: 'The more fool, Madonna, to mourn for your brother's soul, being in heaven' [I.5.65–6]. He is the instrument by which the ideal is divided from the real, the thought from the deed, the signifier from the signified. Even as he smarts from Malvolio's rebuke, he is quick to indicate where the battle lines are to be drawn: Sir Toby, not he, is the antagonist: 'God send you sir, a speedy infirmity, for the better increasing your folly: Sir Toby will be sworn that I am no fox, but he will not pass his word for two pence that you are no fool' [I.5.72–6]. 'Mad' and 'madness' is used more often in this play than any other of Shakespeare's and is the quality that most characterises the inhabitants of Illyria. Viola by virtue of being an outsider and of being disguised, can claim partial immunity until she starts to succumb to her feelings for Orsino, but Feste is a permanent resident, born and bred, who can only escape the plague by the self-immunisation of his folly: 'the fool shall look to the madman'.

Feste's songs are not an escape from this burden of playful sanity but rather a distillation into another key of those same perceptions that separate him from his fellow beings. His choice to perform for Toby and Andrew, for example, besides looking beyond the moment with which the characters are presently preoccupied ('Youth's a stuff will not endure') to picture the skeleton beneath the flesh, also offers a critique of the comic form itself:

> Journeys end in lovers meeting
> Every wise man's son doth know.
>
> [II.3.42–3]

for it is comedies as well as journeys which end in lovers' meeting and Feste (the wise man's son is the fool) aligns himself with the audience in realising that it is not appropriate to speculate on the fate of the lovers as married couples: that way Lady Macbeth lies. Thus the fool's self-awareness not only covers his functions within the fiction of the play, Illyria in this case, but also extends to a meta-theatrical understanding of what falls beyond the boundaries of the play. He operates as guide and co-conspirator with the audience and, in doing so, paradoxically enables us the better to suspend our disbelief. Just because the world of *Twelfth Night* contains the figure of Feste, we are more, not less, likely to accept it as a valid insight into human experience. The character who comes closest to him in self-knowledge is Viola who similarly has to maintain a high degree of self-consciousness in order not to give herself away; so it is fitting that she provides the summary of Feste's function and in so doing offers a sketch of Armin's professional qualities:

> This fellow is wise enough to play the fool,
> And to do that well, craves a kind of wit:
> He must observe their mood on whom he jests,
> The quality of persons, and the time:
> And like the haggard, check at every feather
> That comes before his eye. This is a practice,
> As full of labour as a wise man's art:
> For folly that he wisely shows, is fit;
> But wise men folly-fall'n, quite taint their wit.

[III.1.57–65]

This analysis concerns the ways in which the fool observes society around him and offers no view of the personality of Feste, for in the conventional sense he has no personality: he is his function. In terms of theatre it is an unmediated juxtaposition of actor and role. Whereas those actors undertaking the other parts look for a coming together of their own personalities with the perceived personalities of the character to be portrayed, out of which synthesis comes the impersonation of the role, the actor of the fool has only Feste's function within the action to wear as his mask. The fool is already an 'act' that the actor inherits in the performance of which the audience do not lose sight of the space between actor and role. When Launce performs his stand-up routine in *The Two Gentlemen of Verona*, the moment is barely attached to the rest of the play; a space has been cleared for Kempe to entertain in his own person, quite overwhelming the fictional character. Here it is the opposite process in which Armin brings himself to the role of Feste so that the audience can watch the interaction between actor and role unencumbered by the fiction of character. This is perhaps the most powerful element in Feste's isolation within the play; he is conceived in a generically different way from the rest – as a role which carries with it its own critique almost as if an epic realist performance had inadvertently wandered into a piece of psychological naturalism.

The most complex thread of inversion is perhaps that which tangles itself between madness and sanity when frequently the two states seem either to change over at bewildering speed or else become indistinguishable one from the other. The epicentre of the debate occurs when

Malvolio is confined in 'a dark house' to 'cure' his madness. This appears especially harsh in the context of *Twelfth Night* where almost all the other characters are equally in need of the remedy. Feste who has kept himself well clear of the devices of the carnival faction, is inveigled into contributing to Malvolio's distress because of his skills as an actor and his understanding of the conventions of playing: 'so I being Master Parson, am Master Parson'. In the playhouse the costume makes the person and in the Elizabethan theatre the word must be taken for the thing itself since the visual element, the scene, is painted in words. There's nothing light or dark but saying makes it so, as Katherine discovered in *The Taming of the Shrew*. If Malvolio acquiesces in the practice being played upon him by being persuaded that he is mad, he becomes, like Katherine, dependent upon others for his continued existence. Yet in the theatre whoever commands the scene orders the reality and there seems little he can say in his own defence:

Malvolio: I am as well in my wits, fool, as thou art.
Clown: But as well: then you are mad indeed, if you be no better in your wits than a fool.

[IV.2.85–7]

His next attempt hardly fares any better, given what we have noted of the inhabitants of the country: 'I tell thee I am as well in my wits, as any man in Illyria'. That, unfortunately for him, is the point. Finally, and most pertinently of all coming from one who makes his living by the pretence of madness, is the question of acting:

Clown: But tell me true, are you not mad indeed, or do you but counterfeit?
Malvolio: Believe me I am not, I tell thee true.
Clown: Nay, I'll ne'er believe a madman till I see his brains.

[IV.2.110–12]

If a madman says he is sane, is that further proof of his madness? A regular token of Feste's sanity is his capacity to acknowledge his own madness. The situation of this scene confronts the audience with the inverted countenance of madness and sanity with the added theatrical problem, such as Falstaff presented on the battlefield of Shrewsbury, that in this art form all is counterfeit, and the one who counterfeits most effectively takes control of the situation. Paradoxically it is Malvolio's inability to be anything other than himself, be that festive lover or madman, that saves him from the practices of one who, by contrast, can be all things to all men, depending upon the performance called forth by the situation. Feste underlines the fact that he is engaged in a temptation that could damn Malvolio to eternal darkness by likening himself 'to the old Vice' of the morality plays. But the momentary echo of his ancestry serves as much to remind us how far he has moved away in both form and function; a movement endorsed by his action in providing Malvolio with the means to bring about his release.

The journey of the play ends in the lovers' meeting and we remember Feste's earlier injunction not to look beyond that moment in a comedy of this kind. Resolution in the form of the imposition of order through marriage may be the saving of those who are capable of maturing beyond madness and those who are not are expelled before the conclusion. The extremes of both Carnival and Lent, Malvolio and Toby, cannot be included in the process. This just leaves Feste whose sardonic visions of the fate of man hardly accord with the required jollity of the weddings. Ironically he is too incapable of being festive to warrant inclusion in the party, and his song – a sharp contrast to the jigs of Kempe – takes in the whole scope of mortality well beyond the lovers' meeting. Lurking under the verses and echoing through the refrain of 'for the rain it raineth every day' is a sense that, the humanist and early modern aspirations of Renaissance society notwithstanding, there are elements of the human condition which are beyond improvement. To be human is to suffer a daily dose of bad weather. In the fabulous fiction of romantic comedy there is a golden present which banishes the decaying, carnivalesque past of Sir Toby and Sir Andrew and the violent, intolerant future of Puritanical revenge fostered by Malvolio, but in the world shared alike by Feste and by the listeners to his closing song there is only an unstoppable process of mortality, of decay and renewal, of death inducing and life giving rain.

At the centre of the world of the play, yet at the same time apart from it, Feste most nearly resembles the fool who is the focal figure of Bruegel's painting of *The Fight Between Carnival and Lent*. Like Feste singing his epilogue, this fool too has turned his back on both Carnival and Lent and appears to be leading the couple whom, transposed into the medium of theatre, we might take to be representative of an audience, away from the foreground of conflict towards the more balanced activities that lie between the extremities of body and soul, tavern

and church. If the dominant ideological struggle of the sixteenth century was that between God and the devil, spirit and flesh, the fool is
the figure who comes closest to deconstructing the binary in favour of a
continuous process of becoming in which man's loftiest aspirations can
fall prey at any moment to the promptings of desire. He is at odds with
the society in which he lives, not because he offers a different way of
living, but because he reminds his fellow creatures of their limitations
as animals.

5
Fooling with Kings

> This thing of darkness, I acknowledge mine.
>
> [*The Tempest* V.1.275]

Standing on the brink of the fatal duel with Laertes, Hamlet offers an apology to the man whose father he has killed and whose sister he has driven to suicide, based on the supposed schizophrenia wrought in him by madness:

> What I have done
> That might your nature, honour, and exception
> Roughly awake, I here proclaim was madness.
> Was't Hamlet wrong'd Laertes? Never Hamlet.
> If Hamlet from himself be ta'en away,
> And when he's not himself does wrong Laertes,
> Then Hamlet does it not, Hamlet denies it.
> Who does it then? His madness. If 't be so,
> Hamlet is of the faction that is wrong'd;
> His madness is poor Hamlet's enemy.
>
> [V. 2. 226–35]

As an actor creates a character, so Hamlet has created a mad version of himself; for 'mad' Hamlet can do such things as are beyond the natural scope of normal princely behaviour. In a similar manner Brecht will create, in the two figures of the sober and the drunk Puntila, a man who can simultaneously uphold and transgress the boundaries of accepted social behaviour. However, Hamlet has wilfully adopted the 'antic disposition' as a mask so that his plea of diminished responsibility to Laertes rings somewhat hollow. Madness is wielded throughout the play as a double-edged or, in the case of the duel, an 'unbated' sword. Shakespeare's tragedies place their protagonists in fixed moral and social positions from which they struggle in vain to escape: Hamlet the avenger; Macbeth the usurper; Lear the king. They are held in these places by the expectations others put upon them and by those they put upon themselves. The plays depict the means by which they attempt to evade or equivocate with their destinies. Were Hamlet simply to respond immediately to the Ghost's demand for revenge, to agree to be acted upon by events, ('no delay, no play'), he would have denied himself the space in which to consider his own and mankind's nature. The concept of what is 'natural', that is, in keeping with human nature, is central to Shakespearean tragedy and the major preoccupation of its protagonists:

> Shakespeare's Hamlet does not save time, allay doubts, and protect himself by feigning madness; if anything, his antic pose arouses suspicion. Shakespeare's assimilation of the antic theme, in spite of its relative inappropriateness to his hero's immediate psychological needs or indeed the necessities of plot, suggests that the theatrical tradition of madness must have carried considerable weight.
>
> (Weimann, 1978, p.128)

Hamlet does not adopt this 'pose' to achieve any of the purposes that Weimann ascribes to him. Arousing suspicion is part of his intention, for only by so doing can he mount a challenge to the idea that Claudius' actions and the conduct of the Danish court are normal. The mask of madness is a means of escaping from his designated role within that normality and the 'tradition' to which Weimann refers, as we have noted previously, is one which saw madness as an indissoluble element within human nature. He later redresses the imbalance of his argument by opening the space between character and role but the purpose is still more about Hamlet's attempt to recover his humanity rather than to dissociate himself from the court; an important but secondary motive in the process of folly:

> For Hamlet at such moments releases himself from his own role of the Prince of Denmark: with the help of popular proverb and aside he momentarily dissociates himself from the illusion of the world of the court and revives a late ritual capacity for reckless sport and social criticism.
>
> (Weimann, 1978, p.150)

Claudius' place in the moral scheme is clear. He has committed the most unnatural act conceivable – tearing up the bonds that hold both family and kingdom together. In doing so he has severed himself from his own nature. Hamlet's situation is much less clear-cut. As a member of the same family will his revenge heal the initial breach or compound it by a further unnatural act? Does revenge, in Macbeth's phrase, 'become a man' or does it relegate him to the catalogue of beasts? One of the purposes in putting on the 'antic disposition' is to buy the time in which to work at these questions; by fooling with revenge to render it somehow natural. Like a bull-fighter Hamlet teases and provokes until he reaches the moment when revenge can fulfil its ritual function in the restoration of nature but, since this is tragedy, the bull has a mind to spoil the party. Hamlet's initial encounter with the Ghost, though terrifying and solemn in its implications: 'If thou hast nature in thee, bear it not' [I.5.81], is conducted on another level as a game between two old friends; frequent sparring partners at the centre of the company's fortunes – Burbage and Shakespeare. Hamlet/Burbage refers to the Ghost in the genial terms of 'truepenny' and 'old mole' while Ghost/Shakespeare exploits his familiarity with the below stage areas of the Globe. In this most self-consciously theatrical of plays, Hamlet responds simultaneously on theatrical and metatheatrical levels to the admonitions of the Ghost; both levels united by the function of memory:

> .... Remember thee?
> Ay, thou poor ghost, whiles memory holds a seat
> In this distracted globe. Remember thee?
>
> [I.5. 95–7]

Within the fiction Hamlet highlights the disturbance caused by the Ghost inside his own head and alludes fool-like from outside the fiction to the disturbance created by introducing a supernatural being to the audience inside the Globe. Fittingly for a play which constantly insists on reminding us of its theatricality, the protagonist sees himself from his first appearance as an actor:

> .... These indeed seem,
> For they are actions that a man might play;
> But I have that within which passes show,
> These but the trappings and the suits of woe.
>
> [I.2.83–3]

He is confident of the separation of the performed role from the inner state of being; of the psychological barrier between character and actor. At the outset, at least, secure that he is playing a chosen role rather than being played by that role; an artificial not a natural fool. Such a separation may keep him from being known but also keeps him from revealing what he knows. Eventually in politics, in theatre, or in any form of human relationship 'that within which passes show' must be brought to the surface and shown or else it will die, unused. The 'antic disposition' is the device that Hamlet adopts to translate, at least for the audience if not all his fellow players, inner torment into outer words and actions 'that a man might play'. As Weimann has indicated:

> In its latent meaning, the "antic disposition" in *Hamlet* contrariously expands the field of courtly and humanistic discourses; it resituates the protagonist's secret close intent in the open space of the performer's skill in delivering versions of disguise, disfigurement, and grotesquerie.
>
> (Weimann, 2000, p.168)

He buys a little time and a little space to test how much play there is in the situation but he cannot escape from the contradiction between revenge's demand for action and his adopted role's capacity for infinite equivocation:

> As fluid as his father's ghost and as fast-talking as any Shakespearian clown, Hamlet riddles and bamboozles his way out of being definitively known, switching masks and sliding the signifier to protect his inner privacy of being against the power and knowledge of the court.
>
> (Eagleton, 1986, p.71)

He is drawn by intuition and memory to the situation of the fool who uses his mask to keep himself outside the main ideological currents of the drama. The available positions as laid down in the narrative are either to ignore the accusations of the ghost and participate in the decadent court of Claudius or to trust the ghost and become its active agent as enemy to that court. Either way Hamlet would find himself trapped within a flow of events not of his making or within his control. Paradoxically he opts for a third position in which the suppression of any fixed identity, together with a space apparently outside the discourse, enables him to articulate his sense of self, if only to himself. But even his choice of role contains its own contradiction: if he plays the mask of madness too well, he will lose the fool's ancient ability of exposing the gap between what people seem or profess and what they are in deed; if he does not play it well enough, the mask will slip to reveal too much of the method beneath: 'Though this be madness, yet there is method in't' [II.2.205–6]. Polonius buys Hamlet's masquerade in both its aspects, the madness and the method, but other adversaries offer a sharper wit in their defence. As there are two Hamlets, the mad and the methodical, so there are two of Rosencrantz and Guildenstern, the school friends and the spies. The verbal joust between them is a battle about who will play upon whom; who will know and who will keep from being known. From the outset Hamlet slips into the familiar mode of the fool:

> *Hamlet*:   What news?
> *Rosencrantz*: None, my lord, but the world's grown honest.
> *Hamlet*:   Then is doomsday near. But your news is not true.
>
> [II.2.236–8]

Hamlet anticipates Lear's Fool in depicting a world in which corruption cannot be relied upon as one that is unable to sustain itself. Our relations with one another depend upon the certainty of the imperfection of mankind. But, like Hamlet, we can rest assured, for the very announcement of global honesty is a falsehood in the mouth of the dishonest Rosencrantz. In the verbal interrogation of Hamlet by Rosencrantz and Guildenstern it is the party with the greater mastery of the slipperiness of language who will gain the upper hand. Too blatant a madness will provide Claudius with justification for taking Hamlet out of circulation, too obvious a sanity will run the risk of unmasking his intent. He therefore walks the tightrope of ambiguity with calculated precision:

> I am but mad north-north-west. When the wind is southerly,
> I know a hawk from a handsaw.
>
> [II.2. 374–5]

On one level Hamlet tries to suggest to them that he is partially out of his wits since the distinction between a hawk and a handsaw is one which most half-wits are capable of making. On another level he is telling the audience that he knows precisely what is going on at the court of Claudius since a hawk is also a plasterer's tool and a handsaw is a deliberate mispronunciation of 'hernshaw' or 'heronshaw'. He is neither, as it were, one tool short of a set nor incapable of distinguishing between a bird or prey and a heron. There is a constant double set of meanings running through his words: one set for the other characters within the stage fiction, Horatio excepted, and another for the consumption of the theatre audience. In this way he provides a running, critical commentary upon the action of the drama without entirely detaching himself from the course of events. It is the archetypal position of the fool but in Hamlet's case it is only half a role since he has also been cast as the protagonist in this drama.

Even this degree of subtlety cannot protect him from the surveillance of his former school friends since Guildenstern reports precisely back to Claudius on the strategy that Hamlet employed against them:

> But with a crafty madness keeps aloof
> When we would bring him on to some confession
> Of his true state.

> [III.1.8–10]

and this report is confirmed immediately to Claudius' satisfaction when he spies upon Hamlet's staged encounter with Ophelia:

> Nor what he spake, though it lack'd form a little,
> Was not like madness.

> [III.1.165–6]

However, Claudius is too astute a politician to let pass any advantage that Hamlet's 'madness' might afford him. Hamlet has offered just enough madness to justify Claudius' policy towards him: 'Madness in great ones must not unwatch'd go' [III.1.190]. Madness in *Hamlet* is not a psychological condition but a game, albeit a deadly game; a part of the process of play where, as ever, it is the most skilful player who triumphs. Hamlet knows he is not mad and tries to use the mask to his advantage in playing the role of revenger. Claudius knows Hamlet is not mad but tries to use the mask to shore up his role of usurper. Shakespeare underlines the point throughout by Hamlet's use of playhouse terms, particularly at moments of emotional pressure. He speaks of 'the *motive* and the *cue* for passion' and is '*prompted* to [his] revenge by heaven and hell'.

Fittingly the climax of Hamlet's strategy to expose the gap between Claudius' mask and his reality comes in the form of theatrical action. While conscious that much of his role in the drama of his father's murder lies outside his control, Hamlet revels in the chance to take control of one moment within the wider performance by operating as playwright, director, chorus, audience and even facilitator through his interpretation of Claudius' response to the production of *The Mousetrap*. The one role he does not embrace is that of the fool for here he is the active protagonist rather than the artificial fool reacting to the situations that are put before him. Just as there are multiple contradictions between the roles he attempts throughout the play, so in his manipulation of the poetics of theatre he is caught between the classical and the popular; between Aristotle and Kempe:

> And let those that play your clowns speak no more than is set down for them – for there be of them that will themselves laugh, to set on some quantity of barren spectators to laugh too, though in the meantime some necessary question of the play be then to be considered.
>
> [III.2.38–43]

He repudiates the behaviour he has himself adopted in the play without the play, for he requires no distractions from the scene of crime reconstruction that might provide space in which Claudius could recover his mask. Referring to the additional passage in Q1 Weimann highlights the typical contrary or double action in which Hamlet is engaged with the players:

> The Prince "thus", so "blabbering with his lips", is telling the players what not to do, but he does so by doing it himself. Thereby, he can in one and the same speech collapse two different orders of authority in the purpose of playing. One follows humanistically sanctioned, mimetic precepts associated with Donatus and Cicero, the other – in the teeth of their rejection – the contemporary practices of Tarleton and company.
>
> (Weimann, 2000, p.23)

If the moment does, indeed, mark the time of Kempe's departure from the company on the grounds that his style of comedy is now out of favour with the principal playwright, Shakespeare nevertheless offers several indicators of regret at the demise of a popular tradition that he, himself, helped to hasten from the stage. Like Feste slipping into the role of 'the old Vice' to torment Malvolio, Hamlet alludes to the gamut of folk traditions that are in danger of passing not only from enactment but even from memory, summed up in the line from the popular song: 'For O, for O, the hobby-horse is forgot'. Liebler points to the long struggle between the dominant ideology of church and state and the residual traditions of the people encapsulated in the emblem of the forgotten hobby-horse:

> Given the often frustrated efforts of church and governmental offi-
> cials to suppress various vestigially pagan folk practices such as
> the hobby-horse dance, it would appear that such practices were
> sustained – where they *were* sustained – precisely because they
> were repositories of self-determination and maintenance for popu-
> lations lacking other ways of countering domination by hierarchical
> agencies.
>
> (Liebler, 1995, p.175)

This *motif* is strengthened and deepened in the graveyard scene where Hamlet comes face to face with that past tradition in the form of Yorick's skull. The ironies proliferate when the nostalgic recollections of his fool-ing link him irresistibly to the tumbling and physical comedy tradition of Dick Tarleton, for his bones are being disinterred by the gravedigger; the role performed by Robert Armin who inherited the clown parts from Will Kempe, the disciple of Tarleton, and developed the poetics of folly away from stand-up comedy towards his musical strengths and a verbal wit firmly integrated into the thematic structures of the play as a whole. This is the one moment in the play where the would-be fool encounters the 'real' thing in the person of the professional fool:

Hamlet: Whose grave's this, sirrah?
Gravedigger: Mine, sir.
                      [*Sings*] *O a pit of clay for to be made* –
Hamlet: I think it be thine indeed, for thou liest in't.
Gravedigger: You lie out on't, sir, and therefore 'tis not yours. For my
                      part, I do not lie in't, yet it is mine.
Hamlet: Thou dost lie in't, to be in't and say 'tis thine. 'Tis for the
                      dead, not for the quick: therefore thou liest.
Gravedigger: 'Tis a quick lie, sir, 'twill away again from me to you.
Hamlet: What man dost thou dig it for?
Gravedigger: For no man, sir.
Hamlet: What woman then?
Gravedigger: For none neither.
Hamlet: Who is to be buried in't?
Gravedigger: One that was a woman, sir; but rest her soul, she's dead.

[V.1.115–32]

The fool must have the last word for that is his profession but the fooling of Armin ensures that the wit on display is related directly to the central theme of 'to be or not to be'. Hamlet is good and keeps his end up for a while but, like Simon confronting Azdak in an exchange of proverbs in *The Caucasian Chalk Circle*, he has to cede ground to the master of the genre.

In a play which is consistently characterised by the resort to mask and agency, it is hardly surprising that the *denouement* comes in the form of a mock tournament. The fencing bout and its accompanying rituals are not what they seem for Claudius has invested them with a deadly purpose. The test of skill is understood to be only play with 'bated' foils; the last in a line of mock rituals that emanate from the wedding/funeral that sets the sequence in motion. Hamlet conducts himself according to the rules of play, only to discover that this was earnest. Claudius breaks all the rules of performance just as he broke all natural bonds in murdering his brother and thereby offers an uncanny parallel with the Carnival at Romans in 1580. By transgressing the laws of play, like those who used the Carnival for their own violent ends, he destroys an agreed basis upon which society operates and renders all behaviour possible. He not only pulls destruction down upon his own head but also makes necessary the complete renewal of the society he has poisoned. The fool might evade this fate and remain the digger of others' graves but Hamlet is implicated in the fate of this society. At the very moment of his revenge his role is transformed from avenger to scapegoat. Not mad enough to play the conventional revenger who maintains the cycle of violence, his attempts to broaden the role through the devices of play instead result in him becoming the agent of restoration, the means by which life can be carried on.

Hamlet marks a more sophisticated return to the idea of the protagonist as fool which Shakespeare tried out in *Richard III*. In that instance, Richard was ultimately reclaimed as the vice of the morality tradition. In this case Hamlet tried to play the fool not *instead of* but *within* the role of the revenger. At times he succeeded in creating the revenger's comedy but finally the genre claimed its dues. By now, however, Shakespeare had developed a taste for folly in high places.

Like *Hamlet* before it, *King Lear* begins with the breaking of bonds; the fracturing of the social relations that had knitted together a hierarchical structure. Again, as with *Hamlet*, the condition of the family is the barometer for the state of the nation. Where Hamlet was the victim of the break-up, Lear is both perpetrator and victim; he unleashes that which destroys him. The process starts with the separation of function ('office') from person. What is Lear if he is not fulfilling the function of king? Furthermore the separation of power from the framework of duty and responsibility gives free rein to those left with that power to exercise it merely for the depraved gratification of their own wills. Such people – Goneril, Regan, Cornwall, Edmund – respond to the promptings of nature, understood in the sense of their unfettered, animal natures, and in defiance of their human nature, understood as the proper balance of the socialised human being. Lear's misjudgements, both personal and political, provoke this separation of the two meanings of nature which becomes expressed in conflict on many levels: domestic, civil, national and international.

From the outset, Lear's unkingly behaviour is associated with madness:

> *Kent*: .... be Kent unmannerly,
> When Lear is mad. What would'st thou do, old man?
>
> [I.1.144–5]

Kent's words expose the instant transition in Lear's situation brought on by his dealings with his daughters; he moves at a stroke from King Lear to 'old man'. This change presents the Fool with a serious challenge. Being the fool to a monarch is a designated, well understood role but why would an old man need the services of a truth-teller when he is no longer shielded from confrontations with reality by his social position? The court is the licensed premises of the fool but, denied a courtly function, his playground becomes everywhere and nowhere. Though Lear has given away his office, he is unable to detach himself from the habits of kingship or grasp a notion of how others now view him:

> *Goneril*: Did my father strike my gentleman for chiding of his Fool?
>
> [I.3.1–3]

Goneril's 'gentleman' has a position of some power in the new polity whereas the Fool, uncoupled from the protection of the monarch from whom he received his licence, is now just the companion of an old man. The new situation is especially acute for the Fool who is so defined by his function that he does not, unlike his Shakespearean predecessors, even enjoy the benefit of a name. His identity is both his certainty and his limitation. Despite the change of circumstances he can do nothing but play the fool but, whereas that function was formerly directed towards a king, it now has only an old man as its butt:

> *Fool*: Dost thou know the difference, my boy, between a bitter Fool
>   and a sweet one?
> *Lear*: No, lad; teach me.
> *Fool*: That lord that counsell'd thee
>   To give away thy land,
>   Come place him here by me,
>   Do thou for him stand:
>   The sweet and bitter fool
>   Will presently appear;
>   The one in motley here,
>   The other found out there.
> *Lear*: Dost thou call me fool, boy?
> *Fool*: All thy other titles thou hast given away; that thou wast born
>   with.

> [I.4.134–47]

In divesting himself of a fixed social position Lear has behaved like a fool; he has opened up a space where he can be anything for he is no longer a king, but that space can only be a playground of his imagination since he now has no authority to make it real. The Fool's answer to Lear's question is, however, characteristically ambivalent. Lear, like all other human beings, was born with the capacity for folly and though it may have atrophied through lack of use, not least because the Fool was invested with the function of being Lear's folly so that he could get on with being king, it cannot be given away like titles. On another level the Fool is suggesting that Lear is a 'natural' rather than, like himself, a professional fool. Only a half-wit would do what Lear has done, so presumably Lear was born deficient in some of his faculties:

> thou hadst little wit in thy bald crown when thou gav'st thy golden one away.

> [I.4.159–60]

Even in theatrical terms there is much more stability in the representation of the Fool than there is in King Lear. Not only does the Fool's costume, motley, and behaviour announce him for what he is but his impersonation by the actor Robert Armin consolidates the coherence of actor and role. The opposite is the case with Richard Burbage who was not a king. It is the actor's craft to impersonate but on this occasion Burbage is required to renounce the status almost before he has taken it up, underlining the arbitrary nature of theatrical impersonation where roles and actors cannot always fit comfortably together. While the Fool is an inherently theatrical role for the essence of the professional or artificial fool is his ability to exist entirely in a state of performance, Lear is characterised as a man whose unsuccessful efforts to bring role and performance into coexistence drive him to madness. Paradoxically, if he could play the fool, he might have been able to stave off madness by making of the incongruity a running joke at his own expense. In part we witness his, finally, failed attempt to become a fool, costing him first his wits and then his life. Hamlet adopts a mask of madness in order to create a space in which he can play the fool but the Fool tries to graft a mask of folly onto Lear in order to protect him from the consequences of actual, rather than feigned, madness. Whilst it is necessary to be cautious about using terms like 'actual' and 'feigned' in relation to the pretence of the playhouse, Lear's deteriorating grip on the circumstances surrounding him is clearly of a very different order from Hamlet's 'antic disposition'.

In the first instance, however, we seem to be on the familiar ground of Carnival and Lent. The Fool sees Lear's wilful breach of the natural order in terms of the inversion of social relations commonly associated with carnival: 'thou mad'st thy daughters thy mothers' [I.4.168-69]. The Fool's advice to Lear combines his assessment of what it will take to succeed in the post King Lear world with the more standard dictates of the Puritan ascendancy:

> Have more than thou showest,
> Speak less than thou knowest,
> Lend less than thou owest,
> Ride more than thou goest,
> Learn more than thou trowest,
> Set less than thou throwest;
> Leave thy drink and thy whore,
> And keep in-a-door,
> And thou shalt have more
> Than two tens to a score.

[I.4.116–25]

These are the qualities that Lear singularly lacks and that reveal how uneasily the temper of the age sits upon his weary shoulders. They are aptly summed up by Danby as 'the hypocrite, the canny capitalist, and

the self-denying puritan combined' (Danby, 1949, p.106). Since Lear
has swapped the day to day cares of rule for the holiday pastimes of
retirement, it is perhaps fitting that his modern daughter should align
herself with the virtues of self-made aspiration in being attracted to
Edmund while associating her antiquated father with the carnival riots
of former ages:

> That this our court, infected with their manners,
> Shows like a riotous inn: epicurism and lust
> Makes it more like a tavern or a brothel
> Than a grac'd palace.

> [I.4.240–3]

For Lear the normal state is now a perpetual carnival over which he
presides as an unlikely carnival king of the May, hence his grotesquely
appropriate final appearance before being reclaimed by society *'fantas-
tically dressed with wild flowers'*. This inversion presents the Fool with
some functional difficulties. Within the stratified hierarchies of absolutist monarchies, the Fool as licensed truth-teller is the one figure who
is allowed to play, to expose contradiction through the performance of
multiple roles. But when he plays the Fool to a mockery king in a carnival court he finds himself attempting to negotiate the performances
of others. Nobody's identity or role is fixed or reliable: Lear is not King
Lear; Kent is the servant Caius; Edgar is Poor Tom, the madman. In the
inverted world of carnival, paradoxically, the most stable identity is that
of the fluid, playful Fool. It is, in part, the certainty of his position which
enables him to deconstruct Lear's separation of function from identity:
'I am a Fool, thou art nothing' [I.4.190–1]. In this play so thoroughly is
the principle of inversion applied that even 'nothing' is not a fixed point
or terminus but rather the prerequisite for 'something'. Just as the whole
tragic fall-out of the play emanates from Cordelia's opening 'nothing'
and Lear's typical misreading that events flatly contradict – 'nothing will
come of nothing' – so it is only by reducing himself to nothing that Lear
can reach a place from which any new identity might be constructed.
It is the Fool's belief that this new identity is likely to take the form
of folly, though whether this will manifest itself in the madness of the
'natural' fool or the wisdom of the 'artificial' one is, at this point, an
open question:

Goneril: [*to the Fool*] You, sir, more knave than fool, after your master.
Fool: Nuncle Lear, Nuncle Lear! tarry, take the Fool with thee.

> [I.4.313–15]

As Lear marches off into the void, the vacuum of his identity a prey to being filled by madness and self-harm, the Fool knows that he will only have folly, either in the form of the Fool's own person or by Lear himself putting on the mask of fool, to protect him. The King, now nothing, can be taught to be anything, so the Fool treats him as his apprentice in folly:

> *Fool*: The reason why the seven stars are no mo than seven is a
>   pretty reason.
> *Lear*: Because they are not eight?
> *Fool*: Yes, indeed: thou would'st make a good Fool
>
> [I.5.33–6]

But in the paradox of this insane world, it is the danger of madness that stands between Lear and the attainment of the cap and bells. The Fool is the icon of sanity when value systems have been inverted. But once the human world is given over entirely to the pursuit of power and the satisfaction of individual will at all costs, there is no place for a voice which constantly asserts that such preoccupations constitute a denial of what it is to be human. The office of king may have cut Lear off from the well-springs of his own humanity but there is no certainty that he can rediscover them through the office of Fool. Carnival had made the notion of fool as king a commonplace of late medieval society but rather than revisit that cliché, Shakespeare investigates what play there could be in the idea of king as fool.

Having shown us a world on the move from its fixed positions of ancient certainties towards a fluid, uncertain space where all values proclaim their opposites, Shakespeare begins to explore how the Fool can redraw the boundaries of what might constitute human behaviour where the defining characteristic of mankind, echoing the murderers in *Macbeth*, seems to be the capacity to kill her/his own kind; for the task of despatching the defenceless Cordelia and Lear in their prison is described as 'man's work'.

> Let go thy hold when a great wheel runs down a hill, lest it break thy neck with following; but the great one that goes upward, let him draw thee after. When a wise man gives thee better counsel, give me mine again: I would have none but knaves follow it, since a Fool gives it.
>   That sir which serves and seeks for gain,
>   And follows but for form,

> Will pack when it begins to rain,
>   And leave thee in the storm.
> But I will tarry; the Fool will stay,
>   And let the wise man fly:
> The knave turns Fool that runs away;
>   The Fool no knave, perdy.

[II.4.69–82]

Feste labelled himself Olivia's 'corrupter of words' but in the climate of this play, the Fool's ability to 'corrupt' or render slippery the definitions put upon him are his only means of asserting any remnants of morality. He attempts to play in the gap between the signifier and the signified for otherwise the designation put upon him by Goneril, 'more knave than fool', would close off the playground as a space for the regeneration of the human imagination. His mode is, as ever, 'handy-dandy'; which is the knave? Which the fool? Opinions on where this places the Fool in any wider moral scheme are never likely to coincide. For Danby:

> It is usual to claim that in instances such as this the Fool is submitting the loyalty of Lear's following to a test. He gives advice which he knows will not be taken by the disinterested; he is a hypocrite in a benevolent sense. This view, I think, makes the Fool less ambiguous than he really is. As I see him, he really does believe that to follow Lear to disaster is foolishness. Absolute loyalty is irrational, and the Fool never suggests that there is a supernatural sanction for such irrationality. Folly is an alternative to knavery, certainly. But that does not make it a virtue.
>
> (Danby, 1949, p.105)

Perhaps not; but though no virtue it is perhaps a necessity – a necessary part of being a human trying to balance the different yet ultimately inseparable demands of individual and social survival. The ability to distinguish the knave from the fool and, in an insane world, to invert them, may be the only grounds upon which the continuance of the species can be maintained since the inability leads to the conclusion depicted by Albany:

> Humanity must perforce prey on itself,
> Like monsters of the deep.

[IV.2.48–9]

Though he may occupy no moral high ground, the Fool is the repository of an intuition of what distinguishes mankind from other animals. For Enid Welsford this is best described by the notion of 'fellow-feeling', a capacity upon which, as we saw in the case of Feste, the Fool relies to earn his living:

> Now the Fool sees that when the match between the good and the evil is played by the intellect alone it must end in a stalemate, but when the heart joins in the game then the decision is immediate and final. 'I will tarry, the Fool will stay – And let the wise man fly.' That is the unambiguous wisdom of the madman who sees the truth. That is decisive. It is decisive because, so far from being an abnormal freakish judgment, it is the instinctive judgment of normal humanity raised to heroic stature; and therefore no amount of intellectual argument can prevent normal human beings from receiving and accepting it, just as, when all the psychologists and philosophers have had their say, normal human beings continue to receive and accept the external world as given to them through sense perception.
>
> (Welsford, 1935, p.267)

Though Welsford's language hails us with the despised tones of modernism – 'unambiguous wisdom', 'the truth', and the reiterated refrain of 'normal' – her contention is upheld by the events of the play, both in the sense that the 'evil' characters defeat themselves, and in the way that the loss of the Fool from the action exposes the frailty of Lear's wits. When Lear announces 'O Fool! I shall go mad'[II.4.284], it is simultaneously a statement of intent and a warning that he cannot hold out against the world. Like Hamlet, he is steeped too far in the action of the drama to achieve the unique quality of detachment with engagement that is required of the one invested in motley. If such a quality is the indicator of psychic health, his intense over-engagement may be the cause of his impolitic madness.

When Edward Berry confidently states that 'folly is a liminal state, and the fool a liminal being' (Berry, 1984, p.109), as far as the Fool in *King Lear* is concerned he is in danger of missing the paradox. The breaking of the bonds which loose all the players from their previous fixed positions – Lear becomes a mad old man who is nothing; Goneril and Regan become his mothers; Edmund becomes the favourite son; Edgar becomes Poor Tom; Kent becomes Caius – propels them all into various states of liminality. When the entire condition of society is

'handy-dandy', the Fool holds out as the last embodiment of the former organisation. As we have noted elsewhere, he is usually the one
who holds the memory of former ages as a means of setting the volatile
present in some sort of perspective; under him the hobby-horse still
kicks and prances to the folk tunes. Shakespeare plays with the notion of
folk memory through the joke about Merlin that connects the Fool with
the ancient tradition of the half-wit as prophet while extending the idea
of inversion to time itself. The Fool experiences time as a cycle, a wheel
of Fortune, rather than the linear process of the socially ambitious:

> When priests are more in word than matter;
> When brewers mar their malt with water;
> When nobles are their tailors' tutors;
> No heretics burn'd, but wenches' suitors;
> When every case in law is right;
> No squire in debt, nor no poor knight;
> When slanders do not live in tongues;
> Nor cut-purses come not to throngs;
> When usurers tell their gold I' th' field;
> And bawds and whores do churches build;
> Then shall the realm of Albion
> Come to great confusion:

> [III.2.81–92]

In his note to the Arden edition of the play Kenneth Muir endorses
Warburton's attempt to make sense of the prophecy:

> Warburton pointed out that 81–4 refer to the actual state of affairs,
> while 85–90 are Utopian. He suggested, perhaps rightly, that 91–2
> should be inserted after 84.
>
> (Muir, 1972, p.104)

They have misunderstood the trajectory of the speech in failing to
appreciate the depth of the Fool's irony. He is, as ever, commenting
on what he has seen come to pass. It is Lear who has already brought
Albion to confusion through his inability to read human nature or to
judge motive. Like Mother Courage wrongly relying upon the certainty
of corruption to buy her son's life in Brecht's play, *Mother Courage and her
Children*, the Fool shows how society has become structured around the
reliability of human selfishness and fallibility. Were the Utopian vision

of what mankind aspires to be ever to come to pass, there would have to be a complete redefinition of social relations to reflect the new set of assumptions. It is in the contradiction between what humanity is and what it has the capacity to imagine that the Fool finds the space in which to play with the irony inherent in the human condition:

> He's mad that trusts in the tameness of a wolf, a horse's health,
> a boy's love, or a whore's oath.

> [III.6.18–19]

Lear's journey into madness is, in part, an attempt to create a world in which this trust becomes possible as the basis for human relations. To do this, however, he becomes increasingly remote from the reality around him, signalled by the heart rending discrepancy between his vision of Cordelia and himself telling stories to each other in their prison cell and his next appearance with her corpse in his arms. She is the victim of Edmund's authority to pronounce on the life and death of others; a form of social organisation that Lear himself understands in one of those flashes of insight that punctuate his climactic meeting with the blind Gloucester, like an Alzheimer patient who experiences random recollections of his identity:

> *Lear*:   Thou hast seen a farmer's dog bark at a beggar?
> *Gloucester*: Ay, Sir.
> *Lear*:   And the creature run from the cur? There thou might'st
>   behold
>   The great image of Authority:
>   A dog's obey'd in office.

> [IV.6.152–57]

This is the high point of his understanding; the distance achieved since his dog-like execution of his office in the opening scene. Now he perceives how the functions that women and men ascribe to each other deform their personalities and wreck their relationships. And herein lies the paradoxical function of the Fool; his function is to play with the dangers that emanate from this dependence upon function to define value. He constantly nudges the possibility of another way of being into the consciousness of those trapped by function and in so doing prompts 'mad' thoughts. Both Hamlet and Lear are attracted to these foolish notions and an aspect of their tragedies resides in their inability to escape from their functions or, at the least, to maintain their existence in the face of the discrepancy between function and understanding. But where Hamlet plays, fool-like, with this discrepancy, Lear attempts to live it at a fatal cost.

Because the Fool is the essence of a function, the function of fooling, when others usurp that function he loses his space of existence. The Fool disappears from the play when there is no space left in which to play. As he predicts: 'This cold night will turn us all to fools and madmen' [III.4.77]. Folly is enacted by Edgar who as Poor Tom demonstrates that even a 'natural' fool can be impersonated artificially and by Lear, even though he may lack the critical distance necessary for an effective performance. Tantalisingly, Southworth offers us the possibility that the Fool's disappearance from the play may not have been accompanied by the loss of Armin if, as is almost possible, he doubled in the role of Edgar (Southworth, 1998, p.170). Edgar certainly exhibits in his early appearances the naivety associated with fools, although in his case it seems real rather than feigned. The deprivation of human relationships and material comforts puts him in the same condition as Dario Fo's *jongleur*, driven to seek justice in response to the outrageous injustices he experiences. The actor Armin, a professional fool in his own right, would have been well placed to perform 'madness' and Poor Tom's relationship with Gloucester then echoes that of the Fool to Lear. In both cases the fool is using his function to try to redeem an aging patriarch from their self-inflicted follies. Such double casting would leave Armin, Feste-like, with the last word in the play and his gnomic utterance draws attention to the dialectical relation between character and function that has haunted the action throughout:

> *Edgar*: The weight of this sad time we must obey;
>   Speak what we feel, not what we ought to say.
>   The oldest hath borne most; we that are young
>   Shall never see so much nor live so long.
>
> [V.3.323–6]

The tragedy has come about both as a result of characters speaking according to social obligation and as a result of them speaking according to the dictates of feeling. Whether as Edgar, as the Fool, or as Robert Armin, there is irony about what they have seen, combined with the fool's customary awareness of the transitory nature of existence. The final observation ensures that inversion holds sway until the bitter end.

Previously, in the moment when Lear announces the inversion of the most mundane social habits by which the species lives, the Fool recognises his redundancy:

> *Lear:* We'll go to supper i' th' morning.
> *Fool:* And I'll go to bed at noon.

> [III.6.82–3]

The reply does not only allude to the English wildflower and the Fool's announcement of his own demise but also harks back to the earlier comment about 'Lear's shadow'. The choice of 'noon' refers us to that time of day when the sun is directly overhead and, all other aspects being equal, casts no shadow. If Lear has absorbed his shadow, the Fool who dogs his heels, into his own substantial being, there is, indeed, no place or function remaining to the Fool. The multiple meanings of shadow lie both at the core of Lear's attempts at self-definition and at the heart of the Fool's view of the world as a Pandora's Box of inverted values let loose by Lear's wanton destruction of the bonds that formerly contained social behaviour. His own journey through the play is from the certainty of a fixed function as court fool to the functionless extinction of the 'cold night'. Intimations of the fates of both king and fool are contained in the seminal early exchange between them:

> *Lear:* Who is it that can tell me who I am?
> *Fool:* Lear's shadow.
> *Lear:* I would learn that;

> [I.4.227–9]

At the most direct level Lear's shadow is the Fool who does, indeed, spend most of their dialogues trying to highlight the king's new identity. However, running through the Fool's answer is one of the major tropes of English Renaissance literature, the relationship between substance and shadow. The particular application of the figure to the situation of Lear is made explicit by another king turned out of office, Marlowe's Edward II:

> But what are kings, when regiment is gone,
> But perfect shadows in a sunshine day?

> [V.1.26–7] (Marlowe, 1969, p.508)

e Lear has stripped himself of his own substance, his 'regiment', ... unctional monarch, he has left only the shadow, the two dimensional outward appearance that mocks his former state. His decision to free himself from the cares of state has transformed him into a holiday or May King where he presides over a perpetual carnival. Only Lear's shadow can tell Lear who he is because he has become his own shadow; the shadow of his former glory. As we have noted elsewhere, the fool or clown, or would be fool in the case of Hamlet, is often the performer most aware of the mechanisms of the playhouse since he is both of and not of the dramatic fiction in which he performs. He plays with the conventions that simultaneously enable and limit his performance. So here; the Fool's answer takes us to the centre of the actor's craft. In Elizabethan usage 'shadow' was a term regularly applied to actors (as in Puck's epilogue to *A Midsummer Night's Dream*: 'if we shadows have offended'). Lear's shadow is thus the actor who plays the part of Lear and without whom there can be no impersonation. It is always and only the actor who can announce the character. But here again lurks a paradox of the art form: though the part only has life as the actor breathes into it, the written role is immortal while the actor is transitory. In this context the notion of King is the permanent role while the person of Lear is the actor who inadequately attempts to undertake it. When person and function begin to pull in separate directions the gap between the two becomes apparent. The double paradox suggested by the Fool resides in the fact that the actor, the shadow, finds that the role does not fit the function of king. The playwright is asking for trouble by creating such a part and the Fool is the person most suited to expose the paradox. He is the figure who introduces the juggling with layers of reality for the art which is the staple of his profession is about to become the norm for a king and court who belong to playhouse and carnival rather than the state rooms of office.

Putting the Fool out of his misery, or perhaps out of Lear's misery, is not, however, the end of his story for Shakespeare. At first sight the journey from the deformed Vice Richard III to the deformed slave Caliban may seem a short one but the philosophical distance is vast. In *The Tempest* the alternative vision to the enlightened despotism of Prospero is supplied only by Caliban, performed by the fool of the company representing the actuality of folly, in contrast to its burlesque impersonation by the jester and the drunken butler. Prospero, Miranda and Caliban offer a distorted mirror fragment of Lear, Cordelia and the Fool in another life or on another plane of representation:

> *Caliban*: For I am all the subjects that you have,
>   Which first was mine own King:

> [I.2.343–4]

Caliban, like Lear, has experienced the transition from King to Fool and both have had to find new language in which to record their novel sensations. Where Feste had the freedom to operate as the 'corrupter' of Olivia's words, Caliban is the victim of the corrosive power of Prospero's linguistic control:

> You taught me language; and my profit on't
> Is, I know how to curse. The red plague rid you
> For learning me your language!

> [I.2.365–7]

The theatrical irony is once again typical; the playwright creates a character whose words are not his own, even as all actors of scripted plays must utter the language of another. This announces a key ambivalence of this play where both Prospero and Caliban are alike the products of Shakespeare's pen whilst at the level of the fiction Caliban is, linguistically at least, the product of another character in the story. Prospero's control over the island is exerted through his books; that is by language. Without them he becomes an old man, like Lear without his office, at the mercy of Caliban:

>   Remember
> First to possess his books, for without them
> He's but a sot, as I am, nor hath not
> One spirit to command: they all do hate him
> As rootedly as I. Burn but his books.

> [III.2.89–93]

Prospero upon the island, backed by his 'rough magic', is, like the playwright, able to control the actions of the creatures he brings onto that stage. Their actions and, in Caliban's case his words, are Prospero's to bring forth. He can, however, exert no power over their thoughts even as the playwright's domain ceases at the border of the actors' mind. Prospero's project has been to alter the 'nature' of Caliban and of those who have wronged himself. The question for him is whether the degree of control that he has over his fellow creatures can be converted into a programme for their moral regeneration according to terms laid out for them by Prospero. Caliban's understanding of the significance of the books, Prospero's educative system by which his control over the island is maintained, demonstrates that the latter's assessment will not bear scrutiny:

> A devil, a born devil, on whose nature
> Nurture can never stick; on whom my pains,
> Humanely taken, all, all lost, quite lost.

> [IV.1.188–90]

What is lost, is the possibility of exerting control without coercion and with coercion Prospero is as trapped into his role of master as Caliban is into that of slave. Once more the office, even if a self-appointed one, is simultaneously necessary for the ordering of social relations and the means by which mankind becomes divorced from that nature which is the fullest expression of humanity. It is not that Caliban has failed to learn, rather that he has learnt too well; he knows better than Lear that the costume does not make the office unless it is an emblem of actual power; an icon of substance rather than shadow:

Trinculo: O King Stephano! O peer! O worthy Stephano!
　　　　　 look what a wardrobe here is for thee!
Caliban: Let it alone, thou fool; it is but trash.
Trinculo: O, ho, monster! We know what belongs to a frippery.
　　　　　 O King Stephano!
Stephano: Put off that gown, Trinculo; by this hand, I'll have that gown.
Trinculo: Thy grace shall have it.
Caliban: The dropsy drown this fool! What do you mean
　　　　　 To dote thus on such luggage? Let't alone,
　　　　　 And do the murther first:

> [IV.1.222–32]

As Stephano and Trinculo squabble over who will be May King in the carnival kingdom, Caliban reminds us how far foolishness as the 'other' of the Renaissance model of authority has emigrated from those restrictive realms. Caliban is the emblem of the hopelessness of Prospero's enterprise. As he holds 'the mirror up to nature' it is Caliban's face he finds grinning back at him:

Caliban may be a referent-leaping 'other' to Eurocentric man, but never exclusively; more presciently, he is the mirror of governing rhetoric and ideology, its image and accuser, likeness and inversion.

(Palfrey, 1997, p.168)

Though there can be neither political nor dramatic space for a resolution between order and resistance in either the colonial or the domestic polity, there are, for Prospero, two moments – one as character and one as actor – to realise the limits of his project and to pull back from the self-destruction that emanated from Hamlet's inability to exist outside his role and Lear's to achieve an identity apart from his office. The island/playhouse is the space of dreams and, like Caliban, we may well leave its orbit feeling: 'when I wak'd, I cried to dream again' [III.2.140–41] but outside lurk the political realities of human relations 'for the rain it raineth everyday'. Being human is both aspiration and curse; shadow and substance, and no matter how much art we employ we cannot remove the 'other' from the 'self' for we are our own imperfection, our own folly and our own contradictions:

> *Prospero*: .... Two of these fellows you
> Must know and own; this thing of darkness I
> Acknowledge mine.
>
> [V.1.274–6]

6
Fooling with Reason

That time of year thou mayst in me behold
When yellow leaves, or none, or few, do hang
Upon those boughs which shake against the cold,
Bare ruin'd choirs where late the sweet birds sang.

(Shakespeare, Sonnet 73, 1951, p.1320)

This chapter examines the fate of the stage fool during what may loosely be described as the European Enlightenment or the Age of Reason; that period which stretches variously from 1600 to 1900 depending upon both country and critical inclination. It is my contention that the notion of 'reason', understood as the capacity of humankind to improve their lot progressively through the application of their reasoning faculties, is, at bottom, antithetical to the social function of the fool who is forever pointing to the limitations and fallibility of the species. It is therefore not surprising to find that this period witnessed the gradual erosion of the rituals and social spaces which gave vent to manifestations of the irrational practices that highlighted aspects of human behaviour at odds with the dominant discourse of progress. Whether out of religious, economic or more broadly cultural motives, all over Europe 'folly' was in decline and 'reason' in the ascendant. As Ronald Hutton expressed it:

All over western and central Europe during the sixteenth and seventeenth centuries reformers attacked popular festivity and tried to enforce a stricter standard of sexual morality and of personal decorum. A sharper separation was made between the sacred and the profane and between the sophisticated and the vulgar, and an attempt was made to create a more orderly and sober, as well as

120

a more pious, society. Vagrants, fornicators, and suspected witches were all persecuted with a new intensity, and formal entertainments tended to replace spontaneous and participatory celebrations.

(Hutton, 1994, p.111)

This spirit of separation was felt equally within the aesthetics of theatrical performance. The neo-classical insistence upon the separation of tragedy from comedy and the development of perspective *mise-en-scène* which lead ultimately to the erection of the 'fourth wall' within the theatre, as well as the separation of playful performance from streets and domestic spaces, all conspired to restrict the theatrical as well as the social possibilities of the fool whose operations depend upon the ability to defy genre and to work the spaces between stage and auditorium. The fool is a figure of fluidity and insinuation, at once nowhere and everywhere, intrinsically at odds with classical canons of separation and decorum. For a while at least the period of transition from 'dark' to 'light' ages confronted the playwrights with contradictions that went to the heart of their practices. As an activity whose existence depends upon people's willingness to participate in and to enjoy watching play, there was a strong element of nostalgia for the old ways of 'merry England' that has already been noted in the previous chapters. Yet at the same time developments in formal, commercial staging, the containment of play, put them at the forefront of the new profession of playwright and made them party to the changes in taste that marginalised the fool upon the European stage.

Nowhere in English drama is this ambivalence felt more acutely than in the work of Ben Jonson, striving to appeal at once to the 'new' bourgeois appetite for the neo-classical and to the old-fashioned, popular culture of fairs and carnivals. No play better illustrates the paradoxical relationship between playhouse and carnival than *Bartholomew Fair* (1614), the play that takes as its setting a major London Fair whose representation is then contained within the Hope Theatre and the Palace of Whitehall for its first and second performances. Though a play where social division figures prominently, it is still possible to place it before both monarch and groundlings. However, in so placing it, Jonson is careful to depict the tensions, both social and theatrical, that will ultimately render this 'one world' cultural strategy impossible. Furthermore the Fair, set up in the public highway, has porous borders and free access, whereas the theatre is a fixed place of commercial transaction.

The Induction exposes these tensions before the play proper even begins. The Stage-Keeper represents the traditional, oral, popular view of the theatre ('I kept the stage in Master Tarleton's time') while the Book-Keeper, his antagonist, offers the new view of an art grounded in a text and critically assessed according to tastes that are the prerogative of wealth. The fool, or at least a certain kind of fool is associated with a type of improvised, unsophisticated playing that is being consigned to a former age. Kempe consciously styled himself as a disciple of Tarleton. Though Jonson is attempting to have his cake and eat it too, since both views are the product of his pen, the containment of them within a scripted text aligns him unambiguously with the modern age in which folly is to be contained within institutions and its expression to be associated with popular rather than bourgeois tastes. As Peter Womack puts it:

> As a pedagogic and didactic poet he contributed to the formation of an élite humanist culture; as a historically precocious neo-classicist he stood for perspicuity and the separation of genres against the grotesque mode inseparable from carnival; as a conscious 'dramatic poet' he sought to distance his texts from the 'original dung-cart of popular theatre; and as masque-maker, and poet laureate in all but name, he is arguably the first *official* literary producer in English history. No amount of re-reading could render this cultural trajectory carnivalesque: despite his defence of traditional pastimes against certain kinds of puritan intolerance, he is objectively on the side of 'Lent'. The carnival figures which run through his whole work in the theatre are no less real for that, but they have no access to the fearless and universal gaiety which Bakhtin finds in Rabelais' relations with popular-festive forms.
>
> (Womack, 1986, pp.134–5)

Such a judgement might appear harsh in relation to *Bartholomew Fair* which throngs with the figures of carnival and celebrates the frailty of human desire in the face of misguided attempts at repression, each of whose representatives – Wasp, Busy, Overdo – endure a spell of humiliation in the stocks. However, though the setting and the cast list might persuade us that we are on familiar medieval territory, the manner in which the material is presented by Jonson owes little to the Rabelaisian or even Shakespearean depictions of folly:

> Let us say a few initial words about the complex nature of carnival laughter. It is, first of all, a festive laughter. Therefore it is not an individual reaction to some isolated "comic"event. Carnival laughter

is the laughter of all the people. Second, it is universal in scope; it is directed at all and everyone, including the carnival's participants. The entire world is seen in its droll aspect, in its gay relativity. Third, this laughter is ambivalent: it is gay, triumphant, and at the same time mocking, deriding. It asserts and denies, it buries and revives.

(Bakhtin, 1984, pp.11–12)

This carnival of Bartholomew Fair in the treatment of Jonson offers mockery and derision in large doses and only the occasional, tentative gesture towards gaiety. The case of Justice Overdo is an example of this imbalance. The Fair is introduced to us through Overdo's soliloquy in which he sets out his plan to detect 'enormities', although since we have already been introduced to his family and their associates by this time, the audience peers at him through a veil of irony, as he has obviously missed the enormities that are on his door-step.The disguise he adopts begins the trope of madness which permeates the remainder of the action:

Justice: They may have seen many a fool in the habit of a justice, but never till now a justice in the habit of a fool.

(Jonson, 1995, p.351)

The multiple levels of irony build a distance between Overdo and the audience in the very moment when his asides attempt the opposite. We are watching a fool in the habit of a justice; not a wise fool in the Shakespearean mould, but rather a simpleton ripe for deception. This is a fool in the habit of a justice in the habit of a fool. He 'wears' his judicial habit poorly and is no more effective with his disguise since he insists upon asserting his identity as judge whenever possible. The essential quality of the fool is to be no one and therefore, possibly, everyone but Overdo is always, obsessively, himself. He possesses the farcical capacity to push logic beyond its limits, as announced by his name, but he is presented throughout as farce's victim, the mechanism controlling him. In the following chapters I shall explore examples of fools who disguise themselves as judges in order to exploit the subversive laughter of carnival to destabilise oppressive power structures but Overdo offers an example of the reverse process: a foolish judge who attempts to adopt the mask of folly in order to strengthen his own, petty position within such a structure. We laugh at him not with him as he tries to take us into his confidence:

Justice [aside] My disguise takes to the very wish and reach of it. I shall by the benefit of this, discover enough and more, and yet get off with the reputation of what I would be: a certain middling thing between a fool and a madman.

(Jonson, 1995, p.355)

He does indeed discover more than he is expecting; not about the Fair which he constantly misreads, but about the natures of his nearest and dearest. His aspiration to combine the qualities of the professional and natural fool – a fool and a madman – is thwarted by his inability to convince in either role. As if to highlight his failure, Jonson represents a 'real' natural in the person of Trouble-all and an effective disguised one in the machinations of Quarlous ('I am mad but from the gown outward') who maintains a complete separation between his sense of himself and his adopted role. Overdo expresses some dawning realisation of fallibility whilst in the stocks as a consequence of his encounter with Trouble-all:

Justice [aside] I will be more tender hereafter. I see compassion may become a Justice, though it be a weakness, I confess, and nearer a vice than a virtue.

(Jonson, 1995, p.391)

But any inklings of those insights which might become a fool such as an assertion of the common bonds linking humanity as well as the capacity to read the emotional condition of others, are quickly and utterly dispelled as Overdo propels himself like a swine to the precipice, to the scene of his intended triumph. As in everything else his rhetoric is absurdly overdone:

Justice: Now to my enormities: look upon me, O London! And see me, O Smithfield; the example of Justice, and Mirror of Magistrates, the true top of formality and scourge of enormity. Hearken unto my labours, and but observe my discoveries, and compare Hercules with me, if thou dar'st, of old; or Columbus, Magellan, or our countryman Drake of later times. Stand forth, You weeds of enormity and spread.

(Jonson, 1995, p.431)

Jonson sets him up to be ridiculed, demonstrating that 'dressed in his little brief authority' or whatever other costume he puts on, he is always and irrevocably the butt of both the other characters and the audience.

He is the acme of folly, posing futilely as its opposite. Even aft
been undone by his wife's drunkenness and Quarlous has prom,
to make restitution, he still, cloaking his intents in his fusty Latin, speaks
of his ambition to reform not himself but everyone else. Quarlous, the
other character who adopts the costume of the fool at least possesses
the necessary wit, though it is always used for his own advantage at the
expense of others:

> Quarlous: ...but get your wife out o' the air, it will make her worse
> else; and remember you are but Adam, flesh and blood! You have your
> frailty; forget your other name of Overdo, and invite us all to supper.
>
> (Jonson, 1995, pp.432–3)

The injunction to be mindful of his frailty, recalls Feste and Lear's Fool's
song of the rain that 'raineth everyday'. The fool is the figure who
provides the constant reminder of our imperfections, of our animal
natures, even as the fair is the site where these are variously celebrated or
exploited. The difference between Quarlous and some earlier fools is that
he is not disinterested; as the 'gamester' of the piece he is very much part
of the game. His view of human nature is cynical and there is precious
little sense of gaiety or celebration in the triumph of his machinations.
He can be registered in the roll-call of tricksters, even resorting to shape-
shifting, but there is no moment in the play where his complacency
is threatened or his view of life as a game is challenged. He therefore
represents one element of the fool, stripped of moral ambiguity. He
epitomises the times rather than offering any counter-narrative.

The ancient discourse which links madness with truth-telling, the
licence of the court fool, still lurks around the multiple representations
of the mad in this play, in particular the character of Trouble-all, but
when it is articulated through the mouth of Dame Purecraft, the embodiment of hypocrisy whose craft is anything but pure and whose actions
are pure craft, the signifier and the signified are in terminal danger of
parting company:

> Purecraft: How well it becomes a man to be mad in truth! O that I
> might be his yoke-fellow, and be mad with him! What a many should
> we draw to madness in truth with us!
>
> (Jonson, 1995, p.410)

The hollowness of the rhetoric is underscored by her marriage to
Quarlous: hypocrite and cynic perfectly matched and alike devoid of
madness or truth.

The absence of the celebratory aspect of the Bakhtinian carnivalesque is not confined to the characters who inhabit or visit the fair, but extends to the significance of the fair itself. In this respect Jonson is pre-empting the ultimate demise of the space itself, even though the final abolition of Bartholomew Fair was not until 1855, under pressure from the London City Missions Society. Before the fair is presented to us we learn that

> Grace: Truly, I have no such fancy to the Fair, nor ambition to see it; there's none goes thither of any quality or fashion.
>
> (Jonson, 1995, p.347)

Here is early evidence of what Hutton dubs 'the Reformation of Manners' as bourgeois and popular tastes start to diverge. In the context of *Bartholomew Fair*, however, the statement cannot be read without the accompanying irony since Jonson sets about exposing the true inclinations and behaviour of the bourgeoisie as every bit as wayward and corrupt as those of the fair folk. Nevertheless there is a sense that all is not as it once was, since the audience member is urged in the Induction 'neither to look back to the sword-and-buckler age of Smithfield, but content himself with the present'. Leatherhead who in the puppet finale will come to represent, along with Ursula (the little bear), the very essence of the fair, remarks at the outset that

> The Fair's pestilence dead, methinks; people come not abroad today, whatever the matter is.
>
> (Jonson, 1995, p.352)

The fiercest assault upon the fair and all those ritual pastimes with which it is associated, comes predictably from the Puritan Busy and equally predictably Jonson, as a man of the theatre, sets him up as an object of mockery through the gross hypocrisy of his appetites and his criminal acquisition of personal wealth. It is appropriate that he is defeated by the process of theatre itself and that the character who delivers the *coup de grâce* should be the puppet named Dionysus who represents all those human qualities of joy and communal celebration that the Reformation and Counter-Reformation, 'the Reformation of Manners', and the emerging Enlightenment was beginning to push to the social and cultural margins. Busy's declarations, absurd on his lips, ring ominously down the years of historical hindsight: 'the whole Fair is the shop of Satan!' and he 'sitteth here [in the stocks] to prophesy the destruction of fairs'. Like Malvolio before him he is undone by playing, hopelessly lost in the 'away' territory of the playhouse, the fair within the playhouse and finally the puppet theatre within the fair within the playhouse.

As Jonson's play makes clear, the processes by which carnival and folly beat a slow retreat to the margins of cultural life were not to occur as a simple linear series of events. The 'gentle' characters of *Bartholomew Fair* and those who aspire towards gentility are all undone in various ways through their desire for the experiences offered by the fair. The setting itself becomes a nightmare in which the gentlefolk 'lose' themselves and become transformed into the prostitutes, drunks, madmen and conmen of the fair. Though they may repudiate the manners of the fair, they discover uncomfortably that its substance lurks in their psyches. This interiorisation of the carnivalesque in the eighteenth century is documented and critiqued by Stallybrass and White but, as their references to *Bartholomew Fair* imply, Jonson is a herald of the process:

> It is wrong, therefore, to assume that the attack on popular culture is simply the story of oppression from above. The grotesque body of carnival was being re-territorialized, it was being appropriated, sublimated and individualized to code refined identity, to give the eighteenth-century nobility and the bourgeoisie masks and symbols to think with at the very moment when they were repudiating the social realm from which those masks and symbols came.
>
> (Stallybrass & White, 1986, p.104)

While, in the social sphere, these changes in taste and economic ascendancy among the bourgeoisie brought about the containment, redefinition and, ultimately, marginalisation of the carnival, the fair and all those practices of folly associated with such sites of ritual, so in the theatre comparable changes were gradually redefining the experience of watching plays as well as the scope of the representations on offer. Dryden, the standard-bearer for refinement in the theatre, declares his expectations in his prologue to *Cleomenes*, performed in 1692:

> I think or hope, at least, the Coast is clear,
> That none but Men of Wit and Sence are here:
> That our Bear-Garden Friends are all away,
> Who bounce with Hands and Feet, and cry Play, Play.
>
> (Stallybrass & White, 1986, p.84)

The 'Bear-Garden Friends' are the likes of the audience addressed by Jonson in the Induction to *Bartholomew Fair* for the Hope Theatre alternated as playhouse and bear-baiting arena. Ursula (Little Bear) in that play represents the crossover between the two functions, being the apex of the fair even as the bear was for the baiting. Implicit in Dryden's words is an opposition between sense and play, between reason and folly. Reasonable people, the like of which Dryden wishes to recruit as his audience, are not going to be entertained by fools whose antics would only serve to remind them of their limitations as humans.

The sense of a parallel trajectory between society and theatre is endorsed in Thomas Shadwell's play *The Woman Captain* (1679):

Sir Humphrey: I'll keep no Fool, 'tis out of fashion for great Men to keep Fools.

Fool: Because now adays they are their own Fools, and so save Charges...

Sir Humphrey: I'll have none, 'tis exploded ev'n upon the Stage.

Fool: But for all that *Shakespear's* Fools had more Wit than any of the Wits and Criticks now adays.

(2001, pp.210–11)

'Ev'n upon the Stage' suggests that the theatre was considered the final resting place of the fool after he had been withdrawn from society at large. In expelling the fool after the opening act of his play Shadwell was conforming to fashion by replacing folly with 'sentiment', that keyword of eighteenth century English literature. Perhaps the most famous sentimental comedy of that period is Oliver Goldsmith's *She Stoops to Conquer* where the prevailing taste for a sentimental story is laminated onto earlier notions of comedy where there was a much wider scope for the fool to play. In this instance the adhesive connecting sentiment to folly is the representation of Tony Lumpkin who combines a central role as a character in the plot with the performance of many of the functions traditionally associated with both fool and trickster, natural and professional. Having learnt early on that he is 'a mere composition of tricks and mischief' and that his preferred element is the alehouse and his lower-class drinking companions, the audience is quickly reassured that 'It is a good-natured creature at bottom', a comment which acts as a signal that the outcome will finally conform to the requirements of a sentimental conclusion. Meanwhile, Tony's initial trick of pretending that Mr Hardcastle's 'old-fashioned house' is an inn, plugs into the latter's nostalgia for merry England, perhaps connecting him in the imagination to Oldcastle, the original name of Falstaff, while, at the same time converting the house to licensed premises; that is premises that give licence to Tony's antics as fool. He clearly regards himself as something of a household fool retained by his mother:

> *Tony*: If I'm a man, let me have my fortin. Ecod! I'll not be made a
> fool of no longer.

(Morrell, 1950, p.267)

Whereas in former times he might have been recognised as such and left alone to perform the functions fitting that role, by the eighteenth century this behaviour is seen as a defect of his character attributable to failings of both his nature (Mr Lumpkin) and of his nurture (Mrs Hardcastle). Where it suits him, Tony is happy to go along with the prevailing view of his behaviour:

> *Tony*: Ecod, mother, all the parish says you have spoiled me, and so
> you may take the fruits on't.

(Morrell, 1950, p.305)

From behind the mask of the spoilt child, Tony is able to expose the hypocrisies of polite society, especially those of his mother in matters of wealth ('I can bear witness to that'), while his affable treatment of all, regardless of class, stands in marked contrast to Marlow's dealings with women. When he mistakes Miss Hardcastle for a barmaid his assumption of *droit de seigneur* comes close to tearing the veil of sentiment off the manners of the bourgeoisie. Like fools of old Tony commutes between all classes and remains himself, but the world around him is continuing to fragment into ever widening divisions of class, taste, fashion and economic opportunity.

At times his behaviour reminds us of Puck, as if he is from another world and intent upon demonstrating 'what fools these mortals be'. When the anger provoked by their embarrassment and frustration at last finds its scapegoat in Tony, they do not know how to take him, how to play with him. They are confused by the contradictions which are always embedded in his multiple functions:

> *Marlow*: What can I say to him, a mere boy, an idiot, whose
> ignorance and age are a protection.
> *Hastings*: A poor contemptible booby, that would but disgrace
> correction.

Miss Neville: Yet with cunning and malice enough to make himself
merry with all our embarrassments.

(Morrell, 1950, p.295)

Their responses to Tony hark back to the anthropological roots of the
fool. He is at once both simpleton and trickster and can use either mask
to improvise a response to what is set before him through his ability to
play. The use of the word 'merry' in relation to him, links Tony to the
passing world of 'merry England' where his actions would have been
accepted or at least 'licensed'. Now, however, he has also to pay his dues,
both social and theatrical, to the prevailing taste for sentiment and so
his tricks are turned towards an appropriate outcome for the lovers:

Tony: . . . if you don't find Tony Lumpkin a more good-natur'd
fellow than you thought for, I'll give you leave to take my
best horse, and Bet Bouncer into the bargain.

(Morrell, 1950, p.296)

Tony's skills as a trickster ensure the happy ending according to the dictates of fashion but they cannot disguise the awkward tension between
past and present that lurks beneath the terms in which Mr Hardcastle
announces the conclusion with uncanny echoes of Adam Overdo's
invitation:

Hardcastle: So now to supper. Tomorrow we shall gather all the poor
of the parish about us, and the mistakes of the night shall
be crowned with a merry morning.

(Morrell, 1950, p.311)

Like Overdo before him, he is anxious to assert the possibility of one
'merry' world but the previous action tends to refute his 'old-fashioned'
hope. Tony, unlike Puck, cannot vanish with the dawn or be left to comment sardonically like Feste upon the marriages. Instead he is left to
declare that 'Tony Lumpkin is his own man again!' which presumably
means that he is free to carry on, courtesy of his allowance, playing the
fool in a society that is increasingly unsympathetic to the celebration of
animal desires and that consigns merriment to a bygone era.

   If Tony Lumpkin's efforts at playing the fool are somewhat neutered
by the advent of the desire for a theatre of sentiment, his equivalent
on the continent of Europe, Harlequin, is faring no better. Dario Fo

locates the origins of *Commedia dell'Arte* as 'the result of cross-breeding between the Zanni from Bergamo and farcical, devil-like characters from the French popular tradition' (Fo, 1991, p.46). For Fo it is axiomatic that the genre in general and its most famous representative, *Arlecchino*, in particular, are derived from popular, carnivalesque forms before falling prey to the 'bourgeoisification' of the seventeenth and eighteenth centuries. Referring to two of the best known early actors of *Arlecchino*, Tristano Martinelli and Domenico Biancolelli, Fo writes:

> Both actors resorted to all kinds of provocation. They would wander on stage, assaulting the audience with obscenities and acts of unheard-of scurrility. Martinelli, in the middle of a love scene between a knight and his lady, dropped his trousers and, in perfect peace and tranquillity, began to defecate on the stage.He then picked up the result of his labours with both hands (they were, nearly always, roasted chestnuts) and hurled them at the audience, with a loud chuckle: 'It brings good luck! This is your chance!'
>
> (Fo, 1991, p.46)

Such an incident is the very antithesis of the refinements, both social and theatrical, with which the Age of Enlightenment is associated. The scene depicts the aristocracy and the foolish peasant with no intervening middle-class; the fool is very intimately linked to Bakhtin's 'lower bodily stratum' and he is engaged in physical interaction with the audience. However, in both France and Italy theatrical taste, as in England, was turning against such representations of vulgarity. The key concept in the marginalisation of the fool throughout European theatre in this period is that of character. His various and frequently contradictory interventions amount to a series of functions – social satire, alternative philosophy, tricks contrived like knots in the narrative. But none of these functions depends upon or is derived from character as understood in the modern period. Through the seventeenth and eighteenth centuries theatre demonstrates the gradual fragmentation and marginalisation of the old-fashioned genres, in England associated with Shakespeare's mixed forms which contravene classical prescriptions, and in continental Europe with the older, popular manifestations of *Commedia dell'Arte*. Molière's plays betray this schism between the farces that come out of the *Commedia* tradition with Sganarelle as a French *Arlecchino*, and the 'new' plays of character where a figure such as Alceste, the title character of *The Misanthrope*, delivers the kind of social criticism appropriate to a wise fool without the detachment or self-awareness that might inoculate him against the desire to which he falls prey. The focus of the drama is upon the complexities of his character, the artistry with which Molière realises him as a highly distinct individual, at once part of his time and unique within it.

The most conscious, intentional reformer of *Commedia* is Carlo Goldoni and it is his works which reveal most clearly the 'battle' between carnival and character. For instance, he wrote *The Servant of Two Masters* (1749) as a *tour de force* for the great Harlequin of the age, Antonio Sacchi. Timothy Holme enthuses thus:

> Not only is the play a pure joy from beginning to end, but it is also a perfectly constructed half-way house between the *Commedia dell'Arte* and the new comedy of character containing, it could be argued, the best of both worlds.
>
> (Holme, 1976, p.91)

Harlequin is no longer the generic mask but a specific individual, Truffaldino, who is incorporated into the sentimental happy ending of the play, not only through the revelation of his dual identity but also through his marriage to Smeraldina. He is not excluded from the final social integration and does not proclaim a different, antithetical philosophy in the manner of Feste or an antagonistic religious and political world view in the manner of Malvolio. His manifold tricks and improvisations are the stuff of the archetypal Harlequin but they are now directed not to disturbance and inversion but towards cohesion and sentiment in the emerging bourgeois society:

> But, sir, don't you see, this is a miracle of time management, sir, a thing to be applauded not condemned. There was nothing except a good honest day's graft and had I not fell in love, sir, you would never have known at all. It's all right for you running round with your banker's bonds and your fancy costumes. We've got to fit our love life in between forty years' hard labour. Look, I didn't mean any harm. I've served you both and give or take a few complications when you might have killed yourself and that, it's worked out pretty well, I mean everybody's happy, aren't they. [sic] All I ask now is: you forgive the faults of my performance what I didn't get right, so I can serve Smeraldina, and bid you all good night.
>
> (Goldoni & Hall, 1999, p.98)

Harlequin as Truffaldino still presides over the interface between actors and audience but increasingly he is implicated as a character in the action as the first bricks are cemented into the 'fourth wall'. As in England, so in Italy the changes in theatrical taste were a mirror of, or being mirrored in, broader social changes. The new emphasis on the notion of character, an individual with specific moral qualities who can achieve upward mobility on his (or occasionally her) own merits, serves the purposes of an aspirational bourgeoisie. Dario Fo has drawn attention to the social and political implications of Goldoni's 'reforms':

> Any discussion of Goldoni and his view of Commedia dell'Arte must start from the premise that the author of *Arlecchino, Servant of Two Masters* was a man strongly linked, in modern terms, to his own times. Those times were marked by the new mercantile culture, which meant that the ledger books, no matter how crooked, had always to appear in order. His purpose was to impose order on the chaos of actors' handbooks of outline-plots and to rid the theatre of an ever-present crudeness, or, put more simply, his purpose was to implement a programme of reform. The reform he had in mind could not be merely structural but must also be moral and political.
>
> (Fo, 1991, p.28)

Even allowing for the fact that Fo is using hind-sight to attribute to Goldoni a degree of organisation, purpose and strategy of which he was almost certainly incapable, and that Fo was himself engaged through his own performances in the rehabilitation of an earlier, popular and more 'foolish' representation of Harlequin, it is apparent from references to Goldoni within his own life-time that he was viewed as part of the cultural forces of the Enlightenment. No lesser figure than Voltaire proclaimed in a letter to Goldoni that 'You have rescued your country from the hands of Harlequin' (Holme, 1976, p.147). Such a statement, whether true or not, demonstrates that Harlequin, the archetype of the fool and the trickster, had come to represent all that was backward-looking, old-fashioned and in poor taste in the European theatre of the Age of Reason. One of the most fully realised moments of character development, or perhaps what we would today term psychology, occurs in *The Venetian Twins*. The twins, Tonino and Pancrazio, played by the same actor, together cover the spectrum of functions formerly contained within the contradictory figure of Harlequin. Aspects of his 'character' are psychologically incompatible which would not hitherto have mattered to an audience brought up on functions rather than characterisation. Now, however, in the interests of consistency, the 'problem' of Harlequin is solved by the device of the twins. Unsurprisingly it is the foolish, villainous twin, Pancrazio, who hails from Bergamo, birth-place of Harlequin. As Richard Andrews has pointed out, Goldoni's allegiance is clear:

> Goldoni obviously intended us to be on the side of the *spiritoso*, the witty clown, and to be quite happy to witness the discomfiture of the *sciocco*. It is a characteristic of classical comedy, particularly in Italy, that the fool remains a fool, that he is derided, that the audience has no desire to identify with him, that the public indeed confirms its sense of its own wisdom by the spectacle of just how foolish the fool is. The idea of the 'wise fool', of the paradoxical subversive wisdom which shows up the deficiencies of conventional systems, never took as firm a hold on Italian culture as it did on English culture from the sixteenth century onwards.
>
> (Andrews, 1997, p.188)

As far as Dario Fo is concerned, Andrews' analysis falls short because it does not take account of the popular *Commedia* of the street or those early manifestations of it in the French theatre. In those instances wit and folly are indeed combined in the Harlequin/Sganarelle figure who offers an at least partial parallel with the wise fools of Shakespeare. It is only the subsequent demands of bourgeois taste that divide wisdom from folly as certain moral qualities become the sole preserve of one class. Goldoni's whole *oeuvre* bears witness to the two and fro tensions between the old, popular *Commedia* and the new, bourgeois version which serves the new taste for comedy of character. Goldoni's plays are frequently an attempt to serve two masters but ultimately he is a child of his times; times that fragmented and then marginalised the theatrical space once occupied by the fool.

The process instigated by Goldoni was accelerated in France by the comedies of Beaumarchais, centred on the fool turned protagonist, Figaro. Even in the time between *The Barber of Seville* and *The Marriage of Figaro* there is a significant change in Figaro's representation, as the trickster of the former play assumes the role of hero in the latter one. At the outset of *The Barber of Seville*, Figaro establishes his genealogy as the offspring of Harlequin. From the start he exploits the meta-theatrical relationship with the audience in the manner of fools before him, acknowledging the critics in almost Jonsonian style. After completing his opening song he more or less dares his audience not to like his performance:

When there's an accompaniment to it we shall see, you gentlemen who decide whether a play succeeds or not, we'll see if I don't know what I'm talking about.

(Beaumarchais, 1964, p.41)

Figaro's narration of his past life to Count Almaviva places him squarely within the orbit of the *jongleur*, the travelling player who offers a moving target to authorities and critics alike. He is detached, critical, improvisatory, and able to come up smiling from every adversity:

Figaro: ... I left Madrid and, with my pack on my back, made my way, philosophically enough, through the two Castiles, La Mancha, Estremadura, Sierra Morena, and Andalusia, welcomed in one place and jailed in the next, but always superior to fortune, praised by some and condemned by others, in fair weather and foul, defying all enemies, laughing at my own misfortunes, and playing the barber to anyone who needed me – here you find me at last established in Seville and at Your Excellency's disposal for any duties for which you care to command me.

Count: And what taught you such a cheerful philosophy?

Figaro: Habitual misfortune. I forced myself to laugh at everything for Fear of having to weep.

(Beaumarchais, 1964, p.44)

His past however, aligns him with a tradition from which he is seeking to escape via entry to the household of the Count. Throughout the play there are occasional flashes of the fool, particularly in exchanges with the Pantaloon figure, Bartholo, that set up opportunities for Harlequin-like verbal dexterity:

Bartholo: You are very hoity-toity, my good fellow, but let me warn you that when I'm involved with a knave I face him out to the end.

Figaro: [*turning his back*]: That's where we differ, Sir. I always give way to him.

(Beaumarchais, 1964, p.84)

But the move from contriver of another's happiness to protagonist in the attempt to secure his own robs Figaro of the independence of the fool and puts him at the mercy of the machinations of others. From the opening exchange with his beloved, Suzanne, in *The Marriage of Figaro* it is established that she is his equal in wit and can play upon him because love makes him vulnerable:

Figaro: You are laughing at me, you witch! Ah! If only there were some means of catching out this arch-deceiver, of leading him into a trap and pocketing his money.
Suzanne: Intrigue and money – you are in your element now.

(Beaumarchais, 1964, p.109)

Where, as fool, he might once have commented on the plot, he is now both the maker and the object of the plot. The story of the play concerns whether or not he will succeed in marrying Suzanne, a marriage that will enrol him in the ranks of the gentry. Because his principal obstacle is the Count's desire to exert *droit de seigneur* over Suzanne prior to his wedding, Figaro combines personal animus against him with an increasingly blatant attack on the aristocracy as the spectre of the Revolution draws inexorably nearer:

Count: The servants in this house take longer to dress than their masters.
Figaro: Because they have no servants to assist them.

(Beaumarchais, 1964, p.159)

He retains the fool's capacity for social critique and cynicism at the social climbing which characterises the age but otherwise he is triumphantly absorbed into the social fabric at the conclusion of the play. His final turn to the audience is to seek approbation for himself, not to laugh with him at the follies presented:

Figaro: I was poor and people despised me. I showed some evidence of ability and got myself disliked for it. Now, with a pretty wife and a fortune...
Count: Everyone will be your friend.
Figaro: Can that really be?
Bartholo: I know them.
Figaro: [*to the audience*]: My wife and my fortune apart – You will, I am sure, do me honour...
          [*All join in singing and dancing.*]

(Beaumarchais, 1964, p.216)

Events have socialised Figaro and the fool comes in from the cold. His stay by the hearth will not, however, be long for the emergence of new class divisions in the wake of the Revolution produced a fragmented world torn into sectarian, class interests which could not accommodate the one world vision of the wise fool.

Nineteenth century Europe is marked by a growing awareness of class identity, expressed in terms of what distinguished one group of people from another: aristocracy, middle-classes, working-classes. At the same time it was an age of empiricism where developments in science were fuelled by a sense of the infinite progress available to mankind; a species endowed with God's gift of reason. Neither class factionalism nor a belief in the ultimate perfectability of mankind through the application of reason were likely to produce conditions conducive to the flourishing of fooling. A figure running up and down the social ladder pointing out, without decorum or taste, the imperfections and limitations of the species was unlikely to command much general appeal either in the theatre or in society more broadly. This may partly account, together with the particular circumstances of its writing, for the complete neglect of Georg Büchner's *Woyzeck* which, though written in 1836, was not known until much later in the century. The play has been widely regarded as the major example of revolt, both social and theatrical, of the century and the most significant precursor of twentieth century theatre. Its documentary derivation – the execution of Johann Woyzeck in Leipzig in 1824 and the controversy surrounding definitions of criminal responsibility – together with Büchner's radical reworking of scenic form and narrative development put it in tune with the upheavals in artistic movements which came to characterise the period following the First World War.

My reason for drawing attention to it at this point in my argument, however, is because I offer Woyzeck as an example of a fool and believe that Büchner draws on popular and folk traditions that place Woyzeck within that genealogy. His situation as a fool is not straightforward. Unlike many of his forebears he is the victim of the social forces whose contradictions he highlights. Büchner's medical training drew him to explore the psychopathology of Woyzeck as a particular case even as he comes, simultaneously, to stand as an emblem of humane irrationality, crushed by the prevailing forces of class and reason. Woyzeck 'fools' with class in his exchanges with the Captain and the Doctor and he 'fools' with existence in the remainder of his relationships. In so doing, he paves the way for the emergence of foolish figures from twentieth century theatre who play with class, such as Brecht's Azdak, and those who play with existence, such as the existential clowns of Beckett.

The professional classes in *Woyzeck* derive their morality from the material benefits of their positions and seek to differentiate themselves from those who lack them. In effect being poor comes to be equated with lacking in morals and being comfortably off provides the cloak of 'decency', the key discriminatory word in the discourse. As the Captain puts it: 'Woyzeck, you've got no sense of decency' (Price, 1971, p.107). Woyzeck's response, fool-like, draws attention to the material basis of morality:

> WOYZECK. If you haven't got the money...I mean you can't bring the likes of us into the world on decency. We're flesh and blood too. Our kind doesn't get a chance in this world or the next. If we go to heaven they'll put us to work on the thunder.
>
> (Price, 1971, p.108)

Not only does he expose the hypocrisy of bourgeois social superiority, he also destroys the myth of consolation in the life to come. Paradoxically, though the advance of reason might be expected to sound the death knell of religion, the class interests of the bourgeoisie were best served by recruiting it to maintain social division with the promise of paradise postponed for the peasant and the proletariat. Woyzeck, as an embryonic working-class hero, has no truck with such illusions.

For the Doctor, patient Woyzeck is merely an object on which to perform experiments. There is no longer any link via common humanity from one class to the other. Under the guise of the advancement of science as a core element of the Enlightenment project the Doctor's real motivation is his personal desire for fame at the expense of his rivals. He preaches the central element of Enlightenment doctrine: 'Man is free. Man is the transfiguration of the individual urge to freedom.' (Price, 1971, p.115) This was the conclusion of Dr Clarus who wrote the reports on the historical (hysterical) Woyzeck. It boils down to an issue of responsibility. Büchner suggests here that it suits the professional classes to insist upon all people being responsible for their action, even while the capacity to act, the space within which to act, is so unequally apportioned. As a result of the 'free' actions of the Doctor upon Woyzeck, in this instance the diet of peas, he can no longer even be held responsible for his bodily functions and has to urinate in the street, an act of indecency. The carnivalesque celebration of the 'lower bodily stratum' has become a cause of shame and victimhood. The extremity of his poverty is interfering with his control over the basic drives of his animal nature: food, defecation and sex. The point is highlighted through the comparison with the performing monkey:

> BARKER: Examine this beast as god created him. Nothing to him, you see? Then observe the effect of art: he walks upright and has a coat and trousers. Also a sword. The monkey's a soldier – not that that's much, lowest form of animal life.
>
> (Price, 1971, pp.111–12)

In the world of *Woyzeck* the distinction between the classes is greater than that between the poor and the beasts. When the Showman's astronomical horse defecates during his performance he is intimately linked to Woyzeck, since both are reduced to performing natural functions as a last remaining assertion of independence. As the play progresses, if progression is a useful concept for such a work, the emphasis moves away from Woyzeck's victimisation on grounds of class and poverty and onto his confrontation with the existential void. From seeing heaven as a further site of tribulation he moves on to denying its very possibility. Marie's infidelity, whilst a key element in provoking the specific crisis which climaxes the action, is double-edged in relation to the question of existence. His love for her endows his life with purpose but also misleads him into thinking that he can afford, quite literally, to behave as a responsible partner to her. In a world where all relationships appear to be built on the objectification of the other – the Drum Major is only interested in Marie as a sex object – Woyzeck wants to experience the luxury of mutual subjectivities. In murdering her he both asserts a moral pattern to existence by punishing her for adultery and demonstrates that man is an animal in the grip of irrational passions such as jealousy; at once both more and less than a beast. The futility of Woyzeck's attempts to hold onto the refined abstractions of love and morality are set against the backdrop of the void, articulated by the Grandmother in her tale of the 'poor little boy' who wanders through an empty universe:

> GRANDMOTHER: And when he wanted to go back to earth, the earth was an upturned pot. And he was all alone. And he sat down and cried, and he's sitting there still, all alone.
>
> (Price, 1971, p.128)

The orphan boy of her tale resembles no one so much as Feste, alone on the Renaissance stage to sing of the rain, raining every day. Woyzeck's final attempt to assert a relationship with another human being is bereft of meaning in a meaningless world as his child rejects him and he leaves the baby in the care of Karl, the natural fool, who introduces the child to the arbitrariness of earthly fate through the nursery rhyme of 'this little piggy'.

In the Age of Reason the fool, rather than being cherished as a barometer of social health, is an eccentric, irrational outsider who represents a case study in psychosis and who offers grounds for social exclusion. Folly has not gone away but a society founded upon class distinctions and pride in its reasoning abilities has repressed folly's manifestations by extinguishing its representative. The categories invoked by Stallybrass and White to explain the operation of carnival in the eighteenth century can be extended in both scope and historical period to chart the varying fates of fools upon the European stage for three hundred years. Even these few plays which have been considered in this chapter furnish ample evidence of fragmentation, marginalisation, sublimation and repression. Whilst it can be argued that the fools in each of the examples suffer from all four of these processes, I would also assert that the emphasis down the years moves from fragmentation through marginalisation and sublimation to repression. As Freud observed in his patients, however, the repressed as a tendency to return. The fools repressed by reason, enlightenment and the refinements in theatrical taste return with a vengeance to provoke the disturbances in the most powerful theatre of the twentieth century and, significantly, their authors frequently reach back to the pre-modern period for their inspiration.

7
Fooling with Contradiction

Terrible is the temptation to do good!

(Brecht, 1994. p.165)

It has long been noted that Bertolt Brecht offered several versions of fools as wise men in his plays and that folly itself is frequently worn by such characters as a mask, behind which they can employ irony, paradox and contradiction to discomfort those who represent and benefit from oppressive regimes that operate by separating people from the sources of their own humanity. *In extremis* the ploy is adopted for survival as much as for social critique. This chapter will engage with some of these characters to investigate some of the ways in which their foolishness enables them to operate within violent, pathological societies without fatal consequences to themselves. However, the scope of the analysis of Brecht's relation to fooling is broader than that offered by a few selected types from the collection of his *dramatis personae*. I want to suggest that Brecht's whole evolving dramaturgy is bound up with the notion of folly; that it is, in the terms articulated by Fredric Jameson, a vital part of his method. Both the writing and more especially the performance of his plays constituted a calculated act of folly in the context of the historical and ideological moment of production. There is a sense in which many of the plays are not only about people but also about situations that engender foolish or mad behaviour; about societies, the exposure of whose contradictions shows them to be insane:

> I want to argue that for Brecht, the dialectic – the *'Grosse Methode'* – is defined and constituted by the search for and discovery of contradictions. Perhaps one might even say: by the construction of

contradictions – since it is as a reordering process that it is necessary to grasp the dialectical method in Brecht: as the restructuring
of juxtapositions, dissonances, *Trennungen*, distances of all kinds, in
terms of contradiction as such.

(Jameson, 1998, pp.79–80)

For instance, in *Mother Courage and Her Children* it is not only Kattrin
who suffers the consequences of her folly but also Swiss Cheese, Eilif and
Mother Courage herself. And even beyond their individual madness the
social relations that Brecht depicts in the play are turned so far upside
down, that finally only a foolish response can save them. Consequently
Mother Courage's final, absurd act of pressing on, alone, with her wagon
can be at once both foolish and not foolish enough; at once representing
her victimisation by the system and the continuance of the system itself.
Azdak is the wise fool of *The Caucasian Chalk Circle* but his folly is only
enabled to make an effective intervention because of Grusha's foolish
behaviour in abducting the governor's baby; an act that both defines
and terminates his period in office as carnival judge before disappearing,
like Schweyk into the snowdrifts of Stalingrad, to places where the mask
of madness increases the likelihood of survival.

The other motif that links Brecht's theatre centrally to the concerns
of this book is that of the contradiction between being human and being
the upholder of an inhuman system: be that capitalism, business, war,
fascism or religion, all of which are linked means of enabling the powerful to exploit the powerless. This contradiction is at times the means by
which a play is structured, as in *Mother Courage and Her Children* and
Schweyk in the Second World War; sometimes located within the persona of the protagonist as in *Herr Puntila and His Man Matti* and *The
Good Person of Szechwan* and, in the case of *The Life of Galileo*, both
structural principle and delineation of the protagonist where Galileo
himself embodies the contradictions between science and religion, intellect and sensuality, knowledge and ignorance. In many aspects this
contradiction continues the expression, adapted to reflect societies in
the twentieth century, of the battle between Carnival and Lent. The
weapons in this battle are paradox and irony, since the representatives of
these positions are frequently undone by the presence of their opposite
behind their own lines of defence; the Other that constantly provokes
the redefinition of Self. For instance, the pure researcher, Galileo, must
compromise his science to enable him to satisfy his appetite, and the
selfless, good Shen Te, once pregnant, will be ruthless in pursuit of a
materially secure life for her child.

Inversion, that core principle of carnival, is evoked in the opening lines of *Mr Puntila and his Man Matti*, not only to remind the audience of the state of Europe in 1940 but also to alert it to 'read' the play against the grain of familiar moral precepts:

> Ladies and gentlemen, the times are sad
> When worry's sane, and not to worry mad.

> (Brecht, 1977, p.7)

This balancing of contraries in ways which present them as strange, heralds the opening scene in which Puntila refines the same process. He articulates the familiar Christian platitude: 'for the spirit is willing but the flesh is weak', only to undermine it through an inversion of context where the weakness referred to is the inability to keep pace with Puntila's mammoth drinking binge. The expected connection of the spirit with Lent and the flesh with carnival is defamiliarised through the partial reversal which paves the way for the audience to accept the drunk Puntila as the norm and the sober as an aberration. Typically, no sooner have we adjusted our perceptions to contain this reality than Brecht exposes our naivety by demonstrating how the carnivalesque Puntila is produced by the sober owner of a large estate. Puntila may delude himself into imagining that he is fighting a battle between Carnival and Lent in himself but the audience, aided by Matti, is forced into perceiving the relationship as dialectical. The drunken Puntila enjoys using the wealth of his sober *doppelganger* to foster his delusions of humanity but those who lack the means to escape from the necessity of their role are less fortunate: 'You a human being? Just now you said you were a chauffeur.'(Brecht, 1977, p.9) Ironically, it is Puntila who confuses the two roles, requiring his chauffeur to behave at times like a human being and at other times like a servant. Matti, however, even under the most extreme provocation, never loses his sense of his identity within the social hierarchy:

> *Puntila*: I want to be sure there's no gulf between us any longer. Tell me there's no gulf.
> *Matti*: I take that to be an order, Mr Puntila: there's no gulf.

> (Brecht, 1977, p.13)

Though Puntila is well aware of how the structures of oppression distort human nature, he needs his sober, 'beastly' moments to buy the spaces in which he can perform his carnival role as the shadow or mask of his workaday self. Through the alcohol inspired haze he glimpses another, more humane way, in which human relations might be organised ('I'm practically a communist') but even at these moments he does not quite let go of the *alter ego*. His 'practically' carries all the weight of the Singer's 'almost' at the conclusion of *The Caucasian Chalk Circle* where Azdak's period as Judge is described as 'almost an age of justice'. Where Puntila plays or fools with the social distinctions by which the world is organised, thereby confusing many who are drawn into the orbit of his carnival, Matti prefers the security of unambiguously demarcated positions: 'I once worked in a paper mill where the porter gave notice because the director asked how his son was getting on.'(Brecht, 1977, p.19)

The whole play is constructed as a game, using the idea of the struggle between Carnival and Lent to illustrate the operation of a semi-feudal class structure. The entire district is in on the joke, illustrated by the League of Puntila's fiancées pretending to take up his offer of engagement by appearing at Puntila Hall wearing the curtain rings and straw wreaths. The sober Puntila's response to them disappoints but does not surprise them. They came for a bit of fun on their day off; in fact for a carnival to celebrate Eva's engagement. But Puntila's hierarchical self pointedly separates their humanity from their working function:

> You're the telephonist at Kurgela, aren't you, I'll ring your supervisor and see if that's the sort of laugh that's permitted in the postal service...
>
> (Brecht, 1977, p.60)

Puntila's position allows him to play at carnival on other people's working days but when others wish to enjoy a carnival on their day off, it conflicts with the sober business of marrying off his daughter for social advancement. What should be a carnival celebration is conducted like business, even as business has earlier been turned into a carnival. Puntila plays the fool with the traditional distinction to inaugurate a process of *verfremdung* by which the operation of class is made transparent for the analysis of the audience. In a similar vein Brecht takes the traditional fairy tale of Cinderella and inverts each aspect: the girl is now the 'princess' and the boy of humble origins. It is the upper class person who must undergo the test and, unlike Cinderella, Eva finds that her feet do not fit into the mould of working class domestic slavery. The test is carried out in the spirit of play and so Eva's failure is a failure of performance; she cannot perform working class convincingly or, put another way, class division defeats *jouissance*. Puntila may lament her limitations but his wilder and more extravagant performances also fail to effect his transformation into a communist. Even in his carnival manifestation he is only the carnival version of himself, enjoying food, sex and urinating in the open air. When he tastes the Lenten necessities of the poor ('Welcome, herring, thou meat of the poor!'), he merely enjoys the novelty of a world beyond his regular experience, drunk or sober.

Fittingly for a protagonist and a play structured around the tension between Carnival and Lent, the burst of ferocious sobriety brought on by the engagement of his daughter to the Attaché and his attempt to wrestle with his accounts is countered by the most violent bout of drinking that triggers extremes of sentimentality centred on the seductive charms of the homeland:

> *Puntila:* O Tavastland, blessed art thou! With thy sky, thy lakes, thy people and thy forests! *To Matti:* Tell me that your heart expands at the sight of it all.
>
> *Matti:* My heart expands at the sight of your forests, Mr Puntila.

> (Brecht, 1977, p.91)

The titles of Brecht's plays frequently announce their central tension and this is the case here where Matti indeed remains Puntila's man until the final scene. At the end, though, he is not deceived by Puntila's fooling with internal contradictions that do not change social structures. Puntila is a demonstration of the safety valve theory of licensed carnival, letting off steam where no harm is done to the *status quo*. But the play is not frozen into this paralysis. Where Mother Courage's lonely departure from the stage is the emblem for her failure to learn from the destructive fall-out of her pursuit of business in war, Matti's solitary walk away from Puntila's estate acknowledges the possibility of change:

> So – time your servants turned their backs on you.
> They'll find a decent master pretty fast
> Once they've become the masters here at last.
> *He walks rapidly away.*

> (Brecht, 1977, p.92)

Where Matti can change the central relationship by his departure, Mother Courage does not change her relationship to the war but her relationship to her children whom she sees into their graves before herself, such is the unnaturalness of war. Carnivalesque folly is in short supply in this bleak wartime play but foolish actions that throw into relief the norms by which Mother Courage lives provide two of the major 'gests' of the play: the deaths of Swiss Cheese and Kattrin.

As in *Mr Puntila and his Man Matti*, the notion of inversion is introduced at the outset of *Mother Courage and her Children*. This time, however, the two poles are not Carnival and Lent but peace and war:

> *The Sergeant*: What they could do with round here is a good war. What else can you expect with peace running wild all over the place? You know what the trouble with peace is? No organization. And when do you get organization? In a war.
>
> (Brecht, 1962, p.3)

War is good for business and peace is good for survival; so the tension is formed between those who serve the cause of business and those who serve the cause of humanity, with Mother Courage caught at the apex of the contradiction, mistaking business for survival. In her terms, those who do not adapt their human natures to the laws of business are foolish and she is burdened with foolish children. Her calculations over the likelihood of Swiss Cheese's survival – threatened by his irrational honesty – rely upon his having fallen into the hands of those prepared to do business:

> They're not wolves, they're human and after money. God is merciful, and men are bribable, that's how His will is done on earth as it is in Heaven. Corruption is our only hope. As long as there's corruption, there'll be merciful judges and even the innocent may get off.
>
> (Brecht, 1962, p.38)

But the business of war creates circumstances in which men behave outside the codes of human nature as conceived by Mother Courage. Brecht depicts such circumstances at the extreme edge of human behaviour by constructing a situation which requires her to deny the identity of her son who is thrown into the 'carrion pit' so that business can be continued in a parodied echo of the Young Comrade cast into the 'lime pit' so that revolution can be continued in his earlier *Lehrstück*, *The Measures Taken*.

The figure who most embodies the alienation between human desire and war is, as Alfred White has shown, (White, 1978, p.100-1) the dumb

Kattrin. The war imprints itself upon her body twice; once before the start of the play to deny her voice:

> Even her dumbness comes from the war. A soldier stuck something in her mouth when she was little.
>
> (Brecht, 1962, p.55)

and a second time during the action to leave her with a scar that robs her of the chance to fulfil her desire for a sexual relationship and children, symbolised by her rejection of the red boots denied her by her mother before she was assaulted. War and her mother's involvement in it robs her of every possibility of fulfilling herself in life as a woman and as a human being, leaving her with only one weapon with which she can take her revenge upon it – death. As ever in her comments upon her children, Mother Courage will be proved wrong: 'Be glad you're dumb, Kattrin: you'll never contradict yourself' (Brecht, 1962, p.23). Instead she achieves the ultimate contradiction of dying that others may live in a gesture that, though almost certainly futile, is the only one in the play which shows how poor people can change the circumstances where war seeks to divide them from their natures as human beings. Brecht depicts a world in which totalitarian fascism renders every relationship dangerous, every transaction governed by self-interest. It is, therefore, only the person who is beyond the reach of such considerations; only the person who, like the fool, is outside the orbit of discourse who is free to act in a way that defies the logic of war. Kattrin does not calculate, as her mother might, that she will not be shot since shooting will arouse the town, but uses her remaining expressive powers to assert her humanity in the face of the overwhelming forces of dehumanisation. Paradoxically both in spite of and because of her own suffering, she throws her life down in the defence of the defenceless children sleeping in Halle. In so doing she becomes an emblem for the survival of the human spirit; for the folly of fighting for life in the midst of death, like a seventeenth century harbinger of those who lived through the death camps to tell their stories.

In keeping with a play that depicts the monstrous immorality of a war fought in the name of contending Christian factions, Brecht offers a parody of the medieval morality play through the figures of the Chaplain and the Cook who are rivals for the affections of Mother Courage. Though their respective professions suggest that they represent soul and body, both are equally concerned with the business of their own survival in this world, thereby transposing the morality onto the plane of the material. If this parody conscripts Mother Courage into the role of Everyman, Brecht, as usual, goes against the grain by denying salvation to her in the form of an understanding of the relationship between war (business by other means) and the deaths of her children. She persistently refuses to repent and her parting words: 'Hey! Take me with you!'(Brecht, 1962, p.81) are a plea to be included in the perpetuation of the hell on earth of continuing war. It would take an act of folly beyond the reach of her imagination to change her attitude as a prelude to changing the world.

All the plays of Brecht written after 1933 share a concern with how the world might be changed, by whom and with what consequences. The contradictions of a world organised according to structures that require humans to behave inhumanly in order to survive are quite easy to expose. The more difficult task is, in dialectical terms, to forge the synthesis from the blatant antagonism between thesis and antithesis. Brecht poses the same problem in the fable of *The Good Person of Szechwan*: given the prevailing conditions in human society, whence and in what form can the interventions emerge that produce structural, sustained transformation? Change is held in a static tension produced by the counter discourses of morality and economics: 'The world can stay as it is if enough people are found living lives worthy of human beings.' (Brecht, 1966, p.23) For this play the contradiction is embodied in the single body and dual form of Shen Te/Shui Ta and the familiar opposition of Carnival and Lent has been adapted into goodness and business with goodness firmly associated with Carnival – that which can be indulged in when there are the means and the leisure to take time off from the pursuit of survival – and business with Lent – work, trade, and all the accompanying transactions necessary to ensure present and future prosperity. Shen Te, however, is a fool to her own interests and nowhere more foolish than in her desire to love without regard for economic consequence. She rivals King Lear in the folly of her misplaced love. The problem was starkly articulated in Brecht's original title for the play, *Die Ware Liebe* ('commodity love') with its pun on *Die Wahre Liebe* (true love). For the poor, love which runs counter to business interests is a disaster, but for Shen Te who has previously only experienced the expression of desire as a sex worker, the attraction of Yang Sun is in the very fact that there is nothing in it for her aside from the right to experience love. The alternative is the bourgeois form of prostitution, marriage to the wealthy Shu Fu as recommended by her *alter ego*. Love flatly contradicts business as she well knows: 'He (Shui Ta) doesn't agree with me, I know, but he's wrong'. (Brecht, 1966, p.71) Love, that most profound of human emotional needs, does not exist in some separate compartment outside economic consequence; so Shen Te has to carry its catastrophic effects with her into the negotiating sphere of business:

> All that I have done I did
> To help my neighbour
> To love my lover
> And to keep my little one from want

> (Brecht, 1966, p. 105)

Shen Te plays the fool to Shui Ta who represents the dominant discourse of capitalist business. Like fools before her, she demonstrates the ways in which the need to respond to human instincts and impulses both undermines the operation of the dominant and looks, from its common sense perspective, like an act of madness: to be human in the world of business is to be mad; as mad as Hamlet amid the norms of political corruption. Powerful systems, set up to benefit the few over the many, be they Church, State or Business, have to be structured in ways that deny people the right to be themselves. In *The Good Person of Szechwan*, Brecht reverses the method of the Battle between Carnival and Lent to present the dialectical operation of the struggle in a person who exists simultaneously within and beyond the prevailing ideology.

Fittingly for a man whose opinions on history and social reality were always provisional, always susceptible to change from new realities, the same period of European history which provided the circumstances for his bleakest drama, *Mother Courage and her Children,* also forms the setting for the moment when new astronomical knowledge began the painfully slow process of emancipating people from the unquestioned authority of the church and from those who benefited from obedience to it:

The process of aesthetic autonomization, breaking the action up into its smallest parts, thus has symbolic as well as epistemological meaning: it shows what the act 'really' is, no doubt, but the very activity of breaking it up and 'analyzing' it is itself a joyous process, a kind of creative play, in which new acts are formed together out of pieces of the old, in which the whole reified surface of a period seemingly beyond history and beyond change now submits to a first ludic un-building, before arriving at a real social and revolutionary collective reconstruction.

(Jameson, 1998, p.47)

The 'reconstruction' of the role of Galileo in the development and dissemination of the 'new' science of physics involved a typical act of what Raymond Williams termed 'complex seeing' (Williams, 1976, pp.316–32). Galileo makes possible what he also denies and, in denying, persists in that selfish productivity which will enable future generations to make use of what he withholds from his own. Like fools before him, Galileo is endowed with the gift of prophecy but being a Brechtian fool he is both right and wrong or, more precisely, right while being wrong: 'It is my prophecy that our own lifetime will see astronomy being discussed in the marketplaces' (Brecht, 1980, p.8). Once more Brecht taps into the archetypal pattern of Carnival and Lent with progressive, humane forces associated with the former, and reactionary, conservative forces of the *status quo* with the latter. The sweep of scenes which culminates literally in the marketplace carnival of Scene 10 are immediately followed by the Lenten machinations of the Inquisition, culminating in Galileo giving up his responsibility to enlighten the oppressed for Lent.

Brecht links the hunger of ordinary people for practical knowledge to the processes of fluid exchange and shifting relations, following Bruegel's depictions of the teeming life of public spaces, that Bakhtin associates with the marketplace. When the marketplace is also the site of carnival practices, its subversive potential is doubled. The Ballad Singer's commentary upon the Carnival of 1632 falls into three distinct phases. Firstly he articulates the *status quo*, reminding the people that it is members of the established church who are the chief beneficiaries:

> Around the pope the cardinals
> Around the cardinals the bishops
> Around the bishops the secretaries
> Around the secretaries the aldermen
> Around the aldermen the craftsmen
> Around the craftsmen the servants
> Around the servants the dogs, the chickens and the beggars

> (Brecht, 1980, pp.82–3)

The first effect of Galileo's intervention into this order of being is to produce the chaos and anarchy which result from the inversion of the normal hierarchy that is the special quality of carnival as a time off from restraint:

The serf stays sitting on his arse
This turning's turned his head.
The altar boy won't serve the mass
The apprentice lies in bed.

(Brecht, 1980, p.83)

On this occasion, however, the inversion points beyond holiday to the working world, thereby exceeding its licence. The utopian vision attributed to Galileo is one based in material reality where the application of reason will lead to a more equitable distribution of resources. Writing on the 'gestic' functions of music in the *Short Organon*, Brecht indicates how the significance of this moment can be highlighted in production:

Thus Eisler, e.g. helped admirably in the knotting of the incidents when in the carnival scene of *Galileo* he set the masked procession of the guilds to a triumphant threatening music which showed what a revolutionary twist the lower orders had given to the scholar's astronomical theories.

(Brecht, 1978, p.203)

Galileo's discoveries hold the potential to improve enormously the productivity of working people for their own benefit in a redistribution which prefigures the ending of feudal relations:

The tenant gives his landlord hell
Not caring in the least
His wife now feeds her children well
On the milk she fed the priest

(Brecht, 1980, p.84)

Galileo's carnivalesque creativity – his particular combination of appetite, sensuality and imagination – renders him especially susceptible to the threat of physical pain as the church responds to the provocation with the threat of violence to his own person. If there is an analogy here with Brecht's subsequent situation in East Berlin, that would make the productive laboratory of the *Berliner Ensemble* the equivalent of the house-arrested prisoner of the *Theater am Schiffbauerdam*; Galileo and Brecht alike lying in the gutter but still gazing at the stars:

The theatre can only adopt such a free attitude if it lets itself be carried along by the strongest currents in its society and associates itself with those who are necessarily most impatient to make great alterations there. The bare wish, if nothing else, to evolve an art fit for the times must drive our theatre of the scientific age straight out into the suburbs, where it can stand as it were wide open, at the disposal of those who live hard and produce much, so that they can be fruitfully entertained there with their great problems.

(Brecht, 1978, p.186)

The Carnival/Lent *motif* is once again influential in shaping the course of *Schweyk in the Second World War*. The catalyst for the chain of events which leads to Schweyk's historic encounter with Hitler outside Stalingrad is the Gargantuan, Falstaffian appetite of his friend Baloun. The imposition of strict rationing, a Lenten procedure from which the occupiers exempt themselves, sets up a wartime version of a morality play where Baloun's behaviour ('Eating's his vice'), causes the latter day Everyman, Schweyk, to fall into the clutches of the enemy who with characteristic irony inhabits not hell but 'the higher regions'. As ever, authority is firmly on the side of Lent and opposed to humanity as Schweyk makes clear through his customary torrent of verbal excess. Words are to him what food is to Baloun and in these 'dark times' equally dangerous:

> I'm glad to hear you confirm that the Führer doesn't go for the girls, so that he can reserve his strength for higher matters of State, and that he don't ever drink alcohol. He's done what he has done stone-cold sober, you might say; it's not everyone who'd do the same. And it's lucky too that he doesn't eat anything except a few vegetables and a bit of pastry, because there's not much going, what with the war and all that, and it makes one mouth less to feed.
>
> (Brecht, 1994, p.86)

The antidote to the depravities and inhumanities witnessed and experienced by Schweyk on the circular road to Stalingrad comes in the form of the flashbacks to life in the carnival setting of the tavern. The Song of the Chalice looks forward to a time when its ways are the norm rather than a flickering candle in the storm of hatred and division:

> And we'll find the world's an inn
> Where men come together
>
> (Brecht, 1994, p.133)

Asserting the right to be human becomes an act of resistance in any age in which the dominant group, be that based on religion, race, class or ideology, requires the 'little people' to behave contrary to their own interests. In the Brechtian 'epic' those who resist are not heroes but survivors; not martyrs but idiots:

> *Schweyk*: Long live our Führer Adolf Hitler. Victory shall be ours!
> *Bullinger*: *dumbfounded*: Are you a half-wit?
> *Schweyk*: Beg to report, sir, yes sir. I can't help it, I've already been dis-
> charged from the army on account of half-wittedness. I have been
> officially certified an idiot by a medical board.
> *Bullinger*: Brettschneider! Didn't you see the man's a half-wit?
> *Brettschneider*: *injured*: Lieutenant, the observations of the man
> Schweyk in the Chalice resembled those of a half-wit who disguises
> his defeatist utterances so cleverly you can't prove anything.
> (Brecht, 1994, p.81)

Schweyk puts on an 'antic disposition' as a mask behind which he can give free rein to his propensity to verbal excess. His comments as madman are not, however, directed towards ideological opposition to authority but rather to the revelation of the gaps in the logic of authority; the fissures through which the contradictions that will ultimately undermine it can crawl towards the light:

> Sir, permission to admit that I really was certified, though I was hav
> ing a bit of a joke as well. As the landlord of a pub in Budweis said,
> 'I'm an epileptic but I've got cancer as well', when he wanted to keep
> it dark that he'd gone bankrupt. It's like the old Czech proverb says,
> sweaty feet seldom come singly.
> (Brecht, 1994, p.85)

Paradoxically, only by playing the fool can Schweyk be himself. In a world as dangerous as Nazi occupied Europe it is not safe to operate without the protection of a role that advertises itself as existing outside the discourses of politics. Even then, living or dying at the whim of an external agency usually means that only a short time has been bought by the device. This mask of folly which is adopted in many societies at different times and in different places becomes in Brecht's theatre much more than a local device or isolated effect. It is rather a core contributor to a central aspect of his method as Peter Brooker has commented:

As a new concept the 'naive' united acting and theatre, performance and theory. Thus the actor must 'take up the attitude of a man who just wonders' (*BT*, p. 197), but Brecht's theatre too was 'in a naive sense a philosophical one...', his whole theory 'much naiver than people think' (*BT*, p. 248). The 'naive' therefore fittingly joined together contraries; it was a look, a posture, an attitude of mind; it implied an intelligent simplicity, innocence and shrewdness, joining the conceptual and concrete, the popular and philosophical. A naive attitude would estrange the familiar, and problematise the self-evident, signalling a dialectical movement from the ordinary and everyday to the original and innovatory.

(Brooker, 1994, pp. 198–9)

With the intersecting stories of *The Caucasian Chalk Circle* Brecht combines the type of the 'foolish' woman whose excess of humanity causes her to act against her own interests, with that of the 'naïve' idiot who asserts the cause of humanity from behind the temporary refuge of the mask of folly. The story of Grusha is that of an 'ordinary' girl whose senseless act of humanity propels her into the spotlight of history where she gradually transforms herself from the object into the subject of her own development.

Suddenly Brecht's luminous verse reverses all that ancient tradition of sin and human nature: now it is goodness itself which exerts the baleful force of temptation, which mesmerizes Grusha and is on the point of leading her to do things very much against her own best interests and personal safety. Now the cooperative ideal exerts all the uncanny power of attraction that used to be attributed to vice; and it is the good instincts which seem to have been only momentarily repressed by the process of civilization, and are ready to break out again at the slightest pretext.

(Jameson, 1998, p.174)

'Seduced' into 'stealing' the abandoned baby, Michael, she at first struggles to cope with the burden with which she has landed herself. But when her attempt to pass the burden on to someone else is thwarted by the peasant woman's fear and instinct for self-preservation, Grusha takes a decision to shape her own destiny. The significance of the moment is articulated by the Singer: 'From this moment Grusha Vachnadze decided to be the child's mother.' (Brecht, 1994, p.179) At the historical, though not theatrical, moment of the initial 'terrible temptation' somewhere not too far away a village clerk is also tempted into another senseless act of humanity which we see propelling him onto the front pages of history and a climactic encounter with Grusha. On the point of handing the fugitive Grand Duke over to the village policeman, Shauva, Azdak thinks better of it:

Shauva, go home and repent. No, stop! There's something... *He looks at the fugitive, who stands trembling in the corner.* No, it's nothing after all. Go home and repent.

(Brecht, 1994, p.203)

Though the moment is passed over as swiftly as Grusha's crisis is lingered over, it is a moment of acute contradiction. Does the fool's intuitive humanitarianism defeat his class instincts? Yet, paradoxically, his social intervention is only made possible as a consequence of the exhibition of that humanity. Grusha and Azdak will change the course of history because they have not been entirely estranged from their creative imaginations and productivity as humans by a social system that uses them as objects.

Even before this foolish act Azdak has been firmly located within the Bakhtinian tradition of the popular where the satisfaction of the needs of the flesh takes precedence. His hut is adorned with indicators of his physical appetite while his appearance bears witness to his priorities: '*Azdak, in rags and tipsy, helps a fugitive dressed as a beggar into his hut.*' (Brecht, 1994, p.201) Like Lear's Fool, he can penetrate disguise since role playing and costume are modes that he understands and uses. In a moment with echoes of the Young Comrade from *The Measures Taken*, he berates Shauva in a manner which suggests that he feels the need to disguise his own humanity in such dangerous times, and that Shauva may have seen through him: 'I *don't* have a good heart! How often am I to tell you I'm a man of intellect?' (Brecht, 1994, p.202) His intellect may be real enough while also protecting him from any prolonged engagement with his fellow mortals. He uses this intellect to spy out contradictions that reveal the operation of familiar, normal oppression:

In Tiflis they once hanged a landowner, a Turk. He could prove he quartered his peasants instead of merely cutting them in half, as is the custom. And he squeezed twice the usual amount of taxes out of them. His zeal was above suspicion, and yet they hanged him like a common criminal. Why? Because he was a Turk – something he couldn't do much about. An injustice!

(Brecht, 1994, pp.203–4)

The internal contradictions of the feudal oppressor producing the contending discourses of class and race, are the means by which a form of justice in terms of class analysis comes to pass. The cheerful irony of the fool is the needle with which Azdak unpicks the social fabric of oppression. Two injustices produce a form of justice, anticipating his strategy as judge. Rather than confront injustice head on in open combat and, given the prevailing power structures, lose, Azdak ingratiates himself, accidentally, into the edifice of power where, in the manner of Schweyk after his conscription into the *Wehrmacht*, he can do far more damage.

Azdak, adept at playing the fool, is not tied down by any one characteristic, be that political or personal. His broadcast confession enables him to cover himself against a range of possibilities: he aligns himself with the new regime by this self-abasement but he has also earned credit with the old, for he knew he had abetted the escape of someone important even if, at that moment, he did not know that it was the Grand Duke. The wary East German keeps a Swiss passport in his back pocket. In similar fashion he has seen enough false dawns to view with caution the dawning of a 'new age'. Even before he has stepped into the public, political arena, the revolutionary possibilities of the moment of upheaval have been severely diminished. Nevertheless, this is a time of disorder, a brief moment when the world is turned upside down and, being a figure from carnival, Azdak thrives on inversion. Prince Kazbeki's need to court the favour of the military, pending the capture of the Grand Duke, puts a little play into the normally inflexible system. Azdak's moment of humanitarian madness has resulted in the creation of a performance space whose rules he can command at the expense of the hapless nephew who has never learnt to play. It is, perhaps, more a sense of fun and a thirst for anarchy rather than class solidarity which influences the ironshirts' choice for the new judge but the result is that a flower of the people can briefly bloom amid the rubble of civil war. As the spirit of carnival inversion declares, there never was any justice in the legal system, so there is little to be lost by Azdak's appointment: 'The Judge was always a rascal. Now the rascal shall be the Judge. *The Judge's robe is placed round his shoulders, the wicker from a bottle on his head.'* (Brecht, 1994, p.212) Thus is he placed firmly in the tradition of the Feast of Fools, like Falstaff mocking kingship with cushion and dagger. Unlike Falstaff, the moment of play, the rehearsal, becomes for a while the actual exercise of power. At the court of Judge Azdak carnival is the norm. Since the whole notion of legality has been erected by the powerful to protect their own interests, an inverted procedure requires illegal judgements in favour of the powerless. A counterpoint is established between the material, sensual contingency of Azdak's verdicts in the episodes of his judging, and their relation to any absolute ideal of justice in the verses of the Singer which punctuate each one:

> Beware of willing Judges
>> For Truth is a black cat
> In a windowless room at midnight
>> And Justice a blind bat.

(Brecht, 1994, p. 215)

Azdak is and is not a 'proper' judge. Like a proper judge he accepts bribes. Unlike a proper judge these do not affect his judgement. But since justice is a commodity in an economic system, according to the economic laws of Azdak's system justice goes to those who are in the most need of it, economically. There is a double redistribution: the wealthy pay once for the benefit of the carnival judge and then pay again through the verdict against them. The notion of justice as an act or performance is demonstrated visually by the robe of office struggling to hide the rags of the village clerk beneath. This is a Shakespearean style triple impersonation where the actor remains visible behind Azdak the scrivener who remains visible behind Azdak the judge. The effect was heightened in the original production when Brecht cast Ernst Busch as both the Singer and Azdak, so that as Singer he pronounces history's verdict on his interregnum of people's justice:

> His balances were crooked
>> But they shouted in the streets:—
> 'Good, good, good is Azdak
>> And the measure that he metes!'

(Brecht, 1994, p.217)

In keeping with his strategy of exposing the operation of the law as a corrupt game which usually works to uphold privilege and inequity, he gladly inverts the functions to place the most vulnerable in the seat of judgement and to instantly invest her in a moral authority which endorses the role: 'Little mother, pass merciful sentence on us, the damned!' (Brecht, 1994, p.219) Here he speaks from a position midway between the action of the episode and the Singer's commentary upon it. Fool-like, he is capable of removing himself into a semi-detached position, half in and half out of the scene he has himself generated. As actor he facilitates the action and mediates its meaning for the audience while simultaneously, as Azdak, he performs a role within the scene to reveal motive and expose contradiction. He is the Joker of a Forum that he has generated. His laughter can almost be heard behind the mask of the Singer who delivers the paradox: only by destroying justice can the poor receive their just deserts:

> Two summers and two winters
> A poor man judged the poor
> And on the wreck of justice
> He brought them safe to shore

(Brecht, 1994, p.220)

But when events take a turn for the worse and law and order threaten to call time on Azdak's reign as carnival lord of misrule, he has no desire to be recast as tragic hero. This is no *King Lear* where the figures of tragedian and fool merge into one. Azdak's comment seems addressed as much to the spectators off-stage as to those on it:

> But I'll give no man the pleasure of seeing human greatness. I'll beg on my knees for mercy. Spittle will slobber down my chin. The fear of death is upon me.

(Brecht, 1994, p.222)

The actor of the role of Azdak (Ernst Busch, Ekkehard Schall) prepares himself for the next scene, anticipating the *gestus* which therefore does not need to be played. The self-conscious fool sketches out his act in advance in order that the scene is played according to his script. However, in the best traditions of melodrama, the likely *denouement* is thwarted by a dramatic, unexpected interruption. In this instance, though, it is one which reveals the second consequence of Azdak's initial act of wanton kindness. He becomes judge for the second time but this time by appointment to the Grand Duke. The Biblical echoes which reverberate throughout the text are especially strong at the point where Azdak, Christ-like, undergoes a severe beating at the hands of the soldiers before being saved in order to sit in judgement. The beating also reminds us of the habitual dangers of playing the fool from Socrates onwards.

Various levels of dramatic irony play out through the scene of the chalk circle test which has a strong atmosphere of the game about it. It feels as if Azdak knows all along what judgement he will make; indeed, that judgement is in line with the previous ones. But he orchestrates the trial once more to bring out the contradictions and hypocrisies of the wealthy and powerful as in the admission over the inheritance: 'The Court is touched by the mention of the estates. It's a proof of human feeling.'(Brecht, 1994, p.229) If the Marxist fool keeps his nerve there can be only one outcome. This, however, is a high profile case and his desire for self-preservation might prevail were it not for the boldness lent him by the mask of folly: 'The fool's worst enemy is himself'. (Brecht, 1994, p.231) In fact the test for Grusha comes before the drawing of the circle with the sharpening of the contradiction provoked by Azdak's question to her: 'Don't you want him to be rich?' (Brecht, 1994, p.233) The question drives at the heart of the possibility that her behaviour is selfishly maternal in denying Michael the chance of wealth. But her silence, interpolated by the Singer, expresses the social intervention at the core of the fable. Grusha wishes to interrupt the hereditary pattern of exploitation, to rescue Michael from the burden of oppression in order that he has his own opportunity for transformation. The cycles of violence and counter-violence change nothing in the operation of politics but the removal of a human being from the vicious circle constitutes a small but real change. Grusha's hopes for her child run counter to the iron laws of economics, and, naïve though these are, they will be given an initial start by the support of foolish wisdom. The mode of inversion that has characterised the performance of the carnival judge from his first appearance is maintained until the climax of his judgements:

> The true mother is she who has the strength to pull the child out of the circle, towards her.
>
> (Brecht, 1994, p.234)

Of course, the opposite is, and is not, true. In this case the contradiction is bound up in that solitary, four letter word. Truth, like justice, is an ideal that is bought as a commodity by the rich and powerful. The material fool will have no truck with such idealised abstractions but rather make his judgement on the basis of need and productivity.

As Ronald Speirs suggests, Azdak's criteria break free from the old bonds of inheritance and privilege:

> For Azdak the past therefore carries weight only in as much as it is relevant to the future: he does not decide which woman has the better *right* to 'possess' the child, but bases his judgement on the child's right to a good mother, and so grants Grusha the *privilege* of bearing the responsibility for Michael's further upbringing.
>
> (Speirs, 1987, p.170)

In terms of current preoccupations in the world of development this can be taken as an early instance of a rights-based approach of a kind which is increasingly addressed through the devices of Theatre for Development (TfD). The whole structure of the chalk circle test can be viewed from this perspective with Azdak as facilitator, creating the conditions wherein people can reveal what is in the best interests of the community. The stories of Grusha and Azdak as presented by the Singer are themselves exercises in TfD designed to support the decision arrived at in the debate between the two collectives. The parallels cannot be pushed too far since there is the fundamental difference that this is a meticulously crafted script that has already undergone changes as a result of rehearsal and discussion with the actors. It is not being made through performance in the manner of a Forum improvisation. It is more that the purpose to which the production is being put resembles many of the intentions of Forum Theatre: a rehearsal for revolution or rather, in this case, the more oblique and tentative examination of the conditions without which revolution, as opposed to mere political upheaval, might be made possible. With the possible amending of 'audience' to 'participants' Elizabeth Wright's designation of Brecht's intentions could be applied equally to contemporary practice in the more progressive and radical applications of TfD:

> Brecht's utopian wish was to produce an audience who would rejoice at the contradictions of a necessarily estranged world – the uncanniness of a world in flux, the constant shifting of figure and ground in a dialectical movement.
>
> (Wright, 1989, p.52)

Whether or not that wish is utopian, it is the one which still drives many of the practices that try to use theatre processes to check the many and varied ways in which neoliberal economics distorts human creativity and imagination or, if you will, fool's play. Azdak's legacy of a children's playground is an entirely fitting memorial as a space in which fantasies can be played out; dreams rehearsed.

The play ends in the tradition of Shakespearean comedy with a marriage celebration and a dance. Like Feste, Azdak is once more alone to contemplate the happiness of others but the stagecraft of the ending inverts the final moments of *Twelfth Night*. This time the fool disappears behind the celebrants rather than the celebrants behind the fool. Because 'the rain raineth every day' there can be no perfectability, no time exempt from the process of change – hence a 'brief Golden Age'; no absolutes governing the human condition – hence 'almost just'. Does this constitute failure for Azdak? Is his social intervention pointless in view of the return to the *status quo ante*? Brecht described him as:

> a man of utterly unblemished character, a disappointed revolutionary who plays the part of a man gone to the dogs, just as in Shakespeare wise men play the part of fools.
>
> (Brecht, 1994, p.302)

Plays cannot make social interventions but perhaps they can speak to those who have a mind not to accept the familiar, unjust world into which they are born; perhaps they speak to the 'disappointed' to remind them that they are not alone; not for comfort or therapy but so that the weight of that disappointment eventually leads to an intervention which produces social transformation. If even this claim appears, in an age of neoliberal individualism, to be absurdly utopian, at least fooling with the contradictions within the oppressive structures that govern us enables us to participate more fully, to take more pleasure in the business of being alive:

> The theatre of the scientific age is in a position to make dialectics into a source of enjoyment. The unexpectedness of logically progressive or zigzag development, the instability of every circumstance, the joke of contradiction and so forth: all these are ways of enjoying the liveliness of men, things and processes, and they heighten both our capacity for life and our pleasure in it.
>
> (Brecht, 1978, p.277)

It is the current fashion to suggest that Marxism perished in the rubble of the Berlin Wall, taking with it most of the work of the 'fellow traveller', Bertolt Brecht. But Soviet communism was, from the outset, selective in its use and application of Marx's work and after Stalin took control of the Politbureau, mostly a travesty of it. Brecht's plays, especially those written after 1933, are about the ways in which people, frequently through recourse to acting or being the fool, resist yet survive against the political forces that would reduce them to the objects rather than subjects of their own histories. It does not take a great leap of the imagination to identify the relevance and importance of Brecht's work for a world in which the dominance of a single model of governance is endorsed by ever more sophisticated agents of that prevailing hegemony. The wise fool is positioned on the margins of the hegemonic mainstream from where he can view a world that has predated it and may one day postdate it: in the words of Fredric Jameson:

> This is why a Brechtian conception of activity must today go hand in hand with a revival of the older precapitalist sense of time itself, of the change or flowing of all things: for it is the movement of this great river of time or Tao that will slowly carry us downstream again to the moment of praxis.
>
> (Jameson, 1998, p.4)

8
Fooling with Revolution

> The Son of God is mad!
>
> [Fo, 1988, p.111]

Dario Fo, the highest profile performance clown of the European theatre in the final quarter of the twentieth century, combines many of the threads which have run through the previous chapters of this monograph. Fo's clowning took him back to the Middle Ages and the origins of *Commedia dell'arte* among the street performers who came from the people and performed to the people; the tradition which he identified as being that of the *jongleur* whose 'birth' he celebrates in *Mistero Buffo*. This satirical, popular performance strain runs throughout his theatre work from the earlier *Mistero Buffo* to *Johan Padan* which he created towards the conclusion of his performance career. Both works are vehicles for his unique style of one-man stand-up fooling in which he embodies the satirical and farcical humour that comes from taking every social situation from the perspective of the poor and the powerless. Conventional wisdom, be it of Biblical or colonial history, or twentieth century Italian politics, is stood on its head to reveal the self-interest and corruption usually masked by the smoke and mirrors of the prevailing hegemony.

The other major thread which in his most accomplished work seems effortlessly bound together with that of the *jongleur*, belongs to his Marxist theatrical politics, influencing him via Gramsci whose work directed him towards theories of 'the popular':

> In Gramsci's analysis, a popular culture reflecting the experiences of the subaltern classes existed side by side with the high, aesthetic culture of the patrician and educated classes. It had, however, been the fate of popular culture to be systematically ignored and derided, or,

when it showed some vitality, annexed to the higher culture. In calling for a re-evaluation of popular culture, Gramsci set the intellectual parameters within which Fo later worked.

(Farrell, 2001, pp.17–18)

This combination has resulted in the productive tension which gives Fo's performances their danger, their capacity to disturb. He habitually struts and cavorts along the ragged edge of ideology, simultaneously offering a counter-narrative to the dominant orthodoxy and exposing the limitations of all human behaviour which is grounded in ideology rather than lived experience. Farrell identifies this tension as a 'compromise' but I shall endeavour to show that, rather than compromising anything, Fo's re-incarnation of the jester is the means by which the limits of ideology are delineated while, paradoxically, the demand for social justice constantly, but temporarily, re-energises ideology. In Fo's theatre ideology is humanised by the critique of the *jongleur* who continually pokes and prods the contradictions of the powerful until they are undone by the laughter and play of the popular discourse.

Fo declared himself a Marxist, if an idiosyncratic and unsystematic one, and the jester represented a compromise between political ideology and theatrical aspiration.

(Farrell, 2001, p.78)

The notion of 'compromise' suggests that somehow the requirements for effective theatre, as conceived by Fo, demanded a reining in of the unfettered ideological commitment that he would otherwise be making. This reading, however, does not account for Fo's fundamental attitude of critical scepticism towards any ideology, as exemplified in his dealings with the apparatchiks of the Italian Communist Party. The figure of the *jongleur* is not adopted in order to mask or deflect ideological statements, but rather as the means by which the limits of ideology can be exposed and the contradictions within any ideological formulation explored. He must, perforce, be an 'unsystematic' Marxist because the fool understands that the very notion of the system will eventually run counter to the desires and aspirations of human nature.

Fo's fullest and clearest exposition of the *jongleur* in performance comes in the flexible portfolio of one-man sketches that he performed throughout his acting career, *Mistero Buffo* or 'Clown Mystery'. The title announces the intention: to revisit the medieval Mystery plays from the perspective of the clown. Given Italy's unbroken tradition of

Catholicism, this is perhaps are more plausible enterprise for Fo than it would be for an English equivalent who could not rely upon the audience's grasp of the frame of reference. There are, however, some very strong links between the popular practices of some of the English Mystery plays and the performance strategies of Fo. One of his commonest devices throughout the sketches is the taking of historical leaps from the period of the event being performed to the present day. Fo famously engaged in such a jump when introducing the 'Boniface VIII' sketch via an elaborate demonstration of Pope John Paul II's arrival by aeroplane in Madrid. This is more than a question of Fo seeking contemporary resonances for his 'historical' presentations. By this means he places the audience in an empathetic relationship with the clown. Just as his impersonation offers a grass-roots view of the antics of a rich and powerful pontiff of a former age, so his introduction places the audience in a similar relationship to a pontiff of their own time, thereby positioning them in a clown-like frame from which to comment upon what is presented. The double time scheme operates in a similar way to the one in the *Second Shepherds' Play* where the action is at once both Palestine at the time of Christ's birth and fifteenth century, rural Yorkshire. Here it is both thirteenth century Italy and the moment at which Fo was giving the performance.

Some of the references in other sketches in *Mistero Buffo* create even closer parallels with their medieval forebears. In 'Slaughter of the Innocents' Fo presents the event from the perspective of a woman whose baby has just been massacred. Out of her mind with grief, she imagines her child reincarnated in the form of a lamb:

> There I was in the yard, shouting these curses, as I say, when suddenly I looked round, and there, in the sheep pen, in among all the sheep, I discovered my baby, crying...I recognised him instantly, and took him in my arms, and began to cry, along with him. 'I ask your pardon, merciful Lord, for those bad words I shouted...I didn't mean them...It was the Devil, yes, it was the Devil who put them into my mouth! You, Lord, who are so good, you saved my son...! And you have made it so that everyone takes him for a little lamb; and even the soldiers don't realise it, and they let me go. I shall have to be careful when Easter comes, though, because then everybody starts killing lambs the way they've been killing babies today. The butchers will come to me looking for him, but I shall put a bonnet on his head, with all ribbons in it, and everyone will think that he is a baby...
>
> (Fo, 1988, p.24)

Whilst the tone and style of the delivery are worlds apart, the actual content of the words comes very close to Gill's attempt in *The Second Shepherds' Play* to disguise the stolen lamb as a baby. In both discourses the dramatists depict an attempt by 'popular' forces to disrupt the dominant, conventional narrative by replacing a baby with a sheep; playing literally in typical fool's manner with the idea of the Lamb of God. Ordinary people are shown trying to survive the extremities, in one case of hunger, in the other of grief, of conditions created by the powerful for their own self-interest. The clown, be it Mak or Fo, uses the possibilities of theatre to expose these injustices to the watching, popular audience. The point of this connection is not to show that Fo was trawling through medieval metaphors to plagiarise for his own performances (though he was more than capable of doing just that) but rather to indicate the way in which he put himself in touch with the language and discourses of medieval popular theatre in order to recreate it in his own version, thereby highlighting parallels with contemporary injustice.

In performance Fo draws upon a bewildering variety of dialects as well as the famous *grammalot* which he claimed was first coined by Italian popular theatre artists working in France in the sixteenth century. This ability to draw upon different language registers is used in 'The Marriage at Cana' sketch from *Mistero Buffo* for similar effect to that of the contrast between the Latinate vocabulary of Mercy and the Anglo-Saxon vernacular of the devils in *Mankind*:

> The angel speaks in an aristocratic, elegant, polished Venetian dialect; the drunkard on the other hand speaks in a strong rustic dialect that is crude and highly coloured.
>
> (Fo, 1988, pp.36–7)

Though the strategy is similar in both plays, the outcomes are opposite. Where Mercy finally triumphs over 'the popular' to save mankind according to orthodox morality, here the Drunkard wins the argument with the Angel over the wine and has the last, many last, words on the subject. As with all the sketches, it is the popular perspective which is privileged at the expense of the dominant, as signalled by *buffo* in the title, combining the popular with the clownesque. Ron Jenkins describes the performance effect and affect of the closing gesture of the sketch in terms which suggest that Fo as actor transcends the binary of Angel or Drunkard to offer the audience an image of a holy fool who has unlocked the spiritual potential of humankind:

All of Fo's techniques coalesce in the powerful conclusion to his story of Jesus and the wine. Having just presented Adam's rejection of the Serpent in favour of a glass of wine, the drunk offers a toast to God, the audience, and the earth beneath his feet. Tilting the glass to the public, Fo is graciously thanking them for their involvement. Pouring a few drops on the ground he is paying homage to the earthly impulses that stand in opposition to the repressive censorship of the angel he battled at the beginning of the piece. And raising the glass toward heaven he shifts the focus from the mundane to the spiritual world. This simple, skyward motion is the last gesture of the story, and it is charged with startling eloquence. Having defied the authority of heaven, the buffoon strikes a pose that momentarily transforms him into an angel in spite of himself. The closing sequence epitomizes the spirit of Fo's epic clown in the breadth of its vision, the depth of its feeling, and the generosity with which it embraces the world beyond the stage.

(Jenkins, 1995, p.250)

Besides the constant references and *interventi* which set the present capitalist world of injustice before the audience, Fo also has a dual structure for the 'historical' sketches of *Mistero Buffo*. He presents Biblical scenes from a popular perspective and secular scenes of his own devising, frequently with strong religious overtones. At the core of his approach to Bible stories is the presentation of a people's Jesus; Jesus restored from the clutches of the Catholic Church to perform his role as champion of the peasant. In the Passion Play sketch 'Death and the Fool' the Fool reacts to Death, here in the form of a beautiful virgin, not with fear but with lust, for a key characteristic of the Fool is not to fear death since that fear is the instrument of coercion used by the powerful to keep the peasants down-trodden. This lack of fear is a quality shared with Jesus who is characterised as even more foolish than the Fool since he knows exactly what his fate will be but does nothing to avoid it. This reading taps into the ancient tradition of the foolish Christ whose naivety and love of the common person places him entirely at odds with the discourses of wealth, power and selfishness by which the human world is organised. There is always with the fool a sense in which he stands outside the world as it is in order to open up the possibility of the world as it ought to be, experienced through a different set of ethics and human relationships. In Fo's performances there is always present the double reality of Fo playing the fool and Fo just being Fo who happens to be a fool. In those places in the performance of *Mistero Buffo* where the mask slips, it turns out that there is another beneath it, almost indistinguishable from the first. Another of the sketches is 'The Fool Beneath the Cross' where the same motif of the foolish Jesus is played out in the 'dialogue' that the Fool (Fo) has with him when he is on the cross:

> Oh, I can't believe it ... And they call *me* the Fool, but you beat me by a long chalk, Jesus, my friend!
>
> (Fo, 1988, p.109)

There is, however, an important distinction between this Fool and Christ and that is in the realm of the political function. For the Fool, Christ is even more crazy than himself because he attempts to live an apolitical life in a world that demands resistance to the prevailing politics:

> Now you really are the chief of all Fools! You're a complete lunatic asylum! The only time I liked you was when you turned up in church and all the traders were there, and you began to beat them all with a big stick. Oh, that was so good to see. *That* should be your job, not dying on the cross for people's salvation!
>
> (Fo, 1998, p.110)

Though the Fool and Jesus are linked by a common madness, they are separated by the discourses of politics and religion, whereas, for Fo, religion has become an entirely political matter due to the attempts of the Catholic church down the ages to intervene on behalf of the rich and powerful at the expense of the poor:

> He was never more Gramscian than when he discussed religious practices. The value of the Bible for him lies not in the canonical interpretation handed down *ex cathedra* by bishops or scribes, but in the folk vision of it which had been incorporated into the worship, the festivals, carnival rites and workaday lives of the poor and dispossessed.
>
> (Farrell, 2001, p.184)

The focal point of the satire against the church comes in the sketch, 'BonifaceVIII' and its climax with Jesus delivering a kick to the papal backside. Fo's Jesus is most certainly not the object of the satire for he is the friend of the people. Throughout *Mistero Buffo* he is a force acting to support the oppressed. Fo delivers a bewildering variety of impersonations of both the wicked and powerful and of the poor who are their victims but he does not impersonate Jesus, even when entering into a dialogue with him. The altercation between Boniface and Jesus highlights how far the church has gone on its journey away from Christian values towards greed, lust and depravity:

> Christ! Kicking me?! Me, Boniface! The Prince! Ah, right! Rabble...! Ne'er-do-well...! I tell you, if your father gets to hear of this...Wretch! Donkey of all donkeys! Listen, I don't mind telling you that it will give me great pleasure to see you nailed up; and this very day I am going to get myself drunk! I am going dancing...dancing! And I am going with whores!!! Because I, I am Boniface...I am a prince! Cloak, mitre, staff, rings...and everything! Look how they glisten...Rabble! I, I am Boniface! Sing!
>
> (Fo, 1988, p.84)

The donkey, the beast upon whose back Jesus entered Jerusalem, is always associated by Fo with the peasant, or, in today's terminology, the worker; so much so that Fo ascribes the 'Birth of the Villeyn' to a donkey's fart. Boniface's appeal to Jesus' father draws attention to another motif running through *Mistero Buffo*, that of the implied tension between father and son. If Jesus is positioned unambiguously on the side of the poor, the role of God the Father is much less certain since he is frequently invoked by the powerful to justify their actions. The reference to the crucifixion demonstrates how easily Fo adopts the double time scheme which we saw at work in the English Mystery plays. Here it is more like a triple scheme as he commutes between Jesus' time, Boniface's time and the present of the performance. The anachronism also aligns Boniface with the Hebrew power-brokers who urged Christ's death, while reminding the audience that Jesus, or at least the values he espoused, is constantly at the mercy of the powerful in every age. The final words of the speech offer a typical example of the way in which Fo takes a realist image from Brecht and moves it onto the plane of the grotesque and the satirical. In Scene 12 of *The Life of Galileo* the Pope is gradually costumed in all his pontifical finery throughout the dialogue with the Inquisitor. We see him move slowly from a position of resistance in support of Galileo to a position where he reluctantly upholds the church's *status quo*. The addition of each item of his costume tips the balance from human being to pope. His social function devours his innate sense of justice. Unlike Brecht's Barbarini, Fo's Boniface is unencumbered by any such notions. He is a parody of the papal function, used to mock the normally disguised workings of power relations.

The core of *Mistero Buffo*, both in terms of performance and of function is 'The Birth of the Jongleur' for the *jongleur* is the medieval equivalent of Fo and, in describing his 'birth', Fo reveals both his own intentions as a performer and his sense of his place in a tradition of fooling that harks back to the European Middle Ages and beyond. The desperate tale that the *jongleur* tells of his life before the 'miracle' is particularly significant in two aspects. Firstly, the catalogue of misfortunes visited upon him by the Lord of the Valley results in his passion for justice and his understanding of how this world is run. Secondly, the disappearance of his wife and the death of his children leave him with no personal allegiances in the world. His future actions will not be compromised by a need to look out for the welfare of others. He will be a free agent. Though this condition does not describe Fo himself, it is typical of fools as they appear in the texts of European theatre. From Feste to Azdak we get a sense of the fool as semi-detached in relation to the society in which he lives. From this position he is able to offer a critique that is unencumbered by vested interest or hope of gain or preferment: no mortgage to pay; no children to provide for. Here, too, there lurks a paradox. Much of the fool's behaviour is directed towards revealing the relationships that exist in human society and the need for people to connect with their social natures while, at the same time, this very behaviour is made possible by the absence of personal relationships.

Whilst the *jongleur's* ideological foundations are cemented by his life experiences, his aesthetic strategy is determined by the 'miracle' of the laying on of lips by the people's Jesus. Throughout the *Mistero Buffo* sketches this figure is always close at hand to champion the poor and the oppressed without ever locating himself in any specific or fixed ideological position. Fo is explicit about the significance of the Christian tradition for his own work:

> But in researching medieval texts I came across this Christ figure far too often for me to ignore it. He had been transformed by the people into a kind of hero in opposition to the powerful and ecclesiastical hierarchies, who had on the contrary always tried to monopolise and keep him away from the people. It's sufficient to mention that until well after the year 1000 people were not allowed to read the Gospels, and that their translation into the vernacular took place very late.
>
> (Behan, 2000, p.103)

Given the importance of tradition in Fo's self-fashioning as a contemporary *jongleur*, it is no surprise that he also works in such close proximity to the Christian tradition. For Fo, as with his attitude towards most traditions, this becomes a matter of wresting that tradition away from the stifling embrace of the powerful, be they church or state, and restoring it to its rightful place among the people for whom it was developed. Such a view applies with equal force to Christianity and to *commedia dell'arte*. Political, religious and cultural traditions are each alike susceptible to incorporation by the dominant, following Marx's analysis that the ideas of the ruling class are always the ruling ideas of any given society. Fooling with these ideas is a matter not of resistance but of play; of exposing the contradictions and then playing in the gaps created. The official church is always anxious to present morality as a sphere of human behaviour which is separate from politics in order to disguise its own political function in relation to the state. For Fo this is an entirely false separation as he demonstrates continually in the episodes of *Mistero Buffo*. He suggests that the medieval popular tradition of the morality understood the relationship between morality and politics:

> What is the meaning of the word 'morality'? It means that in the text a moral subject is under discussion, in the sense that the work sets out the indication of a concept of life, of behaviour, of the idea of being and becoming in relation to God and his teaching, but also in relation to the society of men with all their laws and conventions. In other words, the plays contain, in addition to teaching regarding Divine Law, a viewpoint on the proper rules of social life, and a condemnation of injustice and wickedness. Morality, then, also takes in politics. There does not exist in ancient theatre, be it religious or secular, a drama which does not set out to include as a fundamental presupposition the teaching of a principle held to be moral and civil.
>
> (Fo, 1991, p.148)

If Fo, as *jongleur*, is the agent for bringing morality and politics into an angry and farcical juxtaposition in *Mistero Buffo*, in *Accidental Death of an Anarchist*, through the persona of the Madman, he exposes the extremities of corruption when the two lose all contact with each other. Besides drawing our attention to the origins of the character in the figure of Harlequin, Farrell's assessment of the Madman's role carries powerful echoes of *King Lear*. Like Lear's Fool, Fo's Madman is the only reference point of sanity in a world maddened by violence and self-interest at whatever cost:

> His madness, itself a common enough device in Fo's theatre, is madness with method, an outlet for the earthiness, guile and low cunning showed by the classic Harlequin. He is gifted with a wit, perspicacity, divine insouciance and fearlessness denied those of conventionally sound mind. He enjoys a fool's licence to blurt out truths which the authorities would prefer to suppress, but in an upside-down world, where the worldly wise have made their peace with a society of unreason policed by violence, the madman is the only arbiter of decency and reason.
>
> (Farrell, 2001, p.100)

To obtain the privilege of folly, however, as Azdak discovered before him, requires considerable artistry as well as experience in the ways of the world. Like Hamlet he has learned to combine madness with theatre and to use that madness as a mask behind which he can construct his performances: 'I am a lunatic. A certified psychotic!' (Fo, 1980, p.2) Being certified makes him the modern equivalent of the 'natural' of Renaissance theatre. As such he can enjoy some protection from the violence of the law but is also liable to be dismissed and patronised as a simpleton. Any such tendencies are, however, counteracted by the way in which he exploits the potential of theatre for confusions of identity arising from the disjunction between actor and character. As with other aspects of farce, these confusions are pushed to the limit by the Madman's ability to alter identity, including body parts, at bewildering speed, almost in the manner of the shape-shifting trickster. The name given to the role in the Italian is 'il Matto', the same one as was used to designate the Fool in the original version of the Italian Tarot cards. Like the card, Fo's Madman is an absence, a vacuum, until called into an identity to trump the action of another card. Being nothing he can be everything. Through his manipulation of the rules of theatre, he is able to combine the function of the 'natural' fool with that of the professional, even though he describes this aspect as a hobby: '...my hobby, you see, the theatre; and my theatre is the theatre of reality so my fellow artistes must be real people, unaware that they are acting in my productions...' (Fo, 1980, p.2) He is a self-confessed exponent of Augusto Boal's Invisible Theatre, presented paradoxically by Fo within the frame of formal theatre. Thus Fo, through the construction of this character, is able to exert as much control over the subsequent action as the solo performer of *Mistero Buffo* who impersonates every character. He is, in effect, the facilitator of a piece of applied theatre where the Milan police are the participants. In this role he is trying to get them to improve their story; to make it more credible as a piece of theatre to be set before a sceptical public through the medium of court proceedings and their reporting. He is accepted in this role, like Azdak as Judge, because he is able to exploit the panic of the authorities at a moment of social upheaval. He appears at the opportune moment as the straw at which they can clutch while their guard is down. Once in role, he has power over those who normally exert it over others so that the upside-down world is, temporarily, turned through a further 180 degrees, thereby restoring it to its moral compass. The fool, as facilitator, uses the role to expose the ever widening gap between the system as implemented by the police, and notions of justice and truth by which this society purports to live.

Fo, in the introduction to the play, gives a historical reading of the function of satire in Italian society that links to the unbroken thread of Catholicism and power in that country:

> The taste for satire was not suppressed even by fascism – in fact it developed. By good fortune our Italian bourgeoisie has always shown itself to be more stupid than its counterparts in the rest of Europe. It didn't devote as much effort to destroying the cultural forms peculiar to the lower classes and to replacing their traditions, their rituals, their language – in short their 'vulgar' powers of expression and creativity – with the ruthlessness and thoroughness used by the French, German and English bourgeoisie. Perhaps it wasn't able to.
>
> We Italians 'enjoyed' the industrial revolution after a long time-lag. So we are not yet a sufficiently modern nation to have forgotten the ancient feeling for satire. That is why we can still laugh, with a degree of cynicism, at the macabre dance which power and the civilisation that goes with it performs daily, without waiting for carnival.
>
> (Fo, 1980, pp.iv–v)

Fo explicitly connects modernism with the alienation of working class people from their cultural roots; an alienation that has profound political consequences in robbing such people of a vital means by which to express their contempt and anger at the irrational and immoral behaviour of their rulers. His own work intervenes at a crucial moment in the development of the Italian nation-state and operates, through the modes of satire and farce, as a warning of what can happen when the state is allowed to act without the restraint of popular opposition. Many in Italy today may feel that the era of Silvio Berlusconi demonstrates the perspicacity of Fo's concern. The judiciary, the official mechanism for the limiting of state power, may prove less effective than the satire of fools as the Madman suggests as he contemplates impersonating a judge:

> But the frailer and feebler judges get, the more they are elevated to superior and powerful positions. Oh yes, that's the job for me. "Fifty years for you, thirty years for you. Case dismissed. Council can come and corrupt me in my chambers."
>
> (Fo, 1980, p.4)

Here is the echo of Azdak's 'I accept', reminding audiences that justice has been commodified in the modern state and is, therefore, the property of those who can afford it.

The farcical form of the play, rather than being at odds with the content, drives the content on beyond the real to the surreal and thence into a different way of viewing what passes for normality. It is the exuberance of language, the leaping in and out of different registers that causes these transitions to take the audience unawares and transport them in an instant into another world:

> "Crack down on hooligans, drop-outs, drunks, addicts, squatters, demonstrators, infiltrate the union militants, round up activists, fatten up the files, polish your rubber bullets..."
>
> (Fo, 1980, p.19)

Fo leads the policemen down a familiar path of the common clichés before inserting the metaphor of the file fattened for slaughter as a bridge into the fully surreal polished rubber bullet. This is the Madman's tactic throughout. He has the ability to get onto their wavelength by using their own words before turning them on their heads. He projects onto the police the role of White-face – in the terminology of the circus clown – the authority figure whose tyranny is pushed beyond its own irrational logic into absurdity. The police find themselves willingly playing his game so that they are exposed at the point where he, joker-like, changes the rules. He adopts the same ploy when appearing to side with the police in their attempts to concoct a story that will satisfy Maria Feletti, the journalist from the communist paper *L'Unita*. Once they are

entirely dependent upon the speed of his wits to save them from public exposure, he removes the fig-leaf without them realising. Once again
the means is linguistic dexterity as he invents the oxymoronic phrase
'Jesuit dialectics' to explain his strategy:

> Are you trying to get us to admit that instead of chasing idiotic anar-
> chists and relying on informers and agents inside the revolutionary
> left, we should be concentrating our efforts on para-military fascist
> organisations trained and supported by, say, the *Greek junta!* and
> financed by top industrialists both *here and in Spain!*
>
> (Fo, 1980, p.37)

As is usual in Fo's longer political plays, his ideological position moves
into sharper focus as the climax approaches. The different masks
adopted according to the needs of the differing situations of plays such
as *Accident Death of An Anarchist* and *Trumpets and Raspberries* slip to
allow a glimpse of the political artist beneath who uses the platform created by his skill as a *giullare*, from which to launch the broadside against
the system of state capitalism:

> *Maniac*: You are a journalist Miss Feletti, so you want to use your pen
>   to lance the public boil; but what will you achieve? A huge scandal,
>   a heap of big nobs compromised, head of police force shunted off
>   into retirement.
> *Feletti*: Not a bad day's work.
> *Maniac*: It's just another chance for the pristine beauticians of the
>   Communist Party to point out another wart on the body politic
>   and pose themselves as the party of honesty. But the STATE, Miss
>   Feletti, the State remains, still presenting corruption as the excep-
>   tion to the rule, when the system the state was designed to protect
>   is corruption itself. Corruption *is* the rule!
>
> (Fo, 1980, p.38)

Not only do these words demonstrate unambiguously Fo's contempt
for the system and with it, the idea of any system which is conceived
in exploitation, but the choice of metaphor also aligns him with the
carnival body of popular discourse according to the tenets of Bakhtin.
By placing the fool at the heart of the play he is able repeatedly to draw
the audience's attention to a situation, be it the particular one of the
events in the Milan police headquarters, or the general one of the operation of the Italian state. The fool is not concerned with whether other

characters are good or bad but rather with the way in which a given situation manipulates their behaviour by requiring a specific role or action from them. Neither Fo nor any other actor impersonates the murdered anarchist, Pinelli, because the play is not a tragedy of an individual but a farce of the system. As such it requires an 'epic' response from the audience, not a cathartic one. Where *King Lear* aims to achieve both the tragic and the epic, the death of the protagonist and the destruction of the realm, *Accidental Death of An Anarchist* opts only for the epic by presenting a situational farce. It is clear from Fo's own later comments on the success of the play what the criteria were, upon which he asks for the audience's judgement:

> What has been the real reason for the show's success?...It has been above all the way it deals with Social Democracy and its crocodile tears, the indignation which can be relieved by a little burp in the form of a scandal; scandal as a liberating catharsis of the system...The indignation of the good democratic citizen grows and threatens to suffocate him. But he has a sense of satisfaction when he sees, in the end, these same organs of this rotten and corrupt society, pointing the finger at this selfsame society, at its own 'unhealthy parts', and this gives him a sense of freedom throughout his whole being. With his spirit suitably decongested, he shouts, 'Long live this bastard shit society, because at least it always wipes its bum with soft, perfumed paper, and when it burps it has the good manners to put its hand in front of its mouth!'
>
> (Fo, 1992, pp.209–10)

Again bodily functions provide the metaphor that lays bear the pleasures of reform as enemy of revolution. These words offer an insight into the way in which Fo conceives of the dominant bourgeois society as attempting to deny or at least refine the bodily functions that serve to remind its members that they are humans. The system works by alienating people from their intrinsic humanity in order that they can operate successfully as agents of exploitation by refusing to recognise the exploited as fellow members of the human race. The comfort derived from reformism is drawn from the same source as the cliché about capitalism being an imperfect system but the best system that we know. Alongside the political discourse, the Maniac remains structurally true to his function as fool. Having 'defeated' all the protagonists, police and crusading journalist alike, he has only the audience to address directly and, like his forebears in the tradition of folly, does not resolve anything for them but rather presents them with the uncomfortable contradictions of their world: 'Oh Dio! Whichever way it goes, you see, you've got to decide. Goodnight.' (Fo, 1980, p.45) This prioritising of theatre as a tool for the unmasking of contradiction sets Fo firmly within the Brechtian tradition. For both, contradiction is the end of theatrical process and for both the means is fooling, hence 'the joke of contradiction'. Fo clarifies this intention through his own extra-theatrical words:

> I'm interested in discovering the basic contradictions in a situation through the use of paradox, absurdity and inversion. This enables me to transform one reality into another reality, not as a trick, but so people will understand that reality is not flat, but that it is full of contradictions and reversals, and that often absurdity is a reality that is closer to the truth than those things which seem to be sacred and absolute, but are almost always false.
>
> (Fo, 2001a, p.xi)

For the fool there are no absolutes, nothing sacred, and any truth will always be relative, situated, a possibility to be reached for but lost in the act of grasping. Azdak's 'golden age' was 'almost an age of justice' and the Maniac's intervention into the workings of the Milan police almost unravels the coercive arm of the state.

Where the Fo protagonist, the Maniac, exploits a moment of panic to penetrate the power structure, Fo uses the mechanisms of farce for an inversion of this situation in *Trumpets and Raspberries*. In this instance it is power, in the shape of Fiat boss Giovanni Agnelli, that invades the private space of the worker. The dialectical relationship between boss and worker is underlined in performance by Fo's playing of both Antonio and his (now) double, Agnelli. This enables a common humanity to operate in continual tension with the systemic differences of class and wealth. As the less literal but more apposite American title for the play proclaims, the situation is 'about face', where the loss of face is explored on both the concrete and the metaphorical levels. This theme of face is announced at the start of the first act:

DOCTOR: This way please, madam.
ROSA: (*Almost bumping into the bust of Agnelli*): Oh, God, who's that?
DOCTOR: It's a statue of Agnelli. The entire Recovery Ward was built with funds from the Agnelli Foundation.
ROSA: I thought it was a saint.

(Fo, 2001a, p.81)

In this case Agnelli is literally a plaster saint, the modern equivalent of the medieval power-brokers of church and state, but that does not prevent him from becoming the victim of a loss of face in the very institution over which an image of that face presides. His loss of identity is not only a physical deprivation but also extends to the stripping away of language and the ability to perform bodily functions. He is a shell who has to be rebuilt like Brecht's Galy Gay in *Mann Ist Mann*. Further, the struggle to teach him language is layered in ironies about the ideological construction of words, reminiscent of Pelagea Vlasova learning to read in Scene Six c. of Brecht's *Die Mutter* (*The Mother*). In Fo's version there is an added irony in the suitability of the words chosen by the Doctor to a man like Agnelli to whom the vocabulary of the workers is anathema:

> DOCTOR: Silence. And now say: astronaut, manumission, concupiscence.
> ROSA: Hey, doc. Are you crazy? What kind of words are you teaching him. He's a worker. For God's sake, make him say the words he's going to use every day, like wage freeze, layoffs...
> DOCTOR: Listen, I'm doing the teaching here. Come on, Mr. Berardi: astronaut, manumission, concupiscence.
>
> (Fo, 2001a, p. 92)

The farcical situation which Fo creates enables him to embark on an exploration of the social construction of difference as the Double, Agnelli, gradually remembers who he is, moving from the pared down naivety of the fool who is victimised by his situation, to a man so powerful that he can command the actions of the state. As in *Accidental Death of an Anarchist* here too the denouement offers the heightening of the political rhetoric alongside the rising tide of farce. As the furniture closes in on the Double and reveals itself to be agents of secret services, so he reveals himself triumphantly as Agnelli, the embodiment of power in the modern state: the economic dominance of the transnational corporation. Where the state allowed the political elite (Aldo Moro) to perish, it accedes to all terrorist demands, though ironically none were being made, to secure the release of the economically indispensible Agnelli. The state performs an 'about face' as the final twist in this play about face. The construction of the final scene demonstrates how Fo, as both playwright and performer, uses farce to heighten the political significance of the moment, and politics to put a contemporary edge on the farcical. Too often translators and later interpreters have divided these elements, making the farce trivial and the politics sententious. Fo himself insists that the moment of utmost seriousness is the one where the audience's capacity to laugh is most needed. Once power goes beyond laughter, human survival is threatened.

The increasingly surreal actions are set in motion by an unwittingly 'foolish' act as Antonio takes no account of broader class or political implications in rescuing Agnelli from the attempted kidnapping. Like Azdak failing to turn the Grand Duke in, Antonio's instinctively humane behaviour which combats the terrorists, places his own life and that of Rosa, his wife, in danger as victims of state terrorism. The duration of the play resembles the twelve days of Christmas when the fool impersonates his master as Lord of Misrule; in particular the inversion which sees the feudal aristocrat wait upon his own servants at Twelfth Night. Here, however, Fo inverts an inversion so that the lord inadvertently impersonates the fool. The play presents a 'festive' period in which normal power relations do not apply; policemen are rendered impotent and political prisoners are released. Like all such periods the misrule is temporary, the carnival all too soon ended. Agnelli is no King Lear internalising the perspectives of the fool until he becomes him. Rather his experience of folly culminates in his confident assertion of his public identity:

> DOUBLE (*Standing on top of the furniture*): I am Gianni Agnelli. And
> don't let my face fool you. It's only plastic surgery.
>
> (Fo, 2001a, p. 139)

Fooling with faces is over. The binary between boss and worker has been restored. Normal service has been resumed. The meaning of the conclusion is, as often in the writing and performance of Fo, captured and embedded in a concrete, physical image. In this instance it is through Agnelli's command of the furniture which has been hiding the coercive and hegemonic organs of state power: CIA, FBI, CNN (in the US translation). The period between Agnelli's loss of identity and his recovery of himself as boss is like an extended twelve days of Christmas or a time when Bahktin's 'second world' of carnival replaces working life as it is usually experienced. In this way Fo creates a parallel experience for the audience which witnesses the transformations made possible through the ingenuity of his political farce as an interruption to the usual, deadly patterns of social and political life, at the same time as it undergoes an interruption to its normal experience of culture by entering into a performance space that subverts its customary experience of hierarchy and relationship. For performers and audience alike this is a space of carnival where the fool as protagonist can only, ever, be temporary.

This notion of a space which transcends the laws of power as experienced in European history and its colonial exports reaches its apotheosis in Fo's work with the story of *Johan Padan and the Discovery of the Americas*. The play forms a kind of book-end to Fo's performance career with *Mistero Buffo* at the other end. The latter depicts the iniquities upon which medieval European church and state traditions were founded, while the former offers a utopian fantasy of what might have happened if the 'new world' had been able to resist these traditions. In both performance pieces Fo is the story-teller who takes on all the roles as he brings the events he describes to life on stage. He embeds the stories within his own performing persona. The difference in terms of aesthetics is that for the later play, he creates the intermediary character of Johan Padan through whom the story is told. Padan is and is not Fo who can at some moments fully impersonate the figure of his creation while at others he can comment upon the character in the act of presenting him. For the audience immediacy and distance are experienced in a dynamic simultaneity. Padan as a refugee from the Inquisition, is immediately positioned historically as a man at odds with the dominant powers, while his association with his beloved witch introduces him to another way of seeing, a different or uncommon relation to nature which is a vital asset for a fool. But while he is an outsider in the society into which he is born, as a representative of the vicious, colonising force of Europeans, he is hardly likely to be accepted with open arms by their victims. He articulates his dilemma after arriving in the Americas:

> For me it was no fun at all to stay with my comrades, who were only good at getting drunk, playing cards and dice, stabbing one another in scuffles; and then for a sideshow watch them get aroused and throw themselves on the women. Was that a life? The only thing I really enjoyed was trying to communicate with people...you must have guessed by now: I have an obsession for languages, idioms...finding out how people speak...what they think, what they say...trying odd words and discovering ways to say things. But it was difficult to get near the Indians. They were afraid, they were always terrified that afterward, all of a sudden, a horse monster would show up. To put them at ease, I played the clown. When I met them I pretended that I was the one who was scared, before they had a chance to be: "Oh! A savage!...A monster!" And they laughed.
>
> (Fo, 2001b, p.22)

The 'me' of the first line of this quotation is Johan Padan speaking from within his autobiographical narrative but the 'I' of the fourth line and the rest of that sentence is both Padan and Fo; the writer speaking through the mask of the character and reminding his audience of his whole history as a multi-lingual performer of dialect and *grammelot*. So when he comes to the following paragraph the 'I' who plays the clown is both Padan and Fo in a complex perspective where the audience watches the clown, Fo, play the part of Johan Padan who has adopted the strategy of playing the fool in order to use laughter to diffuse hostility and to take the first steps in a process which culminates in the acceptance of the alien by the indigenous community. Using a typical device of facilitation Padan inverts the anticipated power relations by demonstrating, as coloniser, the fear which is the common property of the colonised. The same strategy is repeated further on in the story when he and his companions become slaves of the Indians. The clown unnerves his captors by anticipating the expected reaction and demonstrating its opposite. At all levels, be they in the realm of macro-politics or micro-emotions, the fool masters the art of reversal either as second nature or through the artful rigours of professional practice:

> My companions were seized by unspeakable melancholy and I told them: "Don't let them see how sad you are. Don't make long faces. They don't like it. It annoys our masters to have sad slaves. We're slaves...but we're happy!" So when I met those masters, I played the clown: "Oh...I like being a slave! What a beautiful life! Nobody better try to free me...or I'll murder him!"
>
> (Fo, 2001b, p.36)

As an improvising story-teller Padan/Fo can offer the listener/audience the 'true' sadness of the slaves and the 'false' jollity of the fool whilst simultaneously offering an ironic commentary upon both those states. The gift of prophecy, that traditional attribute of the fool, propels Padan as 'the son of the moon and son of the rising sun' to a place of leadership among the Indians – king, shaman, clown. Before he can justify their faith in him, he must rid them of the Spanish invader whose reputation for extreme violence causes the most visceral of reactions in a tale where the emphasis on bodily needs and functions is, as ever in Fo's work, close to the surface:

> That's it. It's over...you SHIT-IN-YOUR-PANTS COWARDS!" Shit-in-their-pants cowards? I was quick to call them "shit-in-your-pants

cowards"...but what would I have done if we were in Bergamo or Brescia...where I live...and these savage barbarians showed up on horseback covered in metal and killed my children...screwed my women, my daughter, my wife, in front of my eyes, and: "Shut up now...because if you come back we'll bust your ass too!" I'd like to see whether I'd be shitting in my pants. I'd be shitting in my pants, out of my pants, all over the place!

(Fo, 2001b, p.59)

The reference to Bergamo and Brescia invokes the home region of Fo and Padan as well as of Harlequin, and the litany of atrocities follows the same pattern as that depicted in 'The Birth of the Jongleur' in *Mistero Buffo*. Both Fo and his fictional creation Padan are variants of the *jongleur* and both reveal a common motive for their actions in addressing inequality and the violence of power through laughter. In this case Padan's sudden reversal of colonial history acts as a *Verfremdungseffekt* that pitches the self into the experience of the other; thereby causing the audience to change its perspective on the conventional image of colonising self and colonised other. The switch is a typical demonstration of the fool's capacity to see differently.

The climactic confrontation, towards which the whole story tends, between the Indians and the Spanish, is prefigured in *Mistero Buffo*. At its core are fundamental differences about the nature of humankind and purpose of life. In the earlier work the ideological divide is a matter of class with the wealthy and powerful exalting the virtues of denial and misery in this life, whilst the poor and powerless assert the need to enjoy themselves while they can. In *Johan Padan* the divide splits along racial lines with Johan himself as a latter day Jesus, leading the Indians into a 'foolish' battle with the Spaniards where they achieve an unlikely triumph:

You, Lord Governor, who arrived here without having been invited by anyone, you are the big thief! You came with all these armed men covered in metal, and you robbed us of our possessions, our land, the work of our hands, you robbed us of our men, our women, our gold!...and even of our language! You arrived full of self- importance, in plumed helmets...he [Johan Padan] arrived as naked as we were. You arrived triumphantly riding on stallions...he arrived riding too...on the back of a pig. He came here and brought to life men who were dead...you put to death men who were alive! He brought us a religion fashioned from songs, happiness, dances, and joy...you bring us a religion of sadness, melancholy, and death.

(Fo, 2001b, p.92)

As the story moves to its conclusion the character of the story-teller, Johan Padan, begins to merge with that of his creator, Dario Fo. It is as if Fo has discovered in Padan an *alter ego*, who comes to represent all for which Fo's life in the theatre has stood: the assertion of humanity through a stubborn insistence upon enjoying the life of the senses to the full in the face of a violent and repressive authority that constantly tries to steal the people's language and replace it with the deadly discourses of power and control. Finally, Padan is reconciled to spending his life in a foreign land where he is acknowledged as the clown/king and fool/shaman. Fo too, Nobel laureate and international *jongleur*, travelled far from his roots in Piedmont but, like Padan, keeps the memory alive in his imagination to energise his creativity and to remember why we are here:

There are moments when I'm struck by pangs of emotion that wring my heart. My gullet tightens, my heartbeat quickens...and I run desperately to the hammock...stretched out in the hammock I hug the netting...before long two young girls come by...and sing lullabies while they rock the hammock, they rock me slowly, slowly...I close my eyes and they sing me the song from my village that I taught them...with the very same words, the same idiom of my dialect from home.

> *"Oh what joy and oh what wonder*
> *The son of heav'n is still alive*
> *The son of Mary is still living!*
> *The Virgin Mary is full of cheer now*
> *And there's nothing for us to fear now*
> *Not the Turks or stormy winds now*
> *Not the winds or the Christian soldiers*
> *Not the Turks or the Christian soldiers."*

(Fo, 2001b, p. 104)

9
Fooling with Existence

... the time of Becoming, before Being risks to confront one yet again with undefeated despair.

[Beckett, 2007, p.19]

The vision of the world with which the Grandmother left us at the end of *Woyzeck*:

And when he wanted to go back to earth, the earth was an upturned pot. And he was all alone. And he sat down and cried, and he's sitting there still, all alone.

(Price, 1971, p.128)

is the place from which the theatre of Samuel Beckett begins. This is a post-rational universe from which all the former illusory consolations have been withdrawn. The wisdom of the fool in rejecting the promises of progress and the blandishments of an absolute morality has been grimly vindicated. On the stage of Beckett there is only folly. Existence is merely a game by which to pass the time and, as with all games, it requires that the participants play. As Ruby Cohn has demonstrated, playful metatheatricality is the water in which Beckett's fish swim. With an irony typical of the dramatist in the piece entitled *Play*, the characters are unable to play with each other since they are unaware of each other's presence as the light switches their monologues on their past playfulness on and off. Not only do all Beckett's characters realise that they are engaged in play, they also know that when the play is over, the game will be up for them:

CLOV: What is there to keep me here?
HAMM: The dialogue.

(Beckett, 1958, p.39)

184

The act of writing and then performing a play is itself part of the greater game of occupying ourselves, creating distractions to ward off the great silence that will inevitably engulf us sooner or later. This consciousness is a precondition of folly, enabling all the *dramatis personae* to appreciate that they are only fooling around to pass the time. They share this common function that robs them of purpose and therefore renders the notion of character, as traditionally applied in the theatre, irrelevant. Like fools of former ages they have no character because, as Pat Murray pointed out, they are not bound by the dictates of reason:

> There is no underlying assumption that rational discourse is possible between one character and the next, that characters have motives for anything they say or do, that speech and action necessarily reflect personality.
>
> (Murray, 1970, pp.67–68)

Under such conditions the very notion of personality is suspect. The playwright frequently plays with such expectations by luring us into thinking we are starting to detect some pattern of character traits, only to thwart us by having such characters contradict themselves. Just as the fool functions to strip his fellow human beings of all illusions about their natures, for example separating Lear from cosy paternal fantasies, so Beckett withdraws the conventional devices, such as character and history, by which authors dress their creations to disguise their alienation from purpose and meaning:

> Writing was for him, he said, a question of 'getting down below the surface' towards what he described as 'the authentic weakness of being'. This was associated with a strong sense of the inadequacy of words to explore the forms of being. 'Whatever is said is so far from the experience'; 'if you really get down to the disaster, the slightest eloquence becomes unbearable'.
>
> (Knowlson, 1997, p.492)

As far as European theatre was concerned this 'eloquence' had been expressed through the dominant form of naturalism, with an accompaniment of psychological realism in cinema, for the previous hundred years. Beckett's desire to remove the top dressing accords with the deconstructions of naturalism in the dramatic works of Brecht and Fo, even though his preoccupations are existential rather than political. For each in their respective ways the representation of the fool upon the stages they create is a means to arrive at a more 'authentic' view of the human condition.

If the stage and the performance upon it is all there is (in Hamm's words, 'Outside of here it's death!'), characters cannot appear upon it with pre-histories. Like Falstaff or Feste they simply appear fully formed to fulfil their functions. Joel Schechter, while establishing the visual links between Charlie Chaplin's tramp and Beckett's Vladimir and Estragon, also connects them with a notion of spontaneous performance as character:

> Vladimir and Estragon lack a history even when they are on stage – they attempt to create personal histories or recall them throughout the performance – and their entire existence on stage resembles the moment Chaplin describes by saying, "By the time I walked on stage he was fully born". Beckett's tramps live only on stage, in the present tense, creating identities and losing them from moment to moment.
>
> (Schechter, 1985, p.71)

Whilst assigning to Beckett's clowns the critical tag of 'postmodern' (though as Clov might have said: 'they say the earth is postmodern though I never saw it modern'), Donald Perret makes the link with their theatrical genealogy:

> ... Didi, Gogo, Pozzo, and Lucky are close equivalents of the medieval fool: incongruous, liminal characters who, in their ridiculousness, speak or show the truth.
>
> (Perret, 1998, p.81)

This observation places the whole cast of *Waiting for Godot* among the ranks of the foolish – the only possible category in an irrational world – but it does not take account of more subtle differences which manifest themselves between the types or levels of foolishness exhibited by each character. Critics have long noted the contrast between Vladimir the intellectual and Estragon the sensual; some suggesting that the former represents the mind and the latter the body. For instance, Vladimir wants Lucky to think but Estragon, a self-confessed poet, wants him to dance. Estragon means tarragon in French: a bitter herb living in close proximity to the earth but easily damaged. He is therefore immediately associated with the material world of taste and senses, associating him with those earthy, physical qualities highlighted by Bakhtin. Vladimir's name, by contrast, means in Slavic languages, as Eugene Webb pointed out, ruler of the world. Within the very limited means at his disposal, Vladimir is constantly trying to take control of his existence by identifying some possibility of meaning for his life. Beckett employs a conscious echo of an earlier fool, Hamlet, who attempted, fatally, to take control of his existence in Vladimir's expression of purpose:

> What are we doing here, *that* is the question. And we are blessed in this, that we happen to know the answer. Yes, in this immense confusion one thing alone is clear. We are waiting for Godot to come –
>
> (Beckett, 1956, p.80)

Vladimir is the one waiting for the expected consolation of Godot. Estragon does not believe in his redemptive powers and stays with Vladimir out of habit, companionship and the comfort afforded by routine. The likely tensions between them are alluded to at the outset. The best known work of a famous namesake, Vladimir Illich Lenin's *What is to be Done?*, is countered by Estragon's opening line which announces the theme of the play: 'Nothing to be done.' Vladimir is wanting action, purpose and meaning while Estragon, sitting, earth-bound, is caught up in the present, physical problem of his boots. Vladimir associates his efforts at finding a meaning that existence perpetually denies with the mental activity of reason, that quality which once was thought to distinguish mankind from the rest of the animal kingdom:

> ...Vladimir, be reasonable, you haven't yet tried everything. And I resumed the struggle.
>
> (Beckett, 1956, p.9)

His principal ally in 'the struggle' is the consolation offered by the Christian religion, even though that hangs by a thread. He latches onto the only Gospel that mentions one of the thieves crucified with Christ being saved: 'One of the thieves was saved. (*Pause*.) It's a reasonable percentage.' (Beckett, 1956, p.11) Beckett, born on a Good Friday when Christ was dying, an inversion typical of his mode of fooling, reduces the core of the Christian myth to the calculations of the stock-market. For Vladimir the hope of salvation is reasonable but for Estragon who has previously attempted suicide, it is just a story to deceive 'ignorant apes'. Vladimir is markedly less sure and more desperate about his purposes in Act II but even at the close of Act I the hope of progress seems increasingly unlikely:

VLADIMIR: We've nothing more to do here.

ESTRAGON: Nor anywhere else.

VLADIMIR: Ah Gogo, don't go on like that. Tomorrow everything will
be better.

(Beckett, 1956, p.52)

Estragon affirms his place in the long line of material fools by his pref-
erence for confining his horizons to the realm of the senses and of
direct, tangible experience. Unlike Vladimir we see him sleep, eat and
express enthusiasm for the prospect of an erection; as close as anyone
can get to sexual desire in their circumstances. He is also the first to
acknowledge explicitly, albeit ironically, the presence of the audience,
'inspiring prospects'. He is the one who insists that their experience is
worse than the circus and he has the poet's capacity to imagine which
unnerves Vladimir. Because he customarily avoids being sententious,
his rare pronouncement carries the extra weigh signalled in the stage
direction:

> (*aphoristic for once*) We are all born mad. Some remain so.

(Beckett, 1956, p.80)

Not only does the aphorism link him with the wisdom of the mad, it
also connects him through the verbal echo with Lear's Fool:

> *King Lear:* Dost thou call me fool, boy?
>
> *Fool:* All thy other titles thou hast given away; that thou wast born
> with.

(Shakespeare, I,4)

Jan Kott (Kott, 1967, pp.100–33) long since analysed the metaphysical
and verbal links between *King Lear* and *Endgame* and Estragon's view of
the madness of humanity anticipates these.

Following Beckett's declared love of geometry critics have sought to
place the characters in symmetrical patterns, linking Vladimir with
Lucky as fellow intellectuals and Estragon with Pozzo as creatures of
sensuality. That is fine as far as it goes but, as usual with Beckett, it does
not go very far when nothing is certain. Just as plausible is the connection via fooling of Estragon to Lucky. Beckett himself suggested that
Lucky is lucky because he has no more expectations. In this he resembles Estragon more than Vladimir who is continually betrayed by hope

deferred. Likewise Vladimir shares with Pozzo a sense of the arbitrariness of fate which provides a 'reasonable percentage' chance of material comfort if not of salvation:

> *POZZO*: Remark that I might just as well have been in his shoes and he in mine. If chance had not willed it otherwise.
>
> (Beckett, 1956, p.31)

The tension between Vladimir and Estragon is maintained until the end of the play with Vladimir continuing to assert that Godot, should he arrive, will save them, while Estragon stills looks to the possibility of suicide for a material rather than spiritual conclusion to their existence. Knowingly and unknowingly, trousers around his ankles, Estragon fools his way through each passing day.

This quality of dramatic tension between the two principal characters is carried over into *Endgame* where the master servant relationship between Hamm and Clov is complicated by previous events that suggest Clov is Hamm's adopted son. However, such a relationship, if such it be, does not engender affection, merely dependence. Clov serves Hamm's successively reduced bodily needs while Clov receives the dubious benefits of Hamm's place of shelter from a deadly external world. In this manner they resemble Prospero and Caliban rather more strongly than Lear and his Fool. Hamm quotes Prospero ('Our revels now are ended') to drive home the connection. Clov's kitchen, the dimensions of a cell, is where he is, Caliban-like, penned up when not attending upon Hamm whose 'refuge' serves, like Prospero's island, to protect him from the dangerous, perhaps fatal, world beyond. Hamm even shares the chess metaphor ('Me to play'), used both literally and figuratively in *The Tempest*. Clov, with Caliban, shares a murderous intent towards his master: 'If I could kill him I'd die happy' and like his fellow in fooling, Estragon, is scornful of his partner's feeble attempt to deduce significance from their plight:

> *HAMM*: We're not beginning to … to … mean something?
> *CLOV*: Mean something! You and I, mean something! (*Brief laugh.*) Ah that's a good one!
>
> (Beckett, 1964, p.27)

Clov and Caliban are also alike in having to name the worlds they inhabit through the language of their oppressors. Both Hamm and Prospero have attempted to colonise the minds of their servants/slaves by controlling the language available to them, and both discover that their words are flung back in their faces by their ungrateful victims:

> *CLOV*: I use the words you taught me. If they don't mean anything any more, teach me others. Or let me be silent.
>
> (Beckett, 1964, p.32)

Caliban responds to his situation in similar terms:

> *CALIBAN*: You taught me language, and my profit on 't
> Is, I know how to curse: the red plague rid you
> For learning me your language.
>
> (*The Tempest*, I, 2)

Prospero and Hamm are the creators of their stage-play worlds and their main antagonists are the fools, Caliban and Clov, who are less willing to succumb to their allotted parts in the scheme than the other characters. Whereas Caliban is undone by the dull-wittedness of his accomplices in failing to despatch his master, the final tableau of *Endgame* leaves the question of Clov's resistance unresolved. He is dressed 'for the road', knowing what 'belongs to a frippery' but his exit remains locked in the uncertainty of his immobility. The manner in which he imagines his escape might apply equally to Caliban's vision of life after Prospero has set sail from the island. The audience of Shakespeare's play never sees that moment, any more than Beckett's audience gets to see life outside the orbit of Hamm's mind:

> *CLOV*: I open the door of the cell and go. I am so bowed I only see my feet, if I open my eyes, and between my legs a little trail of black dust. I say to myself that the earth is extinguished, though I never saw it lit.
>
> (Beckett, 1964, p.51)

The 'trail of black dust' or the 'thing of darkness' are alike lodged in the souls of the plays' protagonists, and it may be that neither Prospero nor Hamm can maintain an existence without acknowledging their complicity with folly.

Beckett presents the fool grappling with the existential reality of life, outside any overt political context, whereas several British playwrights of the second half of the twentieth century have explored the relationship of folly to politically motivated social change. Such an exploration inevitably highlights the problem of the fool's complicity with an ideological position. Dario Fo's career demonstrates the difficulties that arise when the orthodoxies of any political party threaten to constrain the vision of the fool. Yet that very vision is, itself, born out of anger at systematic injustice that cries out for political action. This contradiction between humanism and revolution within the person of the fool is the dominant subject of Trevor Griffiths' 1975 play *Comedians*.

In Act 1 where the would-be comedians are warming up for their stand-up spots in the local working men's club under the watchful eye of their teacher, Eddie Waters, it seems as though the central conflict will be between Waters' notion of the transformative power of comedy and Challenor's view of it as a commodity, ladled out to an ignorant audience in confirmation of their prejudices. However, it is quickly apparent that this game is loaded against the latter view, with Challenor as an aunt Sally, representing the dominant view of a debased popular culture. The force of Griffiths' writing is directly against such a position and the audience's sympathies are manipulated accordingly. As we hear Waters' manifesto for a comedian, we start to detect the 'authentic' voice of the playwright:

> *Waters*: It's not the jokes. It's not the jokes. It's what lies behind 'em. It's the attitude. A real comedian – that's a daring man. He *dares* to see what his listeners shy away from, fear to express. And what he sees is a sort of truth, about people, about their situation, about what hurts or terrifies them, about what's hard, above all, about what they *want*. A joke releases the tension, says the unsayable, any joke pretty well. But a true joke, a comedian's joke, has to do more than release tension, it has to *liberate* the will and the desire, it has to *change the situation*.
>
> (Griffiths, 1996, pp.211–12)

Thus he articulates social change as the aim of comedy in contrast to Beckett's fools who deny the possibility of change. The nature of this change, as understood by the humanist Waters, is not, however, clear. For Price, the revolutionary, the suspicion is that Waters' kind of change is personal not systemic. The situation of a given individual may change through exposure to folly but does this amount to anything more than the domestication of discontent? Does the postmodernist fool take up the role formerly fulfilled by carnival by enabling his audience to feel better for a little while?

In Act 2 after the other five comedians have fallen predictably into the camps of Challenor or Waters, each occupying separate sides of the stage like the good and bad angels of *Dr Faustus*, the climax is set for Price to reveal himself. He produces a performance which defies categorisation as well as defying his audience. The visual appearance is taken from the Swiss clown, Grock, but the sentiments expressed are the class hatred of a fractured society in which the subject/object relations of the dominant are inverted so that the middle-classes are silenced (literally they are dummies) in the face of the alienation of the previous three hundred years turned back upon themselves. Price professes himself inspired by the anger which occasionally flashes out of Grock's autobiographies:

> But I wonder, shall I be believed when I tell you that sometimes, even now, in the midst of all these plaudits, the old conviction of injustice suffered sometimes comes over me? I would like, when this happens, to rip off the lid of my piano and smash it into pieces. Rage seizes me by the throat to such an extent that I could rush then and there from the footlights and plant the red flag on the roof of every prison and police court in the world.
>
> (Grock, 1931, p.101)

But this is Grock looking back from the heights of his fame, as Eddie Waters might look back on his younger self; the same Grock who was Hitler's favourite. In a *Guardian* interview quoted by Schechter, Griffiths provides an insight into the influence of Grock upon himself while also revealing the extent to which master and pupil deviate in the conclusion of their respective acts:

> Grock used to get a middle-class stereotype on stage and just reduce this person to nothing, to the point where it wasn't even funny, just painful. And the straight man would become so distressed that he would refuse to speak. Then Grock would become incredibly alone; in the fear of the void. And he'd try to make the man laugh, and finally manage it, and then the thing would be sealed and healed.
>
> (Schechter, 1985 p.137)

In Price's act healing has been replaced by hatred and though there is fooling, here there is no fool. Throughout the rest of the play Griffiths has pushed the theatrical genre in the direction of hyper-naturalism, signalled by the clock measuring the time for actors and audience alike. Even the time it takes for an interval is matched by the time the characters need to get from classroom to club. The conventional comedians, both reactionary and progressive, are bound into this convention through which the all-hating fool, Price, bursts in his performance, to confront both fictional and real audiences directly. The stage-directions which introduce Price's performance describe his appearance as 'half-clown' and the missing half is the one which expresses himself through his responses to the people and situations with which he is confronted. Here the transaction is all one-way: Price snarls his clown message at dummies who cannot require him to acknowledge humanity. Though the symbolism is powerful at the level of class warfare, Price cannot learn or develop through the encounter; he is as fixed and immobile as his enemy. Back in the classroom he forces a reluctant Waters to react to his display:

> *Waters*: It was ugly. It was drowning in hate. You can't change today into tomorrow on that basis. You forget a thing called…the truth.
> (Griffiths, 1996, p.266)

Waters recognises that Price wants to enter the business for the same reasons that he did: to change the world through comedic interventions into popular culture, but the youthful simplicities of hatred are now, for the man who, echoing Estragon, experienced the sadism of an erection on a visit to Buchenwald concentration camp, untruthful. Waters inhabits Beckett's post-war world as an existential rather than political fool. Conversely, Waters' fool-like perception that our deficiencies connect us to a common humanity, sound to Price like an old man's evasion of his social mission:

> *Price*: We still don't belong to ourselves. Nothing's changed. You've just forgotten, that's all.
> (Griffiths, 1996, p.267)

The revolutionary tradition with which, somewhat fancifully, Price associates Grock and within which he strives to locate himself, in the England of the 1970s leaves him isolated and impotent to 'wait for it to happen'. He belongs to no party and he has no programme. The origins of his fooling in class conflict and injustice link him directly to the 'birth of the *jongleur*' but, unlike Fo, there is no popular tradition left within which he can express his refusal to 'consent'.

The dramatic force of the play, as Stanton Garner points out, lies in the realisation that neither Waters nor Price, alone, can encompass the folly of social change but their generational locations prevent each from entering into a dialectical relationship with the other.

> *Comedians* approaches its end, therefore, with a set of dialectical possibilities far more difficult to reconcile than those presented by the Challenor-Waters confrontation. Griffiths, who commented in a 1976 interview that "I inhabit the tension between Eddie Waters and Gethin Price," presents the positions of these two protagonists with full awareness of their strengths and inadequacies.
>
> (Garner, 1999, p.141)

Tantalisingly it is the audience rather than the protagonists who perceive the dialectical relationship in which they are contained. Taking up the categories offered by Stallybrass and White once again, Waters and Price are the victims of fragmentation; both the fragmentation of the class divide and the aesthetic fragmentation which has split popular culture from mass culture. However, the play does not simply end in a stand-off. It has a coda in the form of the joke told by Patel to Waters after the 'funny men' have left:

> *Patel*: A man has many children, wife, in the South. His crop fail, he have nothing, the skin shrivel on his children's ribs, his wife's milk dries. They lie outside the house starving. All around them, the sacred cows, ten, twenty, more, eating grass. One day he take sharp knife, mm? He creep up on a big white cow, just as he lift knife the cow see him and the cow say, Hey, aren't you knowing you not permitted to kill me? And the man say, What do you know, a talking horse.
>
> (Griffiths, 1996, p.272)

Patel's joke is rooted in the same soil that gave birth to the *jongleur* and, though it is not the whole answer to the unresolved dialectic of Waters and Price, it offers a different insight into how the ordinary man can use his wit and imagination in the struggle to be human:

> Coming (as it does) at this point in the play, Patel's joke is rich in meanings and implications. More deftly than theoretical argument, it manages to reconcile elements of Waters's and Price's comic visions, rooting itself in the harsh realities of starvation while affirming the

creativity of the human will in subverting the strictures of religious
and class oppression.

(Garner, 1999, p.143)

The joke records one of those small victories of the human spirit over
systems of control that are recorded in the chronicles of fooling that
I have been tracing down the years in the theatre of playwrights such
as Shakespeare, Brecht and Fo. It will not overturn the caste system or
herald the end of class injustice but it might announce the recruiting of
another fool to the cause of being human as Patel and Waters leave, the
latter offering a place to Patel in his next class in May. The fool springs
eternal.

The challenge of establishing a dialectical relationship between the
insights of the fool and the transformative social action of the revolutionary is also a major preoccupation in the theatre work of Edward
Bond. Although human societies organised within the capitalist system are presented as profoundly and dangerously irrational, for Bond,
unlike Beckett, the human condition is not absurd and therefore there
is something 'to be done'. Whilst the fool expresses the absurdities and
irrationalities of society – and there are several such persons in Bond's
plays – the difficulty Bond has with fools is that they do nothing. Therefore his theatrical representations are a continual struggle to go beyond
the situation of Gethin Price who, at the end of *Comedians*, is left in
abject passivity, waiting for the revolution. The humanist constructions
of folly which repudiate the systems that rob people of their freedom to
be human, have to be married to the agents of social activism in order
that people-centred transformation can occur in our societies. Bond does
not pretend that this process is easy and the dramatic action depicts the
always painful and tortuous struggle to secure such a marriage.

This conundrum is explored in terms of light and dark in Bond's play
about John Clare, *The Fool*. The 'unbearable lightness' of Clare's foolish,
poetic being is counterpointed by the abortive social uprising for which
the character nick-named Darkie is hanged. Clare is a fool because he
sees through the madness of his society but he is driven mad because
his only response is words. Bond typically takes the wall or the prison
as the emblem of the oppression of irrational systems and in this play
both the light and the dark of resistance are separated and locked up:

> Clare is light, you see, and I deliberately chose the name Darkie – it's
> an invented name.... Clare the poet, light, understanding, interpreta-
> tion, and he doesn't want to use force because force ... isn't to do with

that side of human behaviour which is to do with kindness and generosity and so on.... Clare knows, for instance, that you can't change the world simply by smiling at it... but if he uses just force... all he will do is simply recreate the problem. And that is his dilemma... and so I showed Clare failing.... [He] is locked up in prison, just as Darkie's locked up in prison... both their lives are wasted and that's simply because the two necessary parts of action – understanding and whatever force is necessary to put that understanding into effect – are not joined.

(Roberts, 1985, pp.35–6)

Perhaps this failure is prefigured in the mummers play of the opening scene where Darkie is cast as Bullslasher, the slayer of Saint George, emblem of the violent, irrational nation, while Clare plays the Doctor who restores Saint George so that nothing changes. The foolish humanity of the poet is responsible for maintaining the system against which he rails. Put another way, the dissenting fool will always be incorporated into the oppressive establishment unless he finds a means to turn folly into action. Besides his traditional role as social commentator, Clare exhibits the sexual appetite associated with the fool, having both wife and idealised mistress, as well as expressing his antagonism for churchmen, reminiscent of both Feste and the impersonations of Dario Fo:

CLARE: Parson aren't you old! Lie in your churchyard soon stead a lyin' in your church. An ol' man's hair's the colour a bone. Seen 'em stack outside the slaughter house. Goo t'be turned t'glue.

(Bond, 1976, p.57)

Clare's madness is the device which enables him to deliver truth in the face of those who inflict the injustices of inequality upon the rural poor. The response of an irrational society is to enlist professional help in silencing the fool by pronouncing him mad: the mark of sanity in the world turned upside down:

DOCTOR (looking at CLARE): Mr Clare should spend a few months with me. At the end of that time I shall begin to know him. Then I can start disentangling the truth from the poetry.

(Bond, 1976, p.58)

This diagnosis echoes the Doctor's treatment of Woyzeck where expertise reduces the patient to the status of an object, 'known' and therefore exposed to the light of reason. The fool's truth is uttered as poetry but reason separates them in order to dismiss dissent as merely poetic; a fanciful deviation from the dominant irrational 'reason' of an insane society. Clare's 'madness' cuts both ways: at once providing the insight from which social truths emerge while also providing the excuse for locking him away and so rendering him voiceless. The point is underlined by the scene in which books of his poems are returned to him because admirers cannot even give them away. Bond constantly employs the same images and motifs throughout his work, the prison, the wall and loss of voice and sight being the dominant ones. The fools, as truth-tellers, are the victims of imprisonment, denied alike an audience and the possibility of social action.

Though the setting is a far cry from Northampton Asylum, the themes of *The Woman* are the same. What becomes of the fool in an irrational, violent society and how to ally the perception of a humanist truth with action that can produce social change? At the start of the play Ismene, the naïve and foolish teller of truths is married to the emblem of the irrational, violent and dominant society: 'The cleverest woman married to the handsomest man, my dear. Not a wise match' (Bond, 1980, p.71). At the end of the play she is married again, this time to a run-away slave, trading the brightness of silver for the darkness of the underground but finding at last her 'right' match. Her initial rejection of power through violence is rewarded with a punishment typical of Bond: first a prison and then cemented into the wall:

> *ISMENE*: I can't pretend now: that's why I'm in prison. In prison you're free to tell the truth.
>
> (Bond, 1980, p.29)

Her foolishness, like Clare's has caused her to be locked away for daring to expose the system that governs men's affairs: 'The good shepherd leads his sheep to the butcher' (Bond 1980, p.44). Unlike Clare, Ismene enjoys the protection of Hecuba, the woman of the title, whose self-inflicted blindness in response to the murder of her grandson opens her mind to the irrationality of violence and the possibility of a different way of ordering the world. In Bond's terms hers is a journey from the darkness of irrational destruction in Troy to the light of reason on a remote Greek island, expressed through her manipulation of the defeat of Heros which paves the way for Ismene's marriage to the Dark Man:

ISMENE: Since you've loved me my mind's began to clear. Even yesterday I was calm.

MAN: I may disgust you.

ISMENE: No, never.

(Bond, 1980, p.108)

At the symbolic level the marriage represents the union of foolish truth with action (the Dark Man kills Heros) that was not achieved in *The Fool*. Bond clarifies the significance in an essay he wrote for the reprinted edition, 'A Socialist Rhapsody':

The play tells a simple story that shows in the characters and their actions the real cause-and-effect of change – especially the stupidity of reaction and the power of the wisdom that opposes it. Because it celebrates that change and those who make it, it is a socialist rhapsody.

(Bond, 1980, p.110)

The journey, however, to this rhapsodic state took the playwright through the agonising violence of his earlier play *Lear*. Bond described Shakespeare's original as 'the greatest play written' but was driven to offer his own criticism of it because it is finally limited by the escapism of tragedy. Bond takes his Lear through the fascism of Heros and on to the understanding of the foolish Clare, before arriving at the place occupied by Hecuba, the marriage of truth with action.

Once again the usual emblems are applied to the unreason of hierarchy:

LEAR: My people will live behind this wall when I'm dead. You may be governed by fools but you'll always live in peace. My wall will make you free.

(Bond, 1972, pp.3–4)

At its simplest the action of the play teaches Lear that he is the fool for equating security with freedom. Echoing his model ('Nothing will come of nothing'), Lear believes initially that '...it's too late to learn anything' (Bond, 1972, p.7) and then embarks on a learning journey across the killing fields sponsored by that belief. At first sight it seems that the Gravedigger's Boy, both in life and as a ghost, occupies the place of the Fool in Shakespeare's play, being the constant companion and

source of fellow feeling for Lear. Like the original, his professional calling has caused him to understand mortality and the vanity of human
wishes, provoking his wife to call him a fool for taking in the politically dangerous Lear in the manner of Azdak, harbouring the fugitive
Grand Duke. As in the original his essentially humanist perceptions are
increasingly internalised by Lear who, like his prototype, uses his time
in prison to imagine a humanist utopia:

> LEAR: The fools will be silent. We won't chain ourselves to the dead,
> or send our children to school in the graveyard. The torturers and
> ministers and priests will lose their office. And we'll pass each other
> in the street without shuddering at what we've done to each other.
> (Bond, 1972, pp.39–40)

In utopia fools would be silent because man would have perfected herself and there would be no call for the function of social criticism.
In *King Lear* it is the Fool whose prophesy of perfection draws the
conclusion that such behaviour would result in 'the realm of Albion'
coming 'to great confusion'. The social relations upon which we currently depend would be disorientatingly dissolved. This vision of Lear's
goes on to be violently dislocated by the scenes to which he bears witness, including his own blinding, leading him to understand where the
actual, rather than the obvious, cause lies:

> LEAR: I have lived with murderers and thugs, there are limits to their
> greed and violence, but you decent, honest men devour the earth!
> (Bond, 1972, p.79)

The Gravedigger's Boy haunts Lear by trying to seduce him into retreat
from the world and the abandonment of the possibility of action. This
is why he has to be 'killed' a second time. Before this Lear launches into
his climactic public statement of a humanist manifesto; the apotheosis
of all the foolish insights collected throughout Bond's *oeuvre*:

> LEAR: You have two enemies, lies *and* truth. You sacrifice truth to
> destroy lies, and you sacrifice life to destroy death. It isn't sane. You
> squeeze a stone till your hand bleeds and call that a miracle. I'm old,
> but I'm as weak and clumsy as a child, too heavy for my legs. But
> I've learned this, and you must learn it or you'll die.... If a God had
> made the world, might would always be right, that would be so wise,
> we'd be spared so much suffering. But we made the world – out of

our smallness and weakness. Our lives are awkward and fragile and we have only one thing to keep us sane: pity, and the man without pity is mad.

(Bond, 1972, p.84)

But however true Lear's understanding, merely to articulate it, to be content with the closet of the artist is to maintain the absurdity of existence. As a representative of the next generation observes:

THOMAS: It's dangerous to tell the truth, truth without power is always dangerous.

(Bond, 1972, p.76)

This is the fate of the fool: dangerous but powerless, and Lear escapes that fate by climbing his own wall and starting to dismantle it; a tiny and futile act in the great ocean of irrationality but a small victory, nonetheless, for humankind over the system. As Bond himself made clear in a programme note for the Liverpool Everyman production of 1975, Lear's action points forward and finishes nothing:

My Lear's gesture mustn't be seen as final. That would make the play a part of the theatre of the absurd and that, like perverted science, is a reflection of no-culture. The human condition isn't absurd; it's only our society which is absurd. Lear is very old and has to die anyway. He makes his gesture only to those who are learning how to live.

(Roberts, 1985, p.25)

This is the challenge that Bond sets up for contemporary theatre: to find ways of combining social critique with social action; to take up the understandings of the fool and then to apply those understandings to the possibility of transformation; to express 'the joke of contradiction' not for its own sake but so that change might be inaugurated.

10
Fooling with Applications

... to speak truth to power through foolish stories

(Julie Salverson)

The tension between social development and social critique identified in the previous chapter lies at the core of the most recent major development in theatre, namely applied theatre. Applied theatre is a process which aims to place the mechanisms of theatre at the service of the social development of individuals and groups. By engaging participants in this process it is hoped that they will emerge as more confident, better socially adjusted human beings who can contribute to the progress of societies, rather than being a dependent drain upon them. Applying theatre to children, prisoners, the homeless, the rural poor, or any other group perceived from the perspective of the dominant culture to be 'oppressed' is good for them in the sense of improving the likelihood of them functioning as useful, active citizens in the present or the future. Applied theatre is judged against social rather than artistic outcomes. Are the participants less anti-social than before they were engaged in the process? There is an unspoken and unwritten assumption that art improves the quality of life and that decent, middle-class people who set the social norms, attend concerts, plays, galleries, libraries, etc. to enrich their life experience and boost their cultural capital. However, there is another category of less fortunate persons to whom the arts must be applied for their necessary development. Applied theatre is based upon the notion of a deficit model. Participants in applied theatre processes are lacking something that 'normal' people do not. This lack may take the form of physical or mental health, social stability, capacity for empathy, freedom in the case of prisoners or experience of life in the case of children. In some sense or other they are victims, hapless or self-willed, of forces and circumstances which have propelled them beyond the pale of normality. A dose of theatre, judiciously applied to their particular ailment, will be good for them.

The applied arts are, therefore, predicated upon a colonial model where the centre prescribes what is good for the periphery. Government initiatives are passed down to local government or third sector organisations to implement a centralised agenda, frequently in the name of 'social inclusion'. This agenda is predicated upon the notion that society, by which is meant the world as we currently know it or the *status quo*, is something in which any right-thinking person would wish to be included. Theatre is applied to the goal of helping the less fortunate back into society through such devices as raising self-esteem, building confidence or, even more ambitiously, changing behaviour. The relationship of the facilitator of this process to the participant is fundamentally a therapeutic one: facilitator as therapist; participants as patients. This must never be articulated openly, however, lest the practice strays into the professional territory of drama therapy. Yet this is frequently the reality. Project implementers and funders are on the lookout for possible victims, like lawyers chasing ambulances or vultures circling above carrion: substance abusers, victims of domestic and sexual violence, prisoners, users of mental health services – these are the grist to the mill of the applied theatre practitioner.

However, this is not the full story of theatre's engagement with the contemporary world and the struggle for social justice. Alongside Vladimir with his almost unshakeable belief in the human capacity for self-improvement, stands Estragon, offering a vision tempered by the bitterness of experience; as Brecht expressed it: 'Taught only by reality can/Reality be changed.' (Brecht, 1977, p.34) The oyster of applied theatre can only transform the grit of human experience into the pearl of a better life by including in its processes all those elements which form part of the human being; irrational, self-destructive and passionate as they may be. In other words a theatrical process which attempts to offer an insight into the workings of society and of the humans who comprise it, must take account of the painful wisdom articulated by the fool. The theatre can represent a space where actuality and imagination enter into a dialectical relationship designed to produce a new reality but it is the presence of the fool which guards against any easy acceptance of a 'magical' solution to injustice, oppression and the crushing of human potential. This tension or potential contradiction is the one which the Brazilian theatre-maker, Augusto Boal, addressed through the creation of the figure of the Joker. In a series of essays written in 1966 on the development of the Arena Theatre in São Paulo, he expounded his notion of a Joker system for the construction of politically engaged theatre:

> The first problem to be solved consists in the presentation within the same performance, both of the play and its analysis.
>
> (Boal, 1979, p.174)

From this ambition it is clear that Boal stands in a direct line from Brecht, alike in seeking to devise an aesthetic which opens up the theatrical narrative to the interventions of social criticism. Within the play, without bringing the action to a dead stop, a means must be found to enable the audience to critique, qualify, perhaps even modify, the representation of it. Initially, like Brecht, Boal addressed the problem from within the aesthetic parameters of formal theatre:

> This Joker, *curinga*, in Portuguese, has a polyvalent role as director, master of ceremonies, interviewer, and exegete, representing the author who knows story, plot development, and outcome as no individual character can. Through all his various roles, the *curinga* was responsible for performing a commentary on the performance within the performance.
>
> (Schutzman, 2006, p.133)

This description comes close to an analysis of the combined roles of the Singer and Azdak as performed by Ernst Busch in the original Berliner Ensemble production of *The Caucasian Chalk Circle*. The process of analysis is begun through the 'loaded' comments of the Singer on the action, supplemented by the 'loaded' interventions of Azdak into the action, but only completed by the interpretation of the action made by the audience who are encouraged to perform this role as a result of the relationship created with it by the Joker:

> We propose a "Joker" who is a contemporary and neighbor of the spectator. For this it is necessary to restrict his "explanations"; it is necessary to move him away from the other characters, to bring him close to the spectators.
>
> (Boal, 1979, p.175)

This positioning of the Joker, at once both inside the fiction of the drama and outside it in the world inhabited by the audience, recalls many of the examples considered in earlier chapters and indicates that Boal was tapping into a tradition as old as the theatrical form itself. Mady Schutzman draws attention to the connection Boal makes with another ancient tradition in the use of the term 'Joker' from Tarot cards; itself allied to the idea of the madman through the Italian name which we saw reprised by Fo, *il Matto*:

> Of particular note is that the joker in playing cards (as well as the fool of tarot, originally a card game as well) are worth nothing unto themselves; their paradoxical power emerges only in the case of a challenge with another card against whom they always triumph (being the highest trump).
>
> (Schutzman, 2006, p.142)

Schutzman reminds us that, by using the label 'Joker', Boal is conceiving of a function not a character. The Joker can adopt the mask of any character which fits the situation since there is no pre-existing character whose features have to be erased. The Joker only comes into being in the moment of challenge as a response to what is offered by the protagonist and, given that his position is fluid, he will always out-manoeuvre an adversary who is trapped in a fixed situation or by an inflexible set of characteristics. In this respect the Joker is essentially the same function as that performed traditionally by the fool who, in turn, recalls the trickster of the founding myths of human societies across the world:

> The Joker of the Joker System was a live theorist and pattern detector with a paradoxical vantage point. He was a trickster of sorts, consciously wielding a strategy of re-articulation to obscure easy answers and to discourage fixed identities.
>
> (Schutzman, 2006, p.134)

This 'vantage point' is exploited to unsettle the audience's understanding of the narrative as presented by those actors whose characters represent fixed places within the story. Not only is the desire for empathy, stimulated by the theatrical process, then qualified or even thwarted by the Joker, but it is also as if the playwright was placing an obstacle in front of his own temptation to present a fictional world in his own image. The paradoxical nature of the Joker or fool in the theatre extends to the aesthetic of his creation, for he is actually written into the play by the playwright and yet is presented as if he has somehow escaped the confines of the creative processes by which the rest of the characters are bound. When Boal writes of the formal or generic freedom accorded by the system, he is somewhat misleading in ascribing the notion of 'function' alike to protagonist and Joker. This suggests that both occupy the same level of reality, whereas one is tied to a single level while the other is free to commute between levels:

> It should be noted that the possibility of great variation in form is offered by the simple presence within the system of two completely opposite functions: the protagonic function, which is the most concrete reality, and the "Joker" function, which is the universalizing abstraction of the other. In them all styles are included and are possible.
>
> (Boal, 1979, p.177)

There seems to be some confusion between form and function in this description since the counterpoint of 'concrete' with 'abstraction' obscures the material basis from which the Joker operates. The protagonist is locked into a world of concrete reality in both the popular and philosophical senses of concrete but the Joker, though able to present contrasting realities, nevertheless still has to play by a set of rules, even if they are of his own making, if he is to maintain his relationship with the audience, without which his function would fail. The Joker only has a function in response to the reality proposed by the protagonist; he is, at it were, drawn into being by the need to unfix the protagonist from a social or psychological stalemate. Whilst he may need to offer a different kind of reality in order to accomplish this task, he must nevertheless provoke an alternative vision grounded in reality, not an abstract fantasy divorced from praxis.

The question of levels of reality and the temptations of magical solutions lies at the heart of the critical debates concerning the evolution of the Joker System into the practice of Forum Theatre, the Boalian system most widely practised, and frequently misrepresented, today. Its first phase is broadly similar to the system originally outlined, with a group of actors under the direction of a Joker/director rehearsing and presenting situations drawn from the contemporary reality of those before whom it is played. The particular stories or series of events are now brought to a point of crisis which is left unresolved, somewhat in the manner of the conclusion of Brecht's *The Good Person of Setzuan* where an epilogue tells the audience that it must come up with an ending, a resolution of the contradiction, for the actors and playwright have done their work in drawing attention to the contradiction. The play is then re-performed with the Joker now inviting any member of the audience to intervene to replace the protagonist if s/he wishes to demonstrate an alternative action to the one offered by the players. Minus the presence of a joker, this is almost the structure arrived at by Brecht in 1930 through his rewriting of *Der Jasager* into *Der Neinsager* in response to feedback from a school class. Boal coined the term 'spect-actor' to describe this role. In this way a new reality is imported onto the stage, not by the Joker but by anyone in the audience who chooses; in effect an entire audience of potential Jokers or, as Boal put it himself, the democratisation of the Joker process:

> *Forum Theatre*: perhaps the most democratic form of the Theatre of the Oppressed and certainly the best known and most practised throughout the world...
>
> (Boal, 2006, p.6)

However, the development of the Joker System into Forum Theatre gave rise to a contradiction which remains unresolved: namely, that between the vision of the fool and those visions of each spect-actor which may or may not be foolish. The grand aim for the Theatre of the Oppressed as the political, social and psychological liberation of those who participate in its process is clearly and unequivocally articulated:

> The Aesthetics of the Oppressed aims at the liberation and fortifi-cation of metaphoric activity, of symbolic languages, of intelligence and sensitivity. It aims at the expansion of the perception that we have of the world. This is done through the Word, the Image, and the Sound, guided by a Humanist Ethic.
>
> (Boal, 2006, p.43)

The audience's guide in the matter of humanist ethics is the Joker; entrusted by Boal with the task of establishing a framework within which the democratic choices of spect-actors can flourish without doing damage to the fundamental social politics of the Theatre of the Oppressed. The eternal contradiction between a progressive aspiration for social justice and an honest appraisal of human nature which has dogged the plays analysed in this book, is present too in both the form and the function of the Theatre of the Oppressed and the Joker is the figure in whom this contradiction is housed:

We should face up to the truth staring us in the face: we are beasts! Let's get that into our heads! Man is the wolf of man – as the poet has it. To which I add, in prose: man eats...and is edible!...This is our huge task: to shake off our savage nature and create a culture where goodness is possible and solidarity sought after.

(Boal, 2006, p.43)

The Joker is charged with the responsibility of acting the fool by confronting the spect-actor with the reality of her/his being, no matter how awkward the confrontation, in order that any transformation achieved by the Forum Theatre process is grounded in the lives of the participants, rather than being a magical solution, satisfying for no longer than the duration of the performance. Frances Babbage is alive to the difficulties inherent in the Forum process:

This is a tension at the very heart of Theatre of the Oppressed: the passion, empathic association and immediacy of participation on which the techniques rely can result in diminution of critical awareness or distance needed to process the results.

(Babbage, 2004, p.64)

For the system to work the spect-actor must be sufficiently provoked by the scene played out in front of her to be propelled by her anger onto the Forum stage. To achieve this state of rage among the audience members all the traditional devices of performers are employed; most of all the arousing of empathy. However, once aroused, empathy can be a difficult beast to channel in realistic, socially productive, humanist ends; hence the care with which Brecht crafted his Epic Theatre so that a theatrical form could become the trigger for socially just transformation. This is where the Joker must come into his own by questioning both spect-actor and fellow members of the company in ways that force a reflection upon the actions and words produced to discover whether they are capable of standing up to the social realities of the world beyond the space of the Forum. Schechter identifies the required behaviour as belonging to that critical space inaugurated by Brecht:

The Joker is less a conventional clown than a Brechtian epic actor.

(Schechter, 1985, p.162)

A difficulty for the Joker is that he may find himself trying to work as an epic actor in an unfolding script which is conceived by a particular spect-actor along other lines. Notions of critique and alternative may be resisted and, by insisting, the Joker may alienate the audience from further participation. Whereas Boal controlled the aesthetic frame of the original Joker System at the Arena Theatre, the global performances of Forum Theatre open up a wide range of other aesthetic practices. The fluency, passion and charisma of his rhetoric, both live and on paper, frequently masks the contradictions encountered in grass-roots practice:

> The theatre is a mirror in which we can see our vices and our virtues, according to Shakespeare. And it can also be transformed into a magic mirror, as in the Theatre of the Oppressed, a mirror we can enter if we do not like the image it shows us and, by penetrating it, rehearse modifications of this image, rendering it more to our liking. In this mirror we see the present, but can invent the future of our dreams: the act of transforming is itself transformatory. In the act of changing our image, we are changing ourselves, and by changing ourselves in turn we change the world.
>
> (Boal, 2006, p.62)

Whilst the political trajectory of the Theatre of the Oppressed is clearly stated, there is a degree of aesthetic confusion here. A Broadway musical might be described in just these terms but, rather than changing the world, its effect upon an audience is likely to be as a 'feel good' tranquiliser, assuring it that change is not necessary and certainly not urgent. The mirror that theatre holds up, like all mirrors, inverts spatial relations (a foolish perspective) and distorts three dimensional reality into two dimensional reflection. It is a picture, an art form. There is in this description a utopianism which borders upon fantasy and is compounded by Boal's extension of the process into the domain of the audience:

> The spectator comes on stage and transforms the images that she sees and does not like – she transforms them into images she likes and desires, images of a just, convivial society.
>
> (Boal, 2006, p.85)

This is simply too easy and the Forum Theatre process, if the Joker is merely a facilitator, becomes facile. Across the world this is all too often the pattern, especially in NGOs' use of the system where its 'success' is frequently measured by the number of spect-actors who respond to the trigger play, regardless of whether any sustainable transformation, macro or micro, occurs as a result. Against all the intentions of Boal himself, Forum Theatre is thus reduced to a technique divorced from any meaningful political context. In this way the Joker, far from fulfilling an epic function, is reduced to a glorified master of ceremonies or keeper of the rules. This is the implication underlying many of the conventional descriptions of the Joker role:

> The rules are explained by the Joker (facilitator), whose function is to invite interventions, assist the transition from spectator to spectator, and encourage the audience as a whole to assess the action unfolding before them.
>
> (Babbage, 2004, p.69)

'Assess' does not do justice to the critical, combative function lurking at the heart of the Joker concept for as long as that concept draws its lineage from the fools of the European theatre. The dilution of function is exacerbated by Babbage's relegation of the Joker to the role of overseer, albeit a playful one:

> At the same time, spontaneous and playful developments occur within a clearly established and essentially simple structure that should ensure that the process – overseen by a careful Joker – remains understandable and accessible to all.
>
> (Babbage, 2004, p.69)

Babbage highlights the democratic essentials of ease of comprehension and access required of Forum Theatre but these qualities are not necessarily ones espoused by the fool in the quest for the contradictions which drive social change. Participation and the search for social justice are neither automatic bedfellows nor necessarily at odds with one another. It falls to the Joker to direct the process in such a way that participation is not at the expense of a social critique grounded in lived experience, and that social critique does not induce a culture of silence in the spectators. The balance of practice away from the guiding hand of Boal himself has been, in my experience, very much towards participation at the cost of critique; as the Joker has been too much the facilitator and too little the fool. The tension is specifically addressed by Boal but in a manner which leaves the contradiction only partially resolved:

It is true that the Joker in a Forum Theatre session, for instance, must maintain his or her neutrality and try not to impose his or her own ideas, BUT *only after having chosen his or her camp!* The Joker's neutrality is a responsible act and arises after having made a choice, after taking the side of the oppressed; the substance of the Joker is doubt, seed of all certainties; the end is discovery, not abstention.

(Boal, 2006, p.104)

The resort to capital letters and italics indicates that there is an anxiety that neutrality might be promoted at the expense of the oppressed. If the Joker is restricted by a rigid adherence to the so-called rules of Forum Theatre, the result is, all too often, the kind of easy, self-satisfying participation that leads only to a magical outcome without validity in the world to which the spect-actors must return beyond the confines of the Forum. If, however, the Joker acknowledges his place in the line of the tradition promoted by the theatrical fools of former ages and disparate cultures, the result may accord more nearly with the picture presented by Schutzman, regardless of the possible discomfort to the participants:

Tricksters and jokers do not belong to any community; as outsiders, they are loyal only to their own will. Following this directive, the TO [Theatre of the Oppressed] Joker might privilege the artistic imperative over explicit political advocacy. Such a Joker would be a communicator not seeking *common* ground so much as maximising possibilities for the articulation (and re-articulation) of *uncommon* beliefs, working toward a vision of community that thrives on constant reformulation. This kind of Joker works for the sake of *artus*.

(Schutzman, 2006, p.143)

This perception brings us to the heart of the paradox. There is a temptation to sacrifice the complexity of the art form to the clarity of a political statement but, in doing so, the effectiveness of that statement is lost. It is the art that remains truest to the bewildering confusions of life, that proves ultimately the most powerful as a political comment. As Brecht observed, politics is the art of living.

This notion that theatrical foolishness can be the means of arriving at levels of human experience normally buried beneath layers of manners, ethics and sensitivity is taken up by Canadian academic, writer and practitioner, Julie Salverson, who has developed the idea of 'foolish witness' as a path along which artists and students might enact Boal's injunction about having 'the courage to be happy'. She most often uses the term 'clown' to represent the figure whose response or witness to stories encompasses the realms of folly, but it is clear from the function ascribed to this figure that the person sits squarely within the tradition of the fool:

> The idea of clown I am drawing on is not the stereotypical circus clown, but one characterized by truthfulness and a willingness to engage in the face of failure. This clown begins with nothing, is in fact ridiculous but is innocent of this fact, innocent of the impossibility of hope.
>
> (Salverson, 2006, p.153)

These features are, by now, familiar qualities from earlier incarnations. Salverson connects her clown with the 'nothing' of the trickster myths, Shakespeare's fools and Fo's Madman, while also exploiting the notion of innocence as an alternative discourse to the prevailing, dominant norms of hopelessness through which passivity and social stasis are engendered. A straight-forward, empathy-based identification with the victims of injustice leads nowhere in relation to social transformation. In a writing and teaching project which she called 'Clown, Opera, the Atomic Bomb and the Classroom' Salverson described her role thus:

> My part of the project is a deliberate investigation into clown and the absurd as an alternate vocabulary to what have become common methods for artists working in community with people's stories: popular-education-based scene development, theatre of the oppressed, storytelling, playback theatre. For years as a community-based playwright I have grappled with the problem of how to tell stories of violence with integrity and a faithfulness to the living and the dead that allows the inevitability of my shaping the telling aesthetically, politically and personally.
>
> (Salverson, 2009, p.34)

It is this action of 'shaping...the telling' which an emphasis upon the neutrality of the Joker as an upholder of the rules of the game, threatens to disguise. In Boal's terms the political is a shared intention between actors, Joker and spect-actors while the aesthetic and the personal are the preserve of the Joker who intervenes with foolishness, being a skilled theatre practitioner and a fool. He insists upon 'the joke of contradiction' not to diminish the significance of the contradictory but rather to force a confrontation between the real and the ideal of the spect-actors in the knowledge that without such a confrontation no social transformation is possible. As ever, the fool comes into being as a function in relation to others; the wild card whose move is a response to what has already been played:

> If we do not bring who we are, including our skills and our vulnerabilities, to the encounter with others, then we are not truly available.
>
> (Salverson, 2006, p.155)

In a competitive, exploitative, neoliberal system to parade one's vulnerability is indeed foolish and this behaviour can only fall to those who are innocent or oblivious of the dangers of exposure. Paradoxically, because they are innocent, it is the fools who pose a threat to the system by showing up its cruelties and limitations in relation to a broader humanist discourse. To be 'available' is to be capable of transcending self-interest, to become nobody in the service of anybody. This is the trajectory mapped out for her students by Salverson:

> In my seminar, I encourage in my students the ability to act in the face of failure, to take risks tempered by the moderating influence of a healthy doubt, and to move beyond the self-enclosing indulgence of a tragic response to existence.
>
> (Salverson, 2008, p.247)

In theatrical terms this means eschewing the role of protagonist or tragic hero in favour of the antagonist in the sense of one who acts in response to the action of the hero. Tragic heroes are undone by the rules of their societies and embrace their nihilistic destinies, whereas the foolish witnesses to their fate invite us to consider what other possibilities may be opened up by changing the rules and accepting failure as a joke:

> The clown is not a hero but she is heroic in her courage, in being available to the possible, no matter how absurd and unlikely. Pleasure, joy and fun in this context are not spectacle or escape, but rather the deadly game of living with loss, living despite failure, living even despite the humiliation of trying endlessly.
>
> (Salverson, 2009, p.39)

The fool always shows us that tragedy is not enough and catharsis must be fooled with, lest it calls survival into question. Crucifixion is always followed by resurrection, winter by spring. Salverson draws on the ethical philosophy of Emmanuel Levinas in support of the notion that we are only fully alive in our response to another and that this capacity of 'availability' is itself foolish:

> Levinas argues that it is only in the encounter with the Other that it is possible to have a self, and to step forward with a 'yes' to the world.... It is this insistence on 'yes' that characterises the foolish witness, but it is not easy nor is it simple. Always we are confronted with our tendency to be overwhelmed, to collapse or at least hesitate under the weight of existence...
>
> (Salverson, 2008, p.248)

Whilst the relational qualities suggested here are redolent of the fool's practices down the ages, the question of self is ambivalent as applied to the fool. On the one hand a sense of self for anyone can only be derived from a comparison with another – I am me because I am not somebody else – but on the other the very notion of 'self' is problematic in relation to the fool who is more accurately defined by function than personality. Salverson implicitly alludes to this difficulty of categorisation by pointing up the paradox of the clown's lack of conventional 'self' being the quality which enables her to witness the selfhood of others most penetratingly:

> The destabilized position of the clown offers a place to consider relationships across difference – relationships of attention without resolution, of respect without capture – that allow for peaceful engagements.
>
> (Salverson, 2006, p.155)

It is the instability of the fool that creates the fluidity and amorphousness that permits him to enter into a particular kind of relationship with the other where the conventional behaviours of social conformity, rather than being defied in the manner of tragedy, are juggled and played with until they offer up transformative possibilities which the fool then hands back to the protagonist other. The experienced fisherman, like the professional fool, is adept at the art of playing. When the angler feels the tug of the fish on the line, he does not let the line go taut, risking it snapping, but instead he plays out the line, giving the fish the freedom to duck and dive until the moment is right to reel it in. Similarly, the fool gives the protagonist the room to experience the contradiction for herself; caught on it only when all other possibilities have been exhausted.

Outside the arena of Forum Theatre the performative possibilities opened up by the fool are today being exploited by some of the more aesthetically adventurous practitioners of Applied Theatre; those who seek to take the application beyond the message-bearing limitations of 'thou shall' and 'thou shall not'. One such is Sharon Muiruri who was the facilitator of a devised play, *Scratchin' the Surface*, initially sponsored by Bournemouth Borough Council's drugs education initiative in 1999. The participants, a group of recovering addicts, subsequently formed themselves into a permanent theatre company, Vita Nova. Muiruri describes how the project got under way:

> The process moved very quickly as group members were like sponges soaking up the drama medium. They poured out their feelings and stories at one moment, and then at another exchanged humorous comments ranging from the childish and adolescent/risky, to the darker side of black humour that would bring us back to reality.

> What we created together as a group was a play *Scratchin' the Surface* that we have shown to over 6000 young people and that has communicated a powerful and emotional story. It is of the journey of a young man, Jay, into the world of dance and drug culture. We discovered in rehearsal, through looking in detail at various situations – firstly alien experience taken from documentary material and then later from personal experiences – that the drama work was giving the group opportunities to gain different meanings, insights and perspectives with which to review their own stories.

> (Muiruri, 2000, p.24)

Thus far the group had created a moving, documentary-style drama along the lines of many similar Applied Theatre projects. In keeping with much of the best of this type of work, the idea of story – the telling of a story rather than the delivering of a message – was paramount in the process. However, Muiruri was conscious of a need to take the play into another realm of deeper reality if it was to convey some of the core experience of addiction. To achieve this deepening a fool was required. Her journal entries reveal how this awareness was activated:

> Something had been missing from our play. Midnight on Sunday, it came to me that we needed this character, alter ego, tempting Jay,

constantly talking to him. I had a vision of Tim sitting on a stepladder very high up. . . . This character of the alter ego developed into the Raven, our addict. Raven symbolically lifts Jay up so he can fly but in the end is dragging his Raven, his burden, his baggage, his addiction. . . . Part of the discovery of the Raven came out of a hot seating session. . . .

Question: Who are you?
Raven [Tim]: You know who I am. . . always the good guy. I never lose.
Question: What does winning mean?
Raven [Tim]: I keep going. . . always plenty to feed on a hunger. I'm never full. I get at people . . . play with them, consume them. It feels good.
Question: What are you?
Raven [Tim]: I am Raven. . .
Question: You never sleep?
Raven [Tim]: I'm not asleep, I never sleep. I am imaginary. I am real. I always will be.

(Muiruri, 2000, pp.25–6)

The actor, Tim, seems to know by intuition that the function of the raven connects with ancient, ubiquitous myths that link the raven to the trickster of the earliest human societies. He summons the associations with appetite, play, and shifting levels of reality as he attempts to pin an identity down in words. Jay, synonymous in the bird world with the flashy and the superficial, cannot achieve release from addiction except by acknowledging the presence of the Raven at the core of his being ('This thing of darkness I acknowledge mine'). The Raven in this play, like Caliban in *The Tempest*, is the spanner in the works of the happy ending; the reality barring the way to the ideal outcome. Until we come to terms with the amoral danger and attraction that is part of being human, that is until we acknowledge our own fools, we cannot know who we are. The place of the raven among the birds mimics that of the fool among humans:

. . . and even the bird's honorary place in Europe was merely a tributary part in a great system of mythologies that entwined the entire hemisphere. The result of all these ancient responses is an extraordinary sweep of reference, from the Gilgamesh epic of the ancient Babylonians to the Book of Genesis, and on through western literature to Edgar Allan Poe's haunting and melancholy classic, 'The Raven'. As imaginative symbol the bird functioned throughout this period as a metaphor for death and evil foreboding divine power.

(Cocker & Mabey, 2005, p.424)

Twenty-first century performers of applied theatre in the schools and clubs of Bournemouth draw inspiration from the most ancient myths of playfulness and folly and from a continuous tradition of the fool in the theatre to invigorate their work with the pain and truth of contradiction. The trickster and, later, the fool are representations of any society's need to expose and explore the contradictions which, left unattended, would undermine and destroy it. Contradiction is the motor that drives social change. At the point where contradictions become intolerable, human behaviour changes to accommodate a new reality and the seed of a new contradiction is planted, ensuring that human relations are forever imperfect and constantly in process. Being in a process of continual change is not comfortable. We are all constantly tempted by the illusions of stability and continuity; illusions which favour those who benefit from any temporary stasis. Because the evidence of change is irrefutable, the myth of progress is the most pernicious accommodation of power to change. The power-brokers concede that societies are in a perpetual state of transformation but seek to assure the rest of us that 'things can only get better'. The very notion of progress is one of those sacred values whose contradictions the fool exposes to the mirror of history. Manifestations alter with the fashions of contemporaneity but the underlying pattern is as old as human societies:

> Individuals who never sense the contradictions of their cultural inheritance run the risk of becoming little more than host bodies for stale gestures, metaphors, and received ideas, all the stereotypical likes and dislikes by which cultures perpetuate themselves.
>
> (Hyde, 1998, p.307)

At moments when a society trumpets its values with the greatest certainty and pride; when it is least interested in alternatives, it is most at risk from the perils of fossilisation. Just as 'the end of history' is being proclaimed by the idealogues of the neoliberal ascendancy, planes are being aimed at the twin towers and financial markets overreach themselves and topple into the abyss of recession. It is the habitual refusal to countenance the *status quo* which pits the fool, sooner or later, against the powers that be. The politician's job is to convince the voters that she has a plan to make everyone's life better; that economic growth will trickle down to all and we can all sleep soundly in our beds, knowing that the government is working in our interests. The fool's job is to cast the searchlight of doubt on such claims; to peer around the corner of the grand designs at the all too fallible humans trying to implement them. The fool is not a subversive in the sense that he is not trying to put a spanner in the works of the five year plan, but he is subversive in the sense that he draws attention to the inevitable tension between human aspiration and human achievement; a tension which at times erupts into outright contradiction. Bertolt Brecht wrote a characteristically ironic poem in response to the workers uprising on the streets of East Berlin in 1953:

> THE SOLUTION
> After the uprising of the 17th June
> The Secretary of the Writers' Union
> Had leaflets distributed in the Stalinallee
> Stating that the people
> Had forfeited the confidence of the government
> And could win it back only
> By redoubled efforts. Would it not be easier
> In that case for the government
> To dissolve the people
> And elect another?
>
> (Brecht, 1976, p.440)

By acting the fool, Brecht draws attention to the limitations of the regime through the traditional fool's ploy of inversion; on this occasion inverting the conventional relationship between electorate and government. Playing with the accepted wisdom about this relationship results in a rethinking of the contradictions between power and freedom, without which social justice becomes impossible. Today as much as ever, there is a need for the fool's wisdom to help us break out of the corrosive, all-embracing grip of the contemporary, neoliberal version of capitalism. Familiarity, common sense, and the limited framings of parliamentary, representative democracy are ripe to be played with in ways which might expose other possibilities for the organisation of societies and nation states:

> We need to rediscover how to talk about change: how to imagine very different arrangements for ourselves, free of the dangerous cant of 'revolution'.
>
> (Judt, 2010, p.153)

One such example is afforded by the self-styled icon of the Zapatista movement of south-eastern Mexico, Subcomandante Marcos. Marcos plays self-consciously with conventional images of revolutionary heroes, deliberately echoing the associations with Che Guevara in balaclava-glad postures struck for post-cards, T-shirts and posters. Yet, in reality Marcos is something else; the antidote to the romantic image of the doomed hero; he is the playful fool. Like fools before him he has no fixed identity, only an image and a series of possibilities. He has consistently defied conventional expectations and avoided the trap of the tragic protagonist by creating a different kind of organisation that enacts the paradox of 'leading by obeying'; the will of the people really, not rhetorically, determining the course of Zapatista action. By playing the fool and resisting the fixed position of the protagonist, Marcos retains the fluidity and amorphousness of ideas and functions, and resists the straight-jacket of personality:

> Marcos is a gay in San Francisco, a black in South Africa, an Asian in Europe, a Chicano in San Isidro, a Palestinian in Israel, an indigenous person in the streets of San Cristóbal... a peasant without land, an underground editor, an unemployed worker, a doctor with no office, a non-conformist student, a dissident against neoliberalism, a writer without books or readers, and a Zapatista in the Mexican southeast. In other words, Marcos is a human being in this world. Marcos is every untolerated, oppressed, exploited minority that is resisting and saying 'Enough!'
>
> (Holloway & Peláez, 1998, pp.10–11)

Today the fool is still implicated in the perennial struggle for social justice and is still looking for ways of engaging in this struggle which do not trap him in the counter-narratives of the dominant. Since the dawn of social living the fool has sought to expose the gaps, absences and contradictions at the core of the ideologies by which societies are governed without himself falling prey to ideological constraints. Can ideology be subverted without the subversion itself planting the seed of a succeeding ideology? Can the fool stand outside the dialectical process (Hegelian or Marxist), or is he the grit by which the pearl of dialectical synthesis is produced?

In his book, *Collapse: How Societies Choose to Fail or Survive*, American biologist Jared Diamond boils his answer down to two factors after an analysis of evidence from civilisations ancient and modern across all the inhabited continents of the earth:

Two types of choices seem to me to have been crucial in tipping their outcomes towards success or failure: long-term planning, and the willingness to reconsider core values. On reflection, we can also recognize the crucial role of these same two choices for the outcomes of our individual lives.

One of those choices has depended on the courage to practice [*sic*] long-term thinking, and to make bold, courageous, anticipatory decisions at a time when problems have become perceptible but before they have reached crisis proportions. This type of decision-making is the opposite of the short-term reactive decision-making that too often characterizes our elected politicians...

The other crucial choice illuminated by the past involves the courage to make painful decisions about values. Which of the values that formerly served a society well can continue to be maintained under new changed circumstances? Which of those treasured values must instead be jettisoned and replaced with different approaches?

(Diamond, 2005, pp.522–23)

Each of these aspects points to the previously documented encounters of the protagonist and the fool. The former is the leader of a society or group who must look ahead and plan in order to safeguard the future of those under her protection. The latter is the fool to whom nothing is sacred and everything susceptible to re-evaluation in the light of fresh contexts. For example, our genetic evolution has endowed the human species with an indomitable drive to reproduce and to adapt to a broad range of environments, resulting in our success in populating almost every part of the globe. This same drive now poses a serious threat to our survival on the exhausted planet through over-population. In a paradox of the kind with which the fool revels, our very success may be the guarantee of our failure to survive. That most sacred of freedoms, the right to conceive children, needs urgent re-examination. Who but the fool will stand up in the crowd and say so?

If not in the crowd, then at least in the playhouse. This book has been written in the hope that the theatre can continue to offer us a place in which to play with difficult notions and to speak the unspeakable. By theatre I mean a space in which reality and fiction, life and art, can meet, play and produce surprising results; not a museum of culture into which a beleaguered species can retreat into the feel-good fantasies of ego massage. One of the leading moral philosophers of our age, John Paul Lederach, has drawn attention to the importance of the playfulness of art for ensuring the quality of our lives and the hope of our survival:

> The greatest artists of all time had a knack for playfulness, for seeing life inside of things. Too much seriousness creates art with a message but rarely creates great art. There is no scientific evidence that seriousness leads to greater growth and maturity, or insight into the human condition than playfulness.
>
> (Lederach, 2005, p.60)

I am tempted to push Lederach's insight a little further and to suggest that, paradoxically, only by not taking ourselves seriously, might we invent the means for our own survival. The fool is a central figure in inviting humans to rediscover the humility to uncrown themselves as kings and queens of the beasts in time to adopt a more modest place of reciprocity in the ecosystem. 'Who is it that can tell me who I am? ... Lear's shadow.'

The fool understands that life unlocks no meaning beyond itself and that attempts to claim immortality for humans are merely an absurd, self-serving fantasy, designed to mitigate the pain of existence. However, since this life is all we have, the fool is a vital agent in the demand for social justice to improve the experience of living for all. The ultimate contradiction of striving to improve an intrinsically meaningless life is the Sisyphus-like task which defined and continues to define the function of the fool, both in the world and in the theatre.

Bibliography

R. Andrews (1997), 'Goldoni's *Venetian Twins*: Whose Side Is the Audience On?' in J. Farrell (ed.), *Carlo Goldoni and Eighteenth-Century Theatre* (Lampeter: the Edward Mellen Press).

F. Babbage (2004), *Augusto Boal* (Abingdon: Routledge).

M. Bakhtin (1984), *Rabelais and His World* (Bloomington: Indiana University Press).

C.L. Barber (1963), *Shakespeare's Festive Comedy* (Cleveland: Meridian).

K. Barber, J. Collins & A. Ricard (1997), *West African Popular Theatre* (Oxford: James Currey).

A.Barton (1984), *Ben Jonson, Dramatist* (Cambridge: Cambridge University Press).

Beaumarchais (1964), *The Barber of Seville and The Marriage of Figaro* (London: Penguin).

S. Beckett (1956), *Waiting for Godot* (London: Faber and Faber).

S. Beckett (1958), *Endgame* (London: Faber and Faber).

T. Behan (2000), *Dario Fo: Revolutionary Theatre* (London: Pluto Press).

C. Belsey (1999), *Shakespeare and the Loss of Eden* (Basingstoke and New York: Palgrave Macmillan).

J. Berger (2007), *Hold Everything Dear* (London: Verso).

E. Berry (1984), *Shakespeare's Comic Rites* (Cambridge: Cambridge University Press).

A. Boal (1979), *Theatre of the Oppressed* (London: Pluto Press).

A. Boal (2006), *The Aesthetics of the Oppressed* (London and New York: Routledge).

R. Boon & J. Plastow (eds) (1998), *Theatre Matters* (Cambridge: CUP).

E. Bond (1972), *Lear* (London: Eyre Methuen).

E. Bond (1980), *The Woman* (London: Methuen).

B. Brecht (1962), *Mother Courage and Her Children* (London: Methuen).

B. Brecht (1966), *Parables for the Theatre* (Harmondsworth: Penguin).

B. Brecht (1976), *Poems 1913–1956* (London: Eyre Methuen).

B. Brecht (1977), *Mr. Puntila and His Man Matti* (London: Eyre Methuen).

B. Brecht (1980), *Life of Galileo* (London: Eyre Methuen).

B. Brecht (1994), *Collected Plays: Seven* (London: Methuen).

M.D. Bristol (1989), *Carnival and Theater* (London and New York: Routledge).

A. Brody (1969), *The English Mummers and Their Plays* (London: Routledge and Kegan Paul).

P. Brooker (1994), 'Key Words in Brecht's Theory and Practice of Theatre' in P. Thomson & G. Sacks (eds), *The Cambridge Companion to Brecht* (Cambridge University Press).

J.R. Brown (1983), *The Complete Plays of the Wakefield Master* (London: Heinemann).

J. Bull (1984), *New British Political Dramatists* (London, Macmillan, 1984).

R. Burton (1994) (trans.), *The Kama Sutra* (London: Penguin).

R. Cave (1991), *Ben Jonson* (Basingstoke: Macmillan).

E.K. Chambers (1933), *The English Folk-Play* (Oxford: Oxford University Press).

L.M. Clopper (2001), *Drama, Play, and Game* (Chicago: University of Chicago Press).

Cochis, S. (1998), 'The Bishop of Fools' in V. Janik (ed.), *Fools and Jesters in Literature, Art and History* (Westport: Greenwood Press).

M. Cocker & R. Mabey (2005), *Birds Britannica* (London: Chatto & Windus).

J. Cohen-Cruz & M. Schutzman (2006), *A Boal Companion* (New York: Routledge).

R. Cohn (1980), *Just Play: Beckett's Theater* (Princeton: Princeton University Press).

J.F. Danby (1949), *Shakespeare's Doctrine of Nature* (London: Faber and Faber).

N. Denny (ed.) (1973), *Stratford-upon-Avon Studies 16, Medieval Drama* (London, Edward Arnold).

J. Diamond (2005), *Collapse* (London: Allen Lane).

K. Duncan-Jones (2001), *Ungentle Shakespeare* (London: Arden Shakespeare).

T. Eagleton (1986), *William Shakespeare* (Oxford: Basil Blackwell).

P. Edwards (1968), *Shakespeare and the Confines of Art* (London: Methuen).

Erasmus (1971), *Praise of Folly* (London: Penguin).

J. Farrell (2001), *Dario Fo & Franca Rame: Harlequins of the Revolution* (London: Methuen).

J. Farrell & A. Scuderi (2000), *Dario Fo: Stage, Text, and Tradition* (Carbondale and Edwardsville: Southern Illinois University Press).

D. Fo (1988), *Mistero Buffo* (London: Methuen).

D. Fo (1991), *The Tricks of the Trade* (London: Methuen).

D. Fo (1992), *Plays 1* (London: Methuen).

D. Fo '*Panorama*, 26 April 1977' quoted in T. Behan, *Dario Fo: Revolutionary Theatre* (London: Pluto Press).

D. Fo (1980), *Accidental Death of an Anarchist* (London: Pluto Press).

D. Fo (2001a), *We Won't Pay! We won't Pay! and Other Plays* (New York: Theatre Communication Group).

D. Fo (2001b), *Johan Padan and the Discovery of the Americas* (New York: Grove Press).

D. Fo & F. Rame (1983), *Theatre Workshops at the Riverside Studios* (London: Red Notes).

S. Garner (1999), *Trevor Griffiths: Politics, Drama, History* (Ann Arbor: University of Michigan Press).

Gash, A. (1986), 'Carnival against Lent: the Ambivalence of Medieval Drama' in D. Aers (ed.), *Medieval Literature; Criticism, Ideology & History* (Brighton: Harvester Press).

C. Goldoni & L. Hall (1999), *A Servant of Two Masters* (London: Methuen).

R. Goldsmith (1974), *Wise Fools in Shakespeare* (Liverpool: Liverpool University Press).

T. Griffiths (1996), *Plays 1* (London: Faber and Faber).

Greenblatt, S. (1985), 'Invisible bullets: Renaissance Authority and Its Subversion', *Henry IV and Henry V*' in J. Dollimore and A. Sinfield (eds), *Political Shakespeare* (Manchester: Manchester University Press).

Grock (1931), *Grock Life's a Lark* (London: Heinemann).

Hall, J. (1998), 'The Evacuations of Falstaff' in R. Knowles (ed.), *Shakespeare and Carnival* (Basingstoke: Macmillan).

P. Happé, (ed.) (1975), *English Mystery Plays* (London: Penguin).

P. Happé (1999), *English Drama Before Shakespeare* (London: Longman).

J. Hetterman (1981), Symbolic Action in the Plays of the Wakefield Master (Athens: University of Georgia Press).

J. Hilton (1982), *Georg Büchner* (London and Basingstoke: Macmillan).

D. Hirst (1985), *Edward Bond* (London and Basingstoke: Macmillan).

J. Holloway & E. Peláez (eds) (1998), *Zapatista! Reinventing Revolution in Mexico* (London: Pluto Press).

T. Holme (1976), *A Servant of Many Masters: The Life and Times of Carlo Goldoni* (London: Jupiter Books).

R. Hutton (1994), *The Rise and Fall of Merry England* (Oxford: Oxford University Press).

L. Hyde (1998), *Trickster Makes This World* (New York: North Point Press).

F. Jameson (1998), *Brecht and Method* (London: Verso).

V.K. Janik (1998), *Fools and Jesters in Literature, Art and History* (Westport, Conn.: Greenwood Press).

Jenkins, R. (1995), 'The Roar of the Clown' in P. Zarrilli (ed.), *Acting (Re)Considered* (London and New York: Routledge).

R. Jenkins (2001), *Dario Fo & Franca Rame: Artful Laughter* (New York: Aperture Foundation).

Jonson (1995), The Alchemist *and Other Plays* (Oxford: Oxford University Press).

T. Judt (2010), *Ill Fares The Land* (London: Penguin).

B. Kershaw (1999), *The Radical in Performance* (London and New York, Routledge).

R. Knowles (ed.) (1998), *Shakespeare and Carnival* (Basingstoke: Macmillan).

J. Knowlson (1997), *Damned to Fame* (London: Bloomsbury).

J. Kott (1967), *Shakespeare Our Contemporary* (London: Methuen).

E. Ladurie (1981), *Carnival in Romans* (Harmondsworth: Penguin).

F. Laroque (1998), 'Shakespeare's 'Battle of Carnival and Lent'. The Falstaff Scenes Reconsidered (*1&2 Henry IV*)' in R. Knowles (ed.), *Shakespeare and Carnival* (Basingstoke: Macmillan).

A. Latham (ed.) (1975), *As You Like It* (London: Methuen).

J.-P. Lederach (2005), *The Moral Imagination* (Oxford: Oxford University Press).

G.A. Lester (ed.) (1981), *Three Late Medieval Morality Plays* (London: Ernest Benn).

N. Liebler (1995), *Shakespeare's Festive Tragedy* (London and New York: Routledge).

S. Longstaffe (1998), 'A Short Report and Not Otherwise': Jack Cade in *2 Henry VI*' in R. Knowles (ed.), *Shakespeare and Carnival* (Basingstoke: Macmillan).

R. Lunney (2002), *Marlowe and the Popular Tradition* (Manchester: Manchester University Press).

A. Lutkus (1998), 'Touchstone' in V. Janik (ed.), *Fools and Jesters in Literature, Art and History* (Westport: Greenwood Press).

D. Mann (1991), *The Elizabethan Player* (London and New York: Routledge).

C. Marlowe (1969), *The Complete Plays* (Harmondsworth: Penguin).

J. Marshall (1997), ' "Oze souens that sytt and ze brothern that stonde ryght wppe": addressing the audience of mankind', *European Medieval Drama*, 1, 189–202.

E. McInnes (1991), *Woyzeck* (Glasgow: University of Glasgow).

R.B. McKerrow (ed.) (1958), *The Works of Thomas Nashe* (Oxford: Oxford University Press).

R. Means (1995), *Where White Men Fear to Tread* (New York: St. Martin's Griffin).

A.Mitchell (1999), *Dario Fo: People's Court Jester* (London: Methuen).

Molière (1959), *The Misanthrope and Other Plays* (Harmondsworth: Penguin).

T. More (1965), *Utopia* (London: Penguin).

J.M. Morrell (ed.) (1950), *Four English Comedies* (Harmondsworth: Penguin).

K. Muir (ed.) (1972), *King Lear* (London: Methuen).

P. Murray (1970), *The Tragic Comedian* (Cork: The Mercier Press).

S. Muiruri (2000), 'Scratchin' the Surface', *Drama*, Volume 8, Number 1, 24–30.

J. Neihardt (1988), *Black Elk Speaks* (Lincoln: University of Nebraska Press).

T. Nelson (1990), *Comedy* (Oxford: Oxford University Press).

H.J. Oliver (ed.) (1971), *The Merry Wives of Windsor* (London: Methuen).

B.K. Otto (2001), *Fools Are Everywhere* (Chicago: Chicago University Press).

S. Palfrey (1997), *Late Shakespeare* (Oxford: Oxford University Press).

A. Patterson (1989), *Shakespeare and the Popular Voice* (Oxford: Basil Blackwell).

Perret, D. (1998), 'Beckett's Postmodern Clowns: Vladimir (Didi), Estragon (Gogo), Pozzo, and Lucky' in V. Janik (ed.), *Fools and Jesters in Literture, Art, and History* (Westport: Greenwood Press).

Plato (1951), *The Symposium* (London: Penguin).

Plato (1954), *The Last Days of Socrates* (London: Penguin).

T. Prentki and S. Preston (eds) (2009), *The Applied Theatre* Reader (London and New York: Routledge).

V. Price (ed.) (1971), *The Plays of Georg Büchner* (Oxford: Oxford University Press).

F. Rabelais (1955), *Gargantua and Pantagruel* (London: Penguin).

P. Radin (1956), *The Trickster* (New York: Schocken Books).

C. Richardson & J. Johnston (1991), *Medieval Drama* (Basingstoke: Macmillan).

P. Roberts (ed.) (1985), *Bond on File* (London and New York: Methuen).

J. Salverson (2008), 'Taking liberties: a theatre class of foolish witnesses' in *Research in Drama Education*, Vol. 13, No. 2, 245–55.

J. Schechter (1985), *Durov's Pig* (New York: Theatre Communications Group).

J. Schechter (2003), *Popular Theatre: a Sourcebook* (London and New York: Routledge).

J.C. Scott (1990), *Domination and the Arts of Resistance: Hidden Transcripts* (New Haven: Yale University Press).

J. Southworth (1998), *Fools and Jesters at the English Court* (Stroud: Sutton Publishing).

R. Speirs (1987), *Bertolt Brecht* (Basingstoke: Macmillan).

B. Spivak (1968), *Shakepeare and the Allegory of Evil* (New York: Columbia University Press).

P. Stallybrass & A. White (1986), *The Politics and Poetics of Transgression* (Ithaca: Cornell University Press).

M. Summers (ed.) (1968) *The Complete Works of Thomas Shadwell* (New York: Benjamin Blom).

S. Taviano (2005), *Staging Dario Fo and Franca Rame* (Aldershot: Ashgate).

E. Webb (1972), *The Plays of Samuel Beckett* (Seattle: University of Washington Press).

R. Weimann (1978), *Shakespeare and the Popular Tradition in the Theater* (Baltimore: Johns Hopkins University Press).

R. Weimann (2000), *Author's Pen and Actor's Voice* (Cambridge: Cambridge University Press).

E. Welsford (1935), *The Fool* (London: Faber & Faber).

A. White (1978), *Bertolt Brecht's Great Plays* (London and Basingstoke, Macmillan).

J. White (2004), *Bertolt Brecht's Dramatic Theory* (Rochester, NY: Camden House).

D. Wiles (1987), *Shakespeare's Clown* (Cambridge: Cambridge University Press).

W. Willeford (1969), *The Fool and His Scepter* (Chicago: Northwestern University Press).

R. Williams (1976), *Drama from Ibsen to Brecht* (Harmondsworth: Penguin).

P. Womack (1986), *Ben Jonson* (Oxford: Basil Blackwell).

E. Wright (1989), *Postmodern Brecht* (London and New York: Routledge).

P. Zarrilli (1995), *Acting (Re)Considered* (London and New York: Routledge).

Index